TRANSFORMATIONAL
POLITICS

TRANSFORMATIONAL POLITICS

THEORY, STUDY, AND PRACTICE

EDITED BY

Stephen Woolpert
Christa Daryl Slaton
Edward W. Schwerin

State University of New York Press

Published by
State University of New York Press, Albany

For information, address State University of New York Press,
State University Plaza, Albany, N.Y., 12246

Production by Diane Ganeles
Marketing by Anne Valentine

Library of Congress Cataloging-in-Publication Data

Transformational politics : theory, study, and practice / edited by
    Stephen Woolpert, Christa Daryl Slaton, Edward W. Schwerin.
        p.   cm.
    Includes bibliographical references and index.
        ISBN 0-7914-3945-3 (alk. paper). — ISBN 0-7914-3946-1 (pbk. :
alk. paper)
        1. Political culture—Philosophy.   2. Political development—
Philosophy.   I. Woolpert, Stephen Brim, 1944–   . II. Slaton,
Christa Daryl.   III. Schwerin, Edward W.
    JA75.7.T73   1998
    306.2—dc21   97–47457
                                                                        CIP

10   9   8   7   6   5   4   3   2   1

Contents

Part II. The Study of Transformational Politics

Part III. The Practice of Transformational Politics

Preface:
Paths to Transformational Politics

The Ecological and Transformational Politics Section of the American Political Science Association was born at the annual APSA meeting in Chicago, 1987. Jeff Fishel of American University organized a "conference group" of political and social scientists, all innovators in a variety of areas—humanistic psychology, futures study, political movements, ecological sustainability, teledemocracy, etc. Most of those in the group had begun their careers in traditional fields and studied at highly reputable institutions—Stanford, New York University, Northwestern, Johns Hopkins, University of Chicago, Brown, University of California at Berkeley, and Massachusetts Institute of Technology. However, many of these scholars had abandoned the conventional fields in which they had established their reputations. Moving from expertise in political participation to sustainability, judicial politics to teledemocracy, urban studies to movement politics, these political scientists had left the safety zones of mainstream political science to explore the unknown. They chose to chart a new course knowing that by leaving the familiar they risked marginalization, misrepresentation—or just being ignored. Yet as explorers and inventors, they sought new challenges when the conventional became to them mundane, obsolete, stifling, self-destructive, and to some, unjust.

This group of "transformational" political scientists grew to become an officially recognized and organized section of the American Political Science Association and generated many innovative and collaborative research projects. The inspiration for this book came out of many panel presentations, workshops, roundtables, discussions, and papers presented at national conferences as the group began to articulate what they meant when they called themselves "transformational political scientists."

Stephen Woolpert, Christa Slaton, and Edward Schwerin were early members of the group and they have participated in the dialogue over the years that has come to define transformational politics. Like other members of this new field of study, each of them came to the group after their intellectual and personal interests surpassed the confines of their graduate training and initial practice of political science.

Woolpert came of age in the 1960s. His personal and professional development were shaped by the social cleavages of that period. In 1966 he entered the Johns Hopkins School of Advanced International Studies, anticipating a career in the foreign service. While there he found his professional training from Washington "insiders" was at odds with his convictions regarding the immorality of United States foreign policy in Southeast Asia. As a result he abandoned the idea of working for the State Department.

In 1967, under the auspices of the Brookings Institution, he worked on a survey research project in Bogotá, Colombia. That experience in the empirical measurement of elite political attitudes led him to a broader interest in political culture and socialization, his focus when he entered the doctoral program in political science at Stanford.

While there, Woolpert again encountered a discontinuity between his professional and personal values: this time between Stanford's rigorous training of empirical social scientific research scholars and the flourishing human potential movement in northern California, inspired by humanistic and transpersonal psychological analysis. Although some of the claims regarding the significance of this latter movement were vague and naively optimistic, he nevertheless became convinced that its impact would not be restricted to the individual level, but would have greater implications for large-scale social processes.

Over time, Woolpert became increasingly dissatisfied with mainstream social science research and more engaged with political paradigm shifts and social transformations. In response to such events as the prison uprising at Attica and related incidents at Soledad and San Quentin prisons in northern California, he made a decision to focus his research on criminal justice issues, where he could apply the human growth perspective to policy questions of practical urgency.

Woolpert's interest in expanded human potentialities, in postpositivist epistemology, and in broadening the political realm to include personal and spiritual dimensions represented a fundamental shift in his study of politics. It also left him a self-exile with no reference group that shared his perspective.

While teaching at the University of Maryland during the late 1970s, he discovered a number of kindred spirits in the Association for Humanistic Psychology and in the Governing Council of an organization called the New World Alliance. This latter group was a short-lived precursor of the North American Greens. It was founded by Mark Satin (author of *New Age Politics*) after a nationwide Delphi-type survey among 500 academics, policy experts, and political activists interested in this emerging political paradigm. These new colleagues, who were also exploring the relationship between personal and political transformation, reaffirmed his commitment to that worldview.

In 1981 he relocated to Saint Mary's College, a liberal arts school in northern California, which values the kind of personalized teaching associated with the humanistic perspective. Within a few years he also found a spiritual community that showed him, finally, how to live life on life's terms. He gave up his grandiose dreams of creating a grand coalition of transformationally oriented organizations, and limited his political involvement to serving on the county Juvenile Justice Commission. Just about then, Fishel (with the help of Satin) initiated the formation of the Transformational Politics Conference Group within the APSA, dedicated to supporting the integration of authentic personal development and political inquiry with the profound changes being experienced in the world. Woolpert participated in the group from the outset in articulating the theory, study, and practice of transformational politics.

Slaton's journey into transformational politics began while growing up in a segregated South. The Jim Crow laws and segregation policies were inconsistent with what she had been taught in her Southern Baptist church about fairness, justice, and compassion. They were also at odds with her early education that extolled the freedom and equality of all citizens in the United States. To her, the justices on the United States Supreme Court seemed to be the salvation of American democracy. Unfortunately, school principals and superintendents, legislators, and power holders throughout the South (with rare exception) sought to maintain segregation and to deny blacks basic freedoms. Worse yet, they did so with a self-righteous zeal that painted the civil rights activists as the villains and the Supreme Court justices as communists bent on destroying the American way of life. Thus began her understanding that true American values were subverted by many who held power in the American political system.

When she entered graduate school in the late 1970s, Slaton had lost much of her naivete about American politics. She came fully of age during Watergate. Originally believing that President Nixon was the victim of a malicious press determined to destroy him, she watched the evidence mount to prove that the president of the United States had lied repeatedly to the American people, had ruthlessly used the power entrusted to him to punish his "enemies," and had helped undermine the political institutions she was taught to respect.

Once again, however, the courts came to the rescue. Judge Sirica and the Supreme Court used the constitution and federal judicial system to ensure that justice was done. Thus, Slaton began her graduate education as a great admirer of the courts and its independence from other political institutions. Yet, as she had discovered at a very early age, although the Supreme Court has enormous power and influence, it has an inability to enforce its decisions and is at times openly defied and condemned by some hypocritical government officials. With a desire to study the impact of Supreme Court decisions, she entered the University of Hawaii to study with two experts on the court system, Glendon Schubert and Theodore Becker. Alas, she found that both had moved on to other areas of study—biopolitics and teledemocracy, respectively. Indeed, nearly the entire department there had chosen dramatically different areas of study from the ones in which they had begun and established their reputations.

With her mentors on the cutting edge of new areas of research, Slaton pursued her study of the courts and judges under the direction of futurist James Dator. She began an extensive investigation on the backgrounds of judges and conducted field work in the federal and state courts in Hawaii. The more she learned and observed, the more she understood what the backgrounds of judges meant. They were politicians in black robes. They were humans with flaws and biases, not saviors with impartial judgment. She also began to see how the judicial system worked—how powerless the parties were in the proceedings; how the process was less about discovery of the truth than obscuring it; how the verdicts often left each side unhappy; and how little justice was produced by the judicial system.

Slaton's in-depth study of the courts paralleled the birth of the mediation movement in the United States. Pilot projects were funded by the federal government during the Carter administration to develop alternative means of dispute resolution. Slaton, in cooperation with Theodore Becker, founded the Community Mediation

Service, the first neighborhood justice center in Hawaii and the first university-based center in the country. Through the volunteers at the center, Slaton began to see the potential that ordinary citizens had to resolve conflict and to use a process that led to higher satisfaction than the adversarial means used by professionals.

That experience led Slaton to conduct research in other areas to examine the capability and the desire of citizens to have more direct control over their lives. For the past two decades Slaton has worked in partnership with Becker to design an original "deliberative" method of public opinion polling (Televote) that seeks to obtain informed and considered opinion and to develop electronic town meetings that use multimedia, two-way communication, and facilitation to achieve consensus and expand democracy. As many had discovered before her, Slaton concluded that too much reliance on the bias of elites was a fatal mistake of democracy. She now operates on the hypothesis that if democracy is to thrive, its citizens need to be empowered. Slaton and her colleagues see their role as political scientists to be designers and experimenters of tools and processes that truly enhance and transform representative democracy into a more participatory state.

Schwerin's interest in transformational politics grew out of his experiences as a graduate student and his community service work in Hawaii. He worked as a research assistant for Rudolph Rummel, who was conducting one of the largest existing political science research projects—the Dimensionality of Nations (DON) project. The goals of the DON project included collecting enormous national data sets, mapping the patterns of nation-states' attributes and behavior over time, testing Rummel's Field Theory, and developing a sophisticated computer model of the world. The computer model was designed to predict international conflict based on field theory and the results of extensive data analysis. The purpose of the model was to be able to anticipate the outbreak of hostilities in time to advise policy makers and perhaps prevent war from occurring. Schwerin was involved in Peace Studies at the time and so the idea that the researchers might be able to apply empirical social science and computer models to bring about a better and more peaceful world was exciting for him.

In addition to the DON project, other interesting and potentially transformational activities were happening in Hawaii. The community was experiencing a rebirth of Hawaiian culture and the beginnings of local—particularly Hawaiian—activism. Environmental groups were struggling with developers to maintain control of access to the beaches. Hawaii held a state constitutional convention that aroused grassroots activity. Local groups organized initiative and recall campaigns to bring important issues directly to the citizens. Hawaiian groups made reparation claims for lands they argued were illegally stolen from them by the United States government. The Green movement and party began to grow out of a coalition of environmentalists, feminists, and other activists in Hawaii.

At the university of Hawaii, scholar-activists like Becker, Dator, and Ira Rohter were active in the community and at the university developing new initiatives in community mediation, teledemocracy, futuristics, and volunteerism. Visiting scholars such as Johan Galtung, who is considered by many scholars, especially in Europe and Latin America, to be the "father" of peace research contributed to the intellectual and political action. Schwerin took several classes from Galtung and learned about the concepts of "structural violence," "negative" peace and the need to empower the oppressed in order to transform the world. But his experience in the community provided the necessary real world grounding for these intellectual concepts as he became more involved in action research and civic work.

Schwerin's interest in empowerment projects and community mediation began in the early 1980s. The unemployment rate was soaring and researchers began to discover that long-term unemployment created serious personal and social impacts in addition to financial problems. Many workers confronting long-term structural unemployment developed major physical and mental health problems. Researchers found that unemployment increases personal stress and lowers self-esteem. In short, they found that unemployment is disempowering. The evidence for this relationship became so clear that President Reagan declared unemployment to be the nation's number one public health problem.

At the time Schwerin was the Executive Director of an action research program that designed and tested empowerment strategies for those attempting to cope with long-term unemployment. He developed an integrated empowerment model that combined training in job search and coping skills with support groups and the provision of material and nonmaterial resources. He soon discovered what others have also learned—helping others is personally empowering work.

Schwerin's program offices were located in a United Way office building that housed several nonprofit service agencies, including the Honolulu Neighborhood Justice Center. He learned about community mediation and became a volunteer mediator and mediation trainer. Like many other citizens, he was initially attracted to mediation work by ideological claims that community mediation was preferable to suing in the formal court system. Advocates of mediation argued that unlike the courts, it was empowering for its participants. They also claimed that community mediation was an important vehicle for personal and political transformation, and that it can contribute to democratic participation and community building as well.

Schwerin realized that although mediation ideology was a powerful symbolic resource for the community mediation movement, its claims were still untested and were taken on faith by mediators, program staff, and advocates. He became aware that, as a new field and an emerging social movement, there were many questions that required research if one were to understand mediation's impact on social, political, and legal issues. Thus began his study of the relationship between mediation training, the mediation process, and theories of empowerment and democratic transformation.

The research interests of the editors of this volume found their paths converging in the Ecological and Transformational Politics section of the American Political Science Association. The members of the section are all unanimous in their view that mainstream political science is stuck in an old paradigm—one that has lost its ability for answering many pertinent and pressing questions of the day. The bulk of political science research is recycled material; its concepts and methods are committed to maintaining the status quo; its language and icons are obtuse and arcane; it is almost totally incomprehensible to even well-educated Americans; and it is irrelevant to many of the major political issues and problems of the day. This volume seeks to move beyond the constraints and limitations of the prevailing paradigm and to offer theory, methods of study, and guidelines for practice as we enter the emerging paradigm.

fered by anonymous reviewers and Richard Couto, who have all offered valuable suggestions to make this a better book.

We are especially indebted to our spouses and partners, Vir-
ginia Logan, Ted Becker, and Jan Barosh, for their intellectual contributions, unrelenting support, unfailing good humor, faith in us,
and enthusiasm for this project.

Introduction:
What Is Transformational Politics?

CHRISTA DARYL SLATON, STEVE WOOLPERT,
AND ED SCHWERIN

The purpose of this anthology is to bring together some of the best and most exciting new scholarship on transformational politics. Each of the fifteen entries in this volume examines a particular feature of the transition currently taking place in political thought and life. The reader will find that there are four major themes treated throughout the text that provide a core of understanding of transformational politics.

*Theme One: The Obsolescence of the Prevailing Paradigm
and the Emergence of a New Paradigm*

The editors and contributors to this anthology share the perspective that the discipline of political science has reached a crossroads. The frequency with which terms such as "postliberal," "postmodern," "postpatriarchal," "postmaterialist," and "poststructural" are used in contemporary political discourse testifies to the pervasive conviction that an era has ended. Similarly, phrases such as "new world order," "new paradigm," "new age," and "third wave" convey the widely-shared expectation that what lies ahead politically will be qualitatively unlike what has gone before.

Symptoms of this fundamental discontinuity between past and future in political affairs are ubiquitous: fragmenting loyalties and multiplying responsibilities; accelerating environmental degradation;

the growing impact of feminism, multiculturalism, and ethnic assertiveness; potent breakthroughs in science and technology; the end of the cold war; and challenges to the sovereignty of nation-states. On a daily basis new dramas unfold of disintegration and convergence, oppression and emancipation, stagnation and creativity.

Intellectually there is a corresponding upheaval in progress, marked by the eclipse of positivism. Both the natural and human sciences are developing a fuller appreciation of the indeterminacy, contingency, and the interpenetration of mental and physical phenomena. A central premise of this collection of readings is that such extraordinarily far-reaching, complex, and interconnected changes require a thorough rethinking of our political condition—a rethinking that moves us beyond the constraints of a paradigm that has become inadequate for understanding the world in which we live.

Transformational politics requires a paradigm that places *major change* at its core. Whether such dramatic change is something we can control or not, desire or dread, plan or resist, we are involved on a daily basis in accelerating processes of change and transformation. Being engaged in the processes of ongoing and profound change, transformational political scientists seek the means to help transform ourselves and our political institutions and policies in positive and peaceful ways. Striving to reach a potential that has not yet been realized is a goal of these social scientists (whether the goal is becoming self-actualized human beings, striving for a more inclusive democracy, or creating a more tolerant and collaborative world). Transformational politics has a value base—one that is compassionate, nurturing, empowering, and democratic. It also values the nexus between being a political scientist and a political activist—one dedicated to embodying these positive transformational values.

In defining transformational politics, however, it is easier to reach consensus on what is wrong or outdated with the old paradigm than to clearly present the new paradigm, which is only emerging. The contributions in this book are the effort by several political scientists who have known each other for years and have been participating in the ongoing dialogue to articulate the theory, study, and practice of the politics of this transformational period, i.e., transformational politics.

Theme Two: Ecological Focus and Systems Thinking

A primary theme of our text is that political thought and action must give greater recognition to environmental well-being. While the behaviorism and anthropocentrism of the prevailing paradigm contribute to the view of nature as a hostile force to be controlled and constrained by humans, transformational scientists see the protection of nature as essential to the survival of humans, who are in a mutually dependent relationship with it. There are several principles related to this perspective.

(1) *Interdependence*

All members of an ecological community are interconnected in a vast and intricate network of relationships. To understand interdependence requires a shift in focus from discrete political actors, whose behavior can be measured, to patterns of political interaction, which can only be mapped.

(2) *Partnership*

Ecological cycles are sustained by pervasive cooperation within an open system. Most species in an ecosystem coevolve through an interplay of creation and mutual adaptation. The pervasiveness of partnership, symbiosis, and permeable boundaries in political communities is often downplayed in the current paradigm, which gives greater attention to the more dramatic but less common instances of conflict and destruction.

(3) *Flexibility*

Ecological cycles, acting as feedback loops, tend to maintain themselves in a flexible state, characterized by continual fluctuations. Ecosystems tend to be "pragmatic" and innovative rather than dogmatic and doctrinaire. Social scientists should experiment with new structures and processes that place more emphasis on feedback and adaptability to the changing environment.

(4) *Diversity*

In diverse, complex communities, stability is increased because of overlapping functions and replacability. Attempts to force homogeneity or to replace cultural diversity with a global monoculture will ultimately lead to enormous instability. It is diversity that enriches complex communities and enhances their viability.

(5) *Sustainability*

The above principles combine to create communities that support their members' growth without diminishing the chances of future generations, but that may, instead, increase their choices.

Ecological literacy is closely related to systems thinking, particularly the principle of interdependence. Systems thinking emphasizes context over content, form over substance, and process over structure. It avoids reducing the operation of complex wholes to one-way, cause-effect explanations and linear relationships. It encourages cross-disciplinary study and awareness of politics' global reach.

Theme Three: Linkage of Personal and Political

"The personal is political" is also a central theme of the anthology. It ties in with a major theme in feminist literature, which reminds us that politics is not just about running for office but also about how we live our lives in the broader sense. It shifts the focus from "power over" to "power with," which points towards the intrapersonal and interpersonal aspects of politics, such as the Greens' group dynamics and Vaclav Havel's consciousness-raising, which are highlighted in the final section of the book. It calls attention to areas of life—the home, the family, the community, the church—that political scientists often overlook in studying politics, influence, and power.

The recurrent emphasis on praxis—placing theory into practice—appears in all sections of the book. This perspective is a challenge to the tenet that political scientists should remove themselves from political activism so that their research is not tainted by their subjectivity. Epistemologically it disputes the belief that the researcher can be purely the detached observer and acknowledges the inseparability of the observer from what is observed.

While recognizing the potential dangers and pitfalls that the scholar-activist faces, transformational political scientists warn of a greater danger when social scientists are not explicit about their values or when they are too reliant on maintaining "detachment" to fully grasp the subtle group dynamics or hidden agendas of their subjects. Those who have studied the Green Movement from within have been able to achieve a greater appreciation of the complexity of the political ironies of the movement. They have been able to identify more clearly leaders, factions, underlying issues, and patterns of inconsistent behavior that outside observers rarely detect. The scholar-activist is explicit about the values that guide the research. Transformational scholarship provides the tools for careful scrutiny and methodical study to allow self-critical reflection of the activist on the activity in which the scholar-activist is engaged.

Theme Four: Inclusion of the Spiritual and Sacred

To most authors in this text the spiritual or sacred dimensions of life are essential components of political life. This view ties in with the shift to postmaterialism, which places a high value on self-actualization and the search for purpose and meaning. Transformational politics strives for a "politics of transcendence" that unites the spiritual and material being (or the inner and outer domains).

While there is broad consensus among transformational political scientists that spirituality and sacredness are an important part of human existence, there is not agreement on exactly what spirituality is and how specifically it informs our theory, study, and practice of politics. There is a distinction, however, that transformational political scientists make between spirituality and religious dogma. Spirituality is not to be confused with rigid adherence to a moral code although morality is an element of spirituality. It is rather a state of being that transcends the material world and that connects us to something greater than us (God, the universe, our ancestors, the earth, all living creatures, etc.). The sacred and spiritual provide inspiration, guidance, and a sense of meaning and purpose that propel us and many political actors beyond the self-interest and self-centeredness of the politics-as-usual world.

Therefore, the questions addressed in this book contain profound implications about political science and political life. Accepting the thesis that a transformation is in process, the authors discuss such questions as: What are the forces driving the transformational process? What is its character and direction? How are we to understand and appreciate its multitude of perils and promises? What are its implications for the evolution of political consciousness, the conduct of political inquiry, the dynamics of political actions well beyond the confines of government, and the self-governance of communities? In short, how can we participate in bringing about a fundamentally better world through this era of uncertainty?

Overview of the Contents

Transformational Politics is divided into three parts: Theory, Study, and Practice. Drawing on a wide array of theories—empowerment, feminist, democratic, communitarian, chaos, quantum, conflict resolution, self-actualization—Part I offers answers to several questions. What are the theoretical components of transformational politics? How does it differ from classic liberalism and positivism embraced by the vast majority of American political scientists? How does it enrich, broaden, supplement, correct, and refine theories of the dominant paradigm?

Part II examines how a transformational perspective guides one's study of politics. Our notion of study entails two complementary components—research and teaching. It is our view that our research informs our teaching and our teaching provides feedback useful for our research.

Part III offers guidance about how we practice our theory and apply our study. As discussed earlier, transformational politics is value-based and concerned with creating a better world. Praxis—theoretically grounded political action that changes both the world and the theory on which it is based—is a fundamental approach of transformational political scientists.

Each section of the book is introduced by an essay from one of the editors to provide a broad view of the complexity of that part of transformational politics. The other contributions in each section offer deeper insights into some of the components of transformational politics. While each introductory chapter incorporates the perspectives presented in the chapters of the section, this is not always done in a linear fashion. Each editor identifies major themes and areas of convergence in articulating transformational theory, study, and practice.

Part I begins with an overview chapter by Christa Daryl Slaton that introduces a theory of transformational politics, described as *a web of theories in the emerging paradigm.* Slaton examines the assumptions of modern political thought that have limited our understanding of politics and have precluded us from identifying and addressing questions of crucial importance in the study of political science. Arising from the growing awareness of the inadequacies of mainstream political theory is a theory of transformational politics that not only challenges components of the traditional orthodoxy, but also offers a theory that is value-based and relatively comprehensive by integrating democratic, ecological, feminist, post-modern, and non-Western thought.

In chapter 2, Louis Herman offers a theory for transforming political science. Herman argues that the crisis of modernity demands that political science reroot itself in the "truth quest." This requires a global, multicivilizational search for the full amplitude of empirical knowledge. Such an extraordinary political science must ask more fundamental questions of history by looking for answers that make contact with our primary, prescientific life experiences. An understanding of a more universal common good is derived by differentiating and integrating such experiences.

Manfred Halpern offers an original theory in chapter 3 to help explain why there are so many partial selves and distorted selves in modern society. He uses the political construct of the nation-state to demonstrate how the existing political power structure retards us and is molded by our understandings (or misunderstandings) of what human beings can become. His theory identifies four interrelated faces of our being: the personal, the political, the historical, and the sacred. Halpern describes the transformational process of the self as an archetypal drama in three acts: Emanation, Incoherence, and Transformation. A major theme of the essay is that transformation is never complete or final. We continuously move through the various acts in the transformational process in order to maximize our potential.

In chapter 4 Barbara Knight explores the potential for recent discoveries in the new sciences of chaos and complexity to provide metaphors with which to reenvision and ultimately transform political community. Reconceptualizing chaos as richly complex information rather than an absence of order, Knight draws a parallel between chaos theory and "feminine" ways of knowing which, she argues, offer vital theoretical contributions to understanding the world more fully and correctly. Knight maintains our public and private lives are interwoven, mutually enriching, and that the boundaries between our public lives and private selves are fluid and responsive to context.

The final chapter in Part I examines the theoretical underpinnings of a global political and social movement, the Greens. Daniel Graham maintains that the democratic left and environmental politics/philosophy have both attempted to transform modern industrial polities. While traditional left movements have focused on issues of equality and justice within human societies, mainstream environmentalism has emphasized planetary sustainability and human/nature conflict. Each has had, at best, very limited success even while they have gained substantial power within some contemporary political systems.

Enter the Greens, with a broader and more inclusive ideology and theory, one that would transform any industrial nation state if this theory were to be implemented. A major aspect of Green thinking is ecofeminist theory. This incorporates issues of gender equality, post-patriarchal thinking, and organizational style and links class, gender, and ecological concerns. Green theory, then, makes a "radical" theoretical contribution in its ecocentric paradigm, which attempts to reevaluate the role of economics, science, technology, and ideology for political and cultural transformation.

Part II begins with an overview chapter by Ed Schwerin that examines various models of transformational research and teaching. Schwerin discusses critiques of conventional approaches to research and teaching and then considers some nontraditional approaches that are potentially more democratic, empowering and consistent with transformational theory. Transformational approaches to research include participant observation by scholar-activists, and various models of "action research." Transformational approaches to teaching include the dialogic/critical thinking model, the collaborative/democratic classroom, service learning, and the Internet classroom.

Marla Brettschneider's chapter offers one example of transformational research to study political and cultural groups. The analysis and evaluation of the social transformation of community groups involves numerous epistemological and methodological assumptions. Brettschneider's analysis focuses on the transformation of the American Jewish community over the last thirty years. She begins with a critique of the standards most often used by political science scholars to evaluate whether groups are successful in their attempts to affect the world. She then discusses how groups seeking transformation themselves define criteria for success. Brettsneider argues that listening to groups articulate their own guidelines gives political scientists a deeper qualitative approach to measurement.

In chapter 8, Betty Zisk examines participant observation as a research strategy of transformational political scientists. While participant observation has been widely used by sociologists, anthropologists, and some political scientists, critics argue that the researcher's personal involvement with his or her subjects often leads to cooptation and lack of objectivity. Zisk provides a thoughtful consideration of the problems and pitfalls, promises and prospects of participant observation, using both the scholarly literature and examples from her own research.

Gale Harrison suggests in the next chapter that "real" education is always potentially transformational. She describes how a pedagogy based on feminist philosophy and epistemology can facilitate the transformational process. Feminist democratic models of pedagogy represent a shift in power relationships in the classroom from control/power *over* to empowerment/power *with*. Drawing on both feminist theory and her own teaching experience, Harrison describes how a professor can foster an environment in which ideas and feelings about fundamental political change can be thoroughly explored and realistically examined while still maintaining personal respect for the participants.

The last chapter in Part II demonstrates how transformational pedagogy uses diverse approaches and perspectives to develop new learning models. Jeff Fishel and Morley Segal suggest how insights from management training, humanistic psychology, and adult education can be used to develop learning communities in the classroom. Their approach attempts to make learning a more active, holistic, and personalized process. They argue that learning involves at least four processes: concrete experience, reflective observation, abstract conceptualization, and active experimentation. Fishel and Segal view classrooms as microcosms of the larger political system and the dynamics of the classroom as an important aspect of effective teaching. For them, learning is a process, not a product. They use techniques of laboratory education to ensure that learning and teaching will be more integrated and meaningful.

Stephen Woolpert's introductory chapter begins Part III, which focuses on the *practice* of transformational politics. This section poses the question: How shall we live our lives? The themes of transformational political thought and study construct and embrace a mosaic of transformational political activities, organizations, and programs. Woolpert's survey of the burgeoning body of literature on the application of transformational political thinking identifies three major motifs.

First, responding to the dangers of environmental deterioration, political transformationalists can be found working towards environmental sustainability in a myriad of environmental organizations and movements, from community recycling to helping convey Native American environmental philosophy to a broader audience. Second, since transformational politics denotes a revitalized democratic spirit and the emergence of a participatory civic culture, political transformationalists can be found working in the politics of institutions and in a wide variety of community organizations and projects. Third, the rethinking of conventional political assumptions in transformational theory and study yields more integrative approaches to political practice. Transformational politics is characterized by a synthesis and transcendence of customary political divisions, such as Left/Right and Democrat/Republican. This review chapter briefly mentions numerous expressions of each motif, which is then supplemented by the specific illustrations in the chapters that follow.

Despite the spread of representative democracy around the globe, powerlessness is a pervasive defect of modern political life. In chapter 12, Theodore Becker addresses the growing chasm that separates representative governments from the general public: powerful elites control the distribution of wealth and influence worldwide. In order to enhance the quality of present systems of representative democracy, new ways are needed to expand and equalize the influence of citizens in the political process, both as voters and as active participants. Do modern information and communication technologies provide an answer? Becker, a leading theorist, researcher, and proponent of sophisticated "Electronic Town Meetings" (ETMs), believes so. He describes the historical development of ETMs and the empowering results of recent projects in Hawaii and Canada that incorporated them into policy making and administrative processes. He also discusses ETMs' role as a bridge between the weak democracy of today and a viable form of direct democracy in the future.

In chapter 13 Robert Gilbert draws insights from the example of a transformational political leader. Vaclav Havel has said that "planetary democracy does not yet exist, but our global civilization is already preparing a place for it." He has earned an international reputation for his holistic and deeply ethical political leadership, first as a catalyst of the nonviolent democratization of a repressive Communist regime and then as President of the young Czech Republic. The integral themes of transformational thought, i.e., the importance of environmental well-being, of the spiritual dimensions of life, and of linking personal and political transformation, have all been eloquently articulated in his speeches and writings. Understanding what lies at the heart of Havel's conduct provides important insights into the qualities that distinguish transformational political leadership from politics-as-usual. Gilbert distills ten principles which inform Havel's praxis and which may be transferable to other political contexts, particularly other representative democratic systems.

Michael Cummings' chapter 14 demonstrates the path to transforming public policy. Many vexing policy conflicts could be ameliorated via the practical application of transformational values. Few, however, have been as persistently divisive as the struggle for equality in the face of prejudice and discrimination. At present, the focus of attention in the United States is on the justice or injustice of affirmative action programs. Cummings' analysis is representative of the transformational approach in that it goes beyond the politically correct arguments of both the right and the left in search of a deeper, contextual understanding of the problem. His analysis of affirmative action's polarizing tendencies and logical inconsistencies, plus his recognition that unearned disadvantages inevitably distort competitive outcomes, lead Cummings to challenge the very system of winners and losers within which the present struggle for equality takes place. He describes steps toward creating a synergistic community in which "fullness of opportunity" (making the pie larger) supplants the competitive search for an "equality of opportunity" (to get a piece of the crust). The diversity, flexibility and interdependence of such a community—principles of healthy ecological communities—are central to the vision of transformational politics.

In the final chapter, Stephen Woolpert examines the political psychology of the Green Movement in exploring the linkage between the personal and the political—a major ingredient of transformational politics. Changing the fundamental rules of the political game involves waking up to a richer perspective of the self, as well as developing healthier processes and procedures within transformationally oriented political organizations. Woolpert agrees with Graham in chapter 5 that the Greens are the political movement most explicitly committed to transformational values. But he goes beyond Graham's discussion of Green theory and policy preferences to explain why the level of Green success has been diminished by certain dysfunctional features of their own group dynamics. Woolpert uses Jung's concept of "The Shadow" to analyze the Green subculture. He describes how the Greens' failure to recognize and come to terms with their own "Shadow" or dark side leads to repression and projection at the group level. This, in turn, contributes to the Greens' difficulties in achieving their goals. Woolpert suggests some innovative methods that transformational groups can use to avoid these dangers and to promote the wholeness of their members.

In conclusion, it will be obvious to the reader that there are substantial differences of opinion, focus, method and style among the contributors to this volume. Therefore, it important to reiterate that diversity (if not paradox) is the *essence* of transformational politics. On the other hand, we believe all the chapters are compatible, synchronistic and highlight the holistic, interdisciplinary and complementary subject of this emergent field. This volume does not attempt to present a comprehensive, step-by-step masterplan of the new paradigm. That is because none can or will ever exist. All we can do is offer guideposts and a glimmer of where we think we are headed as we continue to expand our understanding of ourselves, our work, and the ever-changing, unpredictable universe in which we live. After all, this is the key to what separates transformational politics from much of the rest of the political science discipline.

I

The Theory of Transformational Politics

1

An Overview of the Emerging Political Paradigm: A Web of Transformational Theories

CHRISTA DARYL SLATON

"The Great Question before us is: Can we Change? In Time? and we all desire that Change will come.
. . . And THEORY? How are we to proceed without THEORY? What System of Thought have these Reformers to present to this mad swirling planetary disorganization, to the Inevident Welter of fact, event, phenomena, calamity? . . .
Change? Yes, we must change, only show me the Theory. . ."

Tony Kushner, *Angels in America*

Introduction

We are living in a time of extraordinary change whether we choose it or not. Forces of change act upon us even as we cling to the "security" of the past. Political systems, once powerful and entrenched, are collapsing—often through nonviolent uprisings of masses of citizens, such as in the Soviet Union, South Africa, Iran, and the Philippines. Americans rejoiced at the disintegration of the Soviet Union. Many interpreted the downfall as proof that the American economic and political system was superior to the communist state and that the United States could truly lead the world as the last remaining superpower.

3

For all the feelings of grandeur Americans experienced when they saw the Berlin Wall dismantled, the fact is Americans are extremely disenchanted with their own political system. Only about 50 percent of Americans vote in presidential elections, 35–40 percent in congressional, and turnout for elections at the local level is usually below 30 percent. Lest anyone interpret low voter turnout as voter satisfaction with the status quo, one needs to examine survey data that has indicated consistently for the last three decades that large percentages of Americans believe politicians do not really care what they think. In spite of built-in electoral advantage, a significant number of powerful incumbents suffered defeat or greatly reduced support in the 1994 national elections.

Even conservatives advocate major constitutional reform to address flaws in the political system. Third-party challenges, such as the Green Party and the Reform Party, are gathering strength at the local and national level. Antigovernment groups are gaining strength and getting more bold (and often violently destructive) in their challenges to governmental power and authority.

Public dissatisfaction has been documented and discussed in a variety of recent popular books, such as E. J. Dionne's *Why American's Hate Politics*, David Osborne and Ted Gaebler's *Reinventing Government*, Kevin Phillip's *Arrogant Capital* and *The Politics of Rich and Poor*. It is the contention of this text that public discontent is not merely a reflection of dissatisfaction with policy decisions, political leaders, or political institutions. Its roots are much deeper, even global (Sartori 1994) and its implications are far more profound. Americans themselves are questioning and often rejecting the tenets of liberalism—the philosophical grounding for the American political system and way of life.

The thesis of this book is that the world is in a period of radical transformation—a time of turbulence, change, and uncertainty. Not only are political systems being recreated but deeply held basic values are being reexamined and fundamental epistemological and ontological questions are being posed and answered anew. What do we know? How do we know it? What is the origin and nature of existence? What does it all mean?

This chapter explores the theoretical underpinnings of the politics in this period of upheaval and uncertainty. Briefly addressing some of the inadequacies in the prevailing political theories, the chapter focuses on the components of a nascent theory of transformational politics.

As will be revealed in the following discussion, a theory of transformational politics is a web of theories, ranging from ancient to novel. The theory articulated in this book is a complex network of interwoven parts. As such, it is a theory that is evolving and mutable. Yet it has form and substance that offers a useful guide for understanding where we have been, where we are now, and where we are (or should be) going.

This introductory chapter weaves the theories together to demonstrate connections and integration. Contributions in this section highlight the theoretical approach of scholars who identify themselves as transformational political scientists. While each chapter focuses on particular theoretical nodes in the web, such as chaos, ecofeminism, archetypal analysis, and democracy, all are compatible with each other and provide critical links in the web. And while each scholar embraces a holistic approach to study, each also provides particular expertise to emphasize the intricacy and complexity of the web.

Where Have We Been? Origins of Modern Scientific Thought

"In everything there is a portion of everything."

Anaxagoras, 460 B.C.

As Louis Herman discusses in chapter 2, a theory of transformational politics must consider the democratic underpinnings in our primal past. We learn from the "shamanic religion of Paleolithic and contemporary hunter gatherers and the Socratic search for the 'best way to live.'" In examining where we have been, however, this essay will focus on the origins and influences of modern scientific thought that have profoundly shaped our view of the universe and how we seek answers to questions we pose. It will also emphasize how the tenets of modern thinking have trapped us and precluded us from examining important phenomena, raising new questions, and taking different paths in our journey of discovery.

Nearly four centuries ago, Francis Bacon was at the forefront of a changing worldview or paradigm shift. Writing in a time of the scientific discoveries of Copernicus and Galileo, Bacon challenged the prevailing orthodoxy, which relied on religious leaders and divine guidance as revealed through the church hierarchy for an understanding of the universe and the roles of humans in it. Bacon wanted to discard the theories of ancient and contemporary philosophers and theologians by establishing a naturalistic, materialistic philosophy that would become "a kind of second Scripture" (Bacon 1960, 282).

Knowledge, according to Bacon, can *only* be attained by what the eyes can see. By painstakingly recording observations with great precision, Bacon proposed that one could "proceed regularly and gradually from one axiom to another, so that the most general are not reached till the last" (Bacon 1960, 20). This process would "establish progressive stages of certainty" (33). Using the mind as a controlled "machine," Bacon hoped to "open a new way for understanding" and an "Improvement in *man's* estate and an enlargement of *his power over nature*" (35, 267).

Embracing the patriarchy of the church, Bacon viewed nature as feminine. Nature/She is imperfect, capricious, and dangerous and must be "constrained and molded by art and human ministry. . . . For in things artificial nature [she] takes orders from man and works under his authority, without man, such things would never have been made" (Bacon 1960, 273). Left "free" and unconstrained by man, Nature\She would make "errors" and would not serve the needs of man. Bacon argues that "the main object is to make nature [her] serve the business and convenience of man" (180).

The goal of man's inquiry, according to Bacon, is certainty and the path to certainty must be cleared of the worthless citations of antiquated philosophies, "superstitious stories," unreplicated curiosities, and "experiments of ceremonial magic." His method is to wipe the slate clean and create a new philosophy based on none of the teachings of the past, but founded exclusively on the slow process of induction.

Science throughout the Enlightenment continued to build on Bacon's assumed first principles and presented a comprehensive worldview, replete with laws of nature that include the basic nature of humans, how humans relate to their environment, and how and what kinds of sociopolitical structures humans create. This worldview was also enhanced by Rene Descartes' mind/matter dualism and Sir Isaac Newton's vision of the universe as mechanical and predictable. Knowledge comes through breaking the whole down to its smallest parts and placing the parts in isolation for careful observation to be recorded objectively. Newtonian theory posits that such observation and study will reveal a world of certainty, order, structure, status, and determinism.

Martin Landau argues that this eighteenth century cosmological formula became so powerful that "Newton became not so much the name of a man as of an infallible world outlook" (Landau 1961, 338). The mechanistic Newtonian world with its reductionist strategy, as Gus diZerega argues, came to dominate the social sciences as well as the natural sciences (diZerega 1991, 66). James Dator and several other social researchers maintain that this worldview still prevails in the twentieth century and that it determines not only the methods of study but serves as the foundation of certain political institutions and validates certain predominant political behavior (Dator 1984; Becker 1991; Tribe 1991; Slaton 1992).

The Renaissance Period, however, was a time of more than change in natural scientific thought. In a presentation at a 1992 international conference in Ontario, Nicole Morgan argued in her keynote address that during the Renaissance there was extraordinary chaos and collapse as well as change and innovation. Budding capitalism encouraged global mercantilism and the breakdown of traditional land-based economies. There was widespread social chaos that led to despair and destruction. And of course, a new political philosophy emerged.

Machiavelli wrote his classic advice in the *Prince* about how to succeed in maintaining power. His method of the study of power was to compartmentalize political knowledge as a separate discipline with its own precepts. His precepts were based on a primarily negative view of human nature that saw self-interest as the motivating factor in behavior. While many today find Machiavelli's advise to the prince offensive, many of those active in the political arena embrace it as the "gospel."

One of the more prominent philosophies was developed in the work of Thomas Hobbes. His method à la Bacon, was to establish clarity and certainty in understanding human behavior. Each human emotion was to be defined precisely and explained. Through a meticulous deductive method he took man from the state of nature—"a state of war of all against all"— and led him to the ideal political system—hereditary monarchy. Following his logic, one could arrive at only one conclusion: iron-fist rule by one was the only way to keep the peace.

Later John Locke, a personal friend of Newton's, offered a view of human nature more complex than Hobbes. While humans may be driven by selfish interests, Locke explained that their reason could also lead them to define their interests in broader terms. One may use reason to conclude that the more the good of the whole is advanced, the more one's own selfish interests can be advanced. Locke's views of human nature and his argument that legitimate government is the result of the consent of the governed who decide the role and powers of government are central tenets of present-day liberalism and the theory of modern representative democracy.

Where Are We? Questioning the Certainty of Principles of Modern Science

With such a "scientific philosophy and epistemology, it was not surprising that twentieth century social science became dominated by theories, methodology, and interpretations established in the natural sciences (Uphoff 1992). Rational choice theory, for example, with its roots in utilitarian philosophy and classical economics, presents a model of the self-interested, rational actor (Riker and Ordeshook 1973). The rational actor in this model is a passive information processor who has undistorted knowledge of an objective reality (Woolpert 1984). This social science theory is fundamentally derived from Newtonian physics which, as Laurence Tribe explains, views objects as acting "on each other across the expanse of a neutral, undifferentiated space in an objective and knowable manner, according to simple physical laws that seemed to explain observed reality without requiring much further reflection about the basic structure of the universe" (Tribe 1991, 171). Social scientists studying behavior adopt the empirical approach of the physical sciences. Therefore, "the only external evidence of what people want is what they do . . . When words and actions differ . . . the behaviorist position is to believe the inferences from action" (Riker and Ordeshook 1973, 21) Riker states: "We need no theory of human nature—it only confuses us . . . To bring in psychological considerations . . . distracts us from our business, which is the study of what is said and done, not the study of reasons for saying and doing" (Riker 1962, 22).

In sum, scientists applying rational choice theory have determined the laws of human behavior *a priori*. Such laws allow the application of cause and effect determinism and require purely objective and detached study by the scientist in determining and explaining human behavior. All action of actors that do not fit the rational theory model are actions of irrational actors or deviant cases that do not diminish the validity of the model.

Steve Woolpert counters such theories with Abraham Maslow's self-actualization theory. He argues that to study and understand politics, one must study political motives and recognize that politics is not purely a function of reason, but also of psychological needs (Woolpert 1984). It is clearly oversimplification to say that the desire to win in politics is always rational. For instance, liberation movements are not just attempts to win power, but are also attempts to meet people's need for equal standing, respect, and esteem. Indeed, Woolpert argues that as physical and psychological needs are met, actors' behaviors become less predictable, opportunistic, and expedient.

Democratic theorist Benjamin Barber represents a number of social scientists who argue that Newtonian physics provides a shaky foundation for liberal democratic theories of knowledge and political institutions. Barber posits in *Strong Democracy* that classic liberalism rests on an unprovable axiom—humans are material beings.

Barber argues that the worldview that establishes materialism as an axiom produces some questionable corollaries. Also, challenges to the "givens" of the materialist axiom and its corollaries are ignored or dismissed peremptorily, which has stymied political science and the development of more relevant and significant theory. As a result important, nonmaterial phenomena continue to be ignored, marginalized, or studied in the same way by most scholars without a recognition that the existing theory and methods that fail to explain them arise out of a limited and inadequate paradigm. In fact, in his view liberalism is wrought with "pretensions to objectivity and philosophical certainty that have proven inimical to practical reason and to participatory political activity" (Barber 1984, 29).

So, if modern mainstream political institutions and thought are grounded on erroneous, incomplete dogma, which helps account for their increasing failure, where do we go from here?

Where Are We Going? Towards a Theory of Transformational Politics

The answer is to seek a new paradigm that incorporates change as a major variable. Thomas Kuhn's *The Structure of Scientific Revolutions* discusses how changing paradigms define the growth of scientific study of all natural phenomena. According to Kuhn all sciences transform themselves by transcending a period of "normal science." During periods of "normal science," Kuhn states research is "firmly based upon one or more past scientific achievements, achievements that some particular scientific community acknowledges for a time as supplying the foundation for its further practice" (Kuhn 1970, 10).

While "normal science" prevails, Kuhn argues, scientists do not look for new phenomena, they do not invent new theories, and they are often intolerant of those who do (Kuhn 1970, 24). However, all paradigms, according to Kuhn, have defects in that they narrow the focus of research and drastically reduce vision. Due largely to the defects, all scientific paradigms fail to produce answers to some phenomena. As the number and significance of these failures mount, confidence in the prevailing paradigm is shaken. This is a period "regularly marked by frequent and deep debates over legitimate methods, problems, and standards of solution" (47). Kuhn notes, the emergence of a new paradigm does not end the debates. Thus, it is so here, as we try to seek a "transformational political theory." Manfred Halpern argues in chapter 3 that persons moving through the "core drama of life"—transformation—are throughout their lives accepting the status quo, challenging it, and then creating alternative visions.

We are now in a period where confidence in the liberal paradigm has been undergoing profound challenge to its foundation. While most mainstream democratic theorists continue to hale the advancements of liberal, representative democracy that occurred during the reign of a paradigm and worldview shaped by Newtonian physics, many others have recognized its fundamental limitations and are demanding a dramatic change.

Several major challenges to the validity of that traditional political theory arose in the 1960s. Women demanded more than the right to vote. They demanded equality. African-Americans fought to overturn America's de facto apartheid system. Students took to the streets to challenge the elitist nature of the "establishment." Technology transformed the reporting of news, particularly the coverage of war and civil protest. This upheaval shattered what Samuel Huntington called American society's "broad consensus on democratic, liberal, egalitarian values" (Crozier and others 1975, 112). Huntington concluded that the United States was suffering from an "excess of democracy" and that what was needed was a "greater degree of moderation in democracy" (113). The demands of women, racial minorities, and young were "overloading the political system" and if the democratic system were to function properly, there needed to be some "measure of apathy and noninvolvement on the part of some individuals and groups" (114).

Huntington's views epitomized the intolerance of those tied to an old paradigm or to the "normal science" of the day. The 1960s activists challenged the prevailing definitions and practices of traditional, liberal democracy. Huntington's answer was to return to the normalcy, predictability, and safety of the paradigm that many began to see as obsolete.

Many of those leading the discussion of the antiquated aspects of the political system and identifying emerging trends came outside of the academic community or from those deviants in the academic community whom their colleagues tried to marginalize as being "radical," "unscientific," "emotional," or "demagogues." Best sellers began to emerge that rejected the rigidity and narrowness of "establishment" American political thought. Citizens found intriguing questions, analyses, and directions in books by nonacademics such as Alvin and Heidi Toffler (*Future Shock* and *The Third Wave*); Fritjof Capra (*The Turning Point* and *The Tao of Physics*); Marilyn Ferguson (*The Aquarian Conspiracy*), Hazel Henderson (*The Politics of the Solar Age*); Betty Friedan (*The Feminine Mystic*); E. F. Schumacher (*Small is Beautiful*); John Naisbitt (*Megatrends*), and Mark Satin (*New Age Politics*).

Scholars, too, began to redefine the parameters of study and the methods employed. Many academics with impressive credentials in "normal science" began to break out of the confines of the paradigm. Judicial scholars Theodore Becker (1986) and Glendon Schubert (1989; 1991) focused on teledemocracy and biopolitics, respectively. Lester Milbrath (1989), a major contributor to the study of political participation began to concentrate on environmental sustainability issues. James MacGregor Burns (1978; 1991), a Pulitzer prize winner and extraordinarily successful American government textbook writer, began to develop theories of transformational leadership and to discuss the necessity of redefining "rights." Democratic theorists Ben Barber (1984; 1992), Jane Mansbridge (1980; 1990), and Amitai Etzioni (1993; 1995) launched research in redefining democracy, moving beyond adversarial democracy, and promoting democracy in the age of technology. Feminist theorists, such as Jo Freeman (1995), Catherine MacKinnon (1987; 1989), Carole Pateman (1987; 1988; 1989; 1991), and Irene Diamond (1990) introduced theories that were never given consideration or validity under Newtonian thought. African-American intellectuals Cornel West (1991; 1993; 1994) and bell hooks (1984) followed in the footsteps of W. E. B. Dubois and resisted the confines of traditional liberal intellectualism and broke through boundaries of the academy established by white intellectuals seeing the world only through their particular lenses.

A theory of transformational politics, unlike *all* major political philosophical theories before it, concentrates on the dynamics of change itself and promotes change by challenging all theories and institutions that retard this process of transformation. By doing this, it transforms the worldview that evolved in the seventeenth and eighteenth centuries. Transformational political theory does not replace all that is connected to Newtonian theory and politics. There are occasions when cause-effect determinism exists, predictions are appropriate, order abounds, and inductive reasoning prevails. Indeed as Majid Tehranian points out:

> New scientific metaphors do not replace, and new theories do not refute, the old ones but somehow remake them; even scientific revolutions preserve some continuity with the old order of things. This is as true of theoretical speculations about society as it is of the social system itself. (Tehranian 1979, 141)

The theory of transformational politics that is emerging tries to synthesize the significant political theoretical developments in the last few decades with the theoretical and institutional wisdom of the past, both within and outside of the academy. This nascent paradigm builds on a number of sources, including quantum theory, chaos theory, ecofeminist theory, archetypal theory, empowerment theory, self-actualization theory, participatory democratic theory, and new theories of spirituality to provide guidance to the researchers, theorists, and practitioners of the politics of the twenty-first century.

The Theory of Transformational Politics: Some Patterns
Revealed in the Web of Theories

As stated earlier, the theory of transformational politics is a complex web of connected theories that attempt to supplement and correct the deficiencies in classic liberal theory as we move into a new paradigm. Table 1.1 offers a comparison between the established liberal theory and the ways in which this theory is being transformed by transformational scholars. It is important to note that although the table visually implies contrast, when one carefully examines the components of the transformational theory, one sees that the theory does not entirely reject liberalism. Instead, it merges it with components essential in the emerging paradigm. For in-

Table 1.1
A Comparison of Liberal and Transformational Theories

Liberal Theory	Transformational Theory
cause-effect determinism, certainty, predictability	probability, randomness
objectivity	objectivity/subjectivity
one method of study, or path to Truth	multiple paths to understanding; multiple perceptions of truth
masculine	masculine/feminine
man—master of nature	human—part of nature
constrain and conquer nature	humans nurture and sustain nature as nature nurtures and sustains humans
wipe slate clean and consider only what is proven through scientific method	consider primal past, multi-civilizational approaches to understanding to complement scientific method
induction	induction/deduction/intuition
humans as material beings	humans as material and spiritual beings
individualism	individualism/communitarianism
reason	reason/emotion
self-interests	self-interests/common interests/ self-sacrifice
atomism	interconnectedness
isolation	interaction
ends-oriented	process- and ends-oriented
hierarchy	balance
power = dominance over others	power = empowerment of others
strength = assertiveness and aggression	strength = ability to exercise patience and tolerance as well as assertiveness
stasis	change
representative democracy	participatory democracy
thesis-antithesis	analysis/synthesis
adversarial	consensual/mediated
rational choice theory	self-actualization theory
independence	interdependence
one-way communication	networking
assimilation of differences by dominant culture	cooperation among diverse cultures

stance, whereas modern science offers a masculine vision of the universe, the theory of transformational politics seeks a synthesis of masculine and feminine perspectives. As is revealed in the table, transformational political theory seeks to correct the unidimensionality of mechanistic thought.

Integrating Theories from New Scientific Discoveries

Discoveries in quantum physics and the theory of relativity have led scientists to develop principles that explain the failure of significant progression towards certainty that Renaissance thinkers sought to establish (Tribe 1991). As physicist Fritjof Capra explains in *The Turning Point*, when physicists in the twentieth century began atomic experiments they found the old laws they were following produced paradoxes. It eventually became clear to them that "their basic concepts, their language, and their whole way of thinking were inadequate to describe atomic phenomena" (Capra 1982, 76). Many of the principles derived from quantum theory offer fundamentally improved interpretations and explanations of the world than those advanced by Francis Bacon in the seventeenth century and Sir Isaac Newton in the eighteenth century.

In a similar fashion, some of the more significant quantum principles need to be included as key components of a new social, economic, and political scientific paradigm. Here are several:

UNCERTAINTY. Objects are defined by their environments and their relationship to others. Political theory should question the assumption that humans have a predictable nature and that rationality alone guides the citizen in the pursuit of self-interests. A better explanation is that humans are complex, contradictory creatures that cannot be classified or identified out of the context of relationships or environment.

PROBABILITY. Cause-effect determinism and rational decision making are not at the root of all human interaction, or even primary in human affairs. James Dator concludes that probability and randomness are the norm (Dator 1984, 4). All theories of political behavior must be wary of absolutes and need to embrace probability as being more closely attuned to reality.

INTERCONNECTIONS AND INTERACTION. Dividing the universe, and the political system, into discrete units for analysis will not provide complete understanding. Instead inquiry should recognize the effects of interactions and process. Tehranian points out that democracy is a dynamic, moving process (Tehranian 1979, 52). Democracy is not an institution or an end that can be best understood through mathematical formulas of voting behavior by citizens or legislators, but is a complicated process of interaction and deliberation among citizens (Mansbridge 1980; 1990).

No Objective Reality. The important lesson from quantum theory for political theorists and empirical political scientists is that there is no objective real world apart from one's consciousness. It is essential to keep in mind that our observations, no matter how precise, are affected by our own concepts, thoughts, and values that vary with each individual and under varying circumstances. In other words, subjectivity always influences our objectivity.

Transformational social scientists, who are influenced by the theories of the natural sciences—in particular, quantum and chaos theories—develop metaphors from the models and concepts of the natural sciences to understand, reconstruct, and reenvision politics. Such practice is as old as the organic metaphors developed by ancient Greeks to study the "body politic" and has been useful throughout the centuries as an aid in understanding social as well as physical phenomena. There is, however, extensive criticism of such practice from both natural and social scientists. Criticism ranges from mere warnings to recognize the differences between animate and inanimate objects to ridicule, which calls such efforts "bad pseudoscience" (Beth 1995, 35).

Theodore Becker explains, however, that the political science contributors to his book *Quantum Politics: Applying Quantum Theory to Political Phenomena* do not believe "that the laws of physics strictly govern individual political behavior or should determine its study" (Becker 1991, xii). Nevertheless, each author recognizes the limitations of the Newtonian-inspired paradigm of Western politics and engages in "thought experiments" to apply the principles and concepts of the quantum paradigm. Their value to political scientists is to reconceptualize political science and politics. For instance, my own participatory democratic theory was enriched by applying the quantum principles of interactivity and interconnection rather than merely focusing on participation opportunities and examining barriers to participation. I also began to experiment with random selection of representatives rather than restrict my study to maintaining the highly unrepresentative electoral system designed under a Newtonian paradigm (Slaton 1992). In chapter 4 Barbara Knight discusses how social scientists use models and metaphors from chaos theory to bring feminist principles to the fore and to incorporate them in understanding the transformation of political community.

Constitutional scholar Laurence Tribe addresses the caution most social scientists use when they apply lessons of the physical sciences to social phenomena. He states he is not determined to bring science into law and does not believe there is an "epistemological hierarchy with law perched on a lower rung looking up to its superiors [quantum physics] for guidance" (Tribe 1991, 169). Instead Tribe states:

> I borrow metaphors from physics tentatively . . . to explore the heuristic ramifications for the law; my criterion of appraisal is whether the concepts we might draw from physics promote illuminating questions and direction. I press forward in this endeavor because I believe that reflection upon certain developments in physics can help us hold on to and refine some of our deeper insights into the pervasive and profound role law plays in shaping our society and our lives. (Tribe 1991, 169)

Richard Rubenstein states that "good theory" should make sense of everything around us and tie together events that may seem to have no connection (Rubenstein 1990, 317). Sound theory "reevaluates change-over-time, illuminating the connection and disconnections between past and present, and indicating to what extent the present can be projected into the future. It redefines relationships between thought and its objects and between oneself and others. And, of course, it stimulates new thinking" (317). Theory needs to help us understand the world. And even if theory does not rely on predictability or certainty, after unforeseen events happen, social theory should continue to reformulate to help explain and to more accurately anticipate events of the future.

Linking Past, Present, Future to Sustain the Planet

While transformational political theory integrates scientific discoveries and theories of the seventeenth through the twentieth century, it also reconnects us to our primal past. Louis Herman argues that our quest for understanding must connect us with our "primary pre-scientific life experiences" (chapter 2). Our search for truth must be global as well as multicivilizational. Similarly, Steve Sachs (1993) maintains that in reconceptualizing politics for the twenty-first century, theorists need to consider the pre-Western thought and way of life of Native Americans that Western scientific thought dismissed. In other words, Herman and Sachs emphasize that transformational political science can benefit from looking to the past as well as the future, particularly to overlooked and denigrated cultures that emphasize synthesis and offer a basis for a continuing dialectic on where we have been and where we are going.

While warning against romanticizing Native American culture (or any other culture), Sachs argues that modern theory needs to examine traditional Native American tribal and band societies and recognize the value of their ideas and practices that Western thought rejected—particularly the belief that humans are a part of the natural harmony of the whole of nature, not the masters of nature. Traditional Native American politics is about finding consensus within community. Tribal leaders see power as a means to empower others, not as a vehicle for control. Sachs maintains: "At the heart of [Native American tribal] politics is a set of communal relationships based upon mutual respect emphasizing both the community and the individual, so that in a very important sense the whole is equal to the part" (Sachs 1993, 1).

Biologist Mary Clark's writings consistently argue that Euro-American values have threatened the sustainability of the planet and that what we need to do to survive is to move towards decentralization and local self-sufficiency. Her global vision sets us on "a path emphasizing cooperation rather than competition, diversity rather than uniformity, social bondedness rather than self-centeredness, sacred meaning rather than material consumption" (Clark 1989, xx). Similar themes are echoed in Lester Milbrath's *Envisioning a Sustainable Society* and Vice President Al Gore's *Earth in the Balance: Ecology and the Human Spirit.*

Valuing the Feminine and Seeking Balance

Essential to the concept of harmony in Native American thought is "balance," not homogeneity or uniformity. Scholars learning from primal cultures and those concerned with sustainability are often in agreement with many feminist scholars who dispute modern theories that discount or devalue intuition, spirituality, and subjectivity (Spretnak 1986; Starhawk 1993; Armstrong and Botzler 1993; Warren 1993; Lahar 1993; Russell 1993; Shiva 1993).

The mechanistic world of Bacon and Newton valued the masculine dominance of nature and the feminine and discounted subjectivity and spirituality. This imbalanced worldview has encouraged the exploitation of the planet for man's convenience, and established a hierarchy of values and worths. It is a worldview that, mostly unchecked and unchallenged, has resulted in serious threats to the sustainability of life on the planet. In this world we find that: (a) aggression and force are tools of the strong, whereas humility and accommodation are the trappings of the weak; (b) selfish ambition is prized and leads to power and wealth, whereas selfless generosity often subjects one to exploitation by the greedy; and (c) profit, expansion, money, and power are the ends of those who lead rather than spiritual growth, empowerment of followers, and harmony among equals.

Ecofeminism contributes to transformational theory by addressing the unidimensionality and pitfalls of patriarchal thought and systems and by offering a more balanced worldview that incorporates the value of the feminine. Susan Armstrong and Richard Botzler explain that ecofeminism is a form of feminism that not only seeks to end masculine oppression of women, but also rejects the patriarchy of western science that leads to destruction of nature. Ecofeminism strives to bridge the gap between nature and culture; mind and body; female and male; reason and feeling; theory and practice (Armstrong and Botzler 1993, 432).

Barbara Knight argues in chapter 4 that whereas Newtonian science defined itself with masculine characteristics and identified the male intellect as the objective observer who must manipulate and tame unpredictable nature (feminine), chaos theory is intrigued by the feminine and develops far more complex models that abandon the either/or dualism central to the Newtonian paradigm. The Newtonian approach values only the masculine (equated with order and predictability) and deprecates the feminine (equated with chaos and unpredictability). Knight posits that chaos is not an absence of order, but instead is characteristic of complexity, diversity, interdependence, multiplicity, and cyclic processes. By recognizing feminine ways of knowing and understanding the world (intuition, contextual thinking, collaborative discussion, visions of life as a web of interconnections), chaos theory contributes to transformational political theory, which offers a vision of peaceful change and wholeness.

Recognizing Common Interests and Interdependence

The importance of individuals and their *relationships* is also stressed in ecofeminism. There is a rejection of the dualistic dichotomy between egoism and altruism, and between the self as atomistic or merged. Instead, ecofeminists argue, the self should be understood as being embedded in a network of essential relationships with distinct others (Armstrong and Botzler 1993, 433).

Stephanie Lahar argues that ecofeminism works to bring together the personal, social, and environmental issues in order to transform society (Lahar 1993, 445). As an integrated moral philosophy that combines humanity and nonhuman nature, Lahar points out that ecofeminist theory should be viewed as a living process. In the process of acting politically, ecofeminists should both deconstruct and reconstruct (Lahar 1993, 449–451). This distinguishes transformational political theorists from critical theorists or deconstructionists. While the crits and deconstuctionists do a thorough job of dismantling liberalism, they leave only the debris and cynicism from their destruction. They offer no hope, no vision, no alternative, no improvement.

Emphasizing Creativity and Innovation through Synthesis of Objectivity and Subjectivity

Louis Herman's contribution to transformational political theory, challenges academics to end the "unremitting critique" that leads only to destruction (chapter 2). Transformational theorists need to develop a dialectic between critique and creation; between analysis and synthesis. Manfred Halpern emphasizes the necessity in utilizing creativity in transformation (chapter 3). As we move through the various "Acts of Life"—defined by Halpern as Emanation (Act I), Incoherence (Act II), and Transformation (Act III)—Halpern contends we need to remain critically conscious as well as creative and caring in choosing what we accept and reject from the past and developing new strategies for moving into the future.

Transformational theorists make no pretense to pure objectivity. Indeed, they argue for a value-based (Rensenbrink 1992; Rohter 1992), morally-grounded (Lahar 1993) theory guided by compassion (Halpern chapter 3) that seeks to define the "good life" (Herman chapter 2). Yet description and definition alone are inadequate in transformational theory. Praxis—the wedding of theory and action—is also central to theories of transformation.

Developing Praxis that Enhances Democracy and Moves Towards Consensus

In chapter 5 Daniel Graham discusses a nascent international political movement, the Green Movement, that exemplifies how one acts politically when embracing the theories of transformational politics. Graham states: "The ecocentric paradigm of the Greens creates a 'new' (renewed) framework to evaluate the role of economics, science, technology, culture, epistemology, ideology, and spirituality in political/social transformation." His chapter discusses how the Green Movement (and later the Green political parties) began with the formulation of basic values that provided the foundation for political action.

It is noteworthy that several of those most active in Green Party politics in the United States have been political scientists who have rejected the classic liberal illusion of the detached scientist studying political phenomena. Theorists John Rensenbrink, Irene Diamond, and Louis Herman develop political strategies based on their theories and fine tune their theories through what they learn in their political activism. Likewise, Betty Zisk uses her in-depth knowledge of the history, key figures, and peak events to analyze Greens and other political activists to present a richness rarely found by the "detached" (and often clueless) observer. Green political scientists Tony Affigne, Ira Rohter, and Christopher Jones have lived in the "real" political world and understood it through their intellectual as well as activist lenses. When they teach students about politics, they have the "real world" experience to enrich the discussions.

The organized section on Ecological and Transformational Politics in the American Political Science Association states that its purpose is to "explore those trends in contemporary life that are challenging the viability of traditional divisions in political science and political life (normative/empirical; personal/professional; theory/practice; Liberal/Conservative; Left/Right; global/local; secular/spiritual . . . *We are committed to examining alternatives that seek a new synthesis*" (Schwerin 1995, 3). Members of the section seek concrete alternatives that would transform political systems and processes. Theodore Becker's discussion of teledemocracy in chapter 12 explores how modern technology can be used to develop a more democratic, interactive, and consensus-oriented political system—one that would go beyond reform by truly empowering citizens.

In the last few years, Becker and I have worked alongside others—Hazel Henderson, Duane Elgin, Amitai Etzioni—to develop electronic town meetings that are based on the democratic values of the traditional New England town meeting. Rather than seeing technology as an evil to be resisted, our research has focused on ways in which community, participation, dialogue, respect for diversity, and enlightened policy-making can be developed through technology that is employed by neutral facilitators working towards consensus.

Balancing Rights and Responsibilities

One of the strongest held tenets of liberalism is individualism. Yet how does one build community essential to democracy, according to theorist John Dewey, when each citizen is pursuing his or her self-interests? In a paper presented to the 1995 American Political Science Association Annual Conference, William Caspary astutely utilizes Dewey's theories to direct transformational political scientists on this topic. The task is daunting in an American society that has overwhelmed its court system with citizens asserting their rights.

Amitai Etzioni (1993; 1995), an early advocate of electronic town meetings, has worked with other scholars and leaders recently in developing the burgeoning communitarian movement in the United States. One of the major principles of communitarianism is that in democratic societies, citizens not only have rights, but also responsibilities. Communitarians contribute to transformational political theory by helping us understand that if we want the benefits of government, and we want a say in how government is run, we must be responsible citizens who recognize we also have obligations to others. The American Greens echo the same theme in the pillars of their philosophy that emphasizes social and personal responsibility and respect for diversity.

The United States is the homeland of many diverse cultures. Except for Native Americans who were displaced, all Americans are descendants of immigrants. No one nation or culture can legitimately claim title to the land or dictate to others. Earlier in our history we embraced the image of "the melting pot," where diverse cultures blend into one. This metaphor was never really accurate. In the 1990s, transformational social scientists are arguing it is not even desirable. Our diversity is our richness. Through respecting diversity we can open our eyes to new understandings and develop creative ways of dealing with difficulties. As Halpern points out in chapter 3 our multiculturalism helps us become whole, rather than partial, selves. Halpern argues that transformation entails our learning to open ourselves to others—to the unfamiliar.

Empowering Ourselves and Others

Edward Schwerin's book *Mediation, Citizen Empowerment and Transformational Politics* analyzes several political movements and their theoretical grounding to develop a theory of empowerment that is a "core concept or value" of transformational theory and politics (Schwerin 1995, 6). The synthesis that leads to his definition of empowerment emerges from theorists in quantum theories (Becker 1991; Slaton 1992); transformational leadership (Burns 1978; Fishel 1992; Couto 1993); individual transformation (Halpern 1991; Abalos 1993); communitarianism (Bellah 1985; Barber 1992; Etzioni 1993); teledemocracy (Becker 1991; Slaton 1992); strong and mass partici-patory democracy (Barber 1984; Mansbridge 1993); and spirituality (Spretnak 1986; McLaughlin and Davidson 1994) .

He also examines political movements and trends that began to emerge in the 1960s to challenge the prevailing paradigms and polit-ical institutions. Empowerment is found at the heart of many of these movements—Green (Capra and Spretnak 1984; Slaton and Becker 1990; Rensenbrink 1992; Rohter 1992); environmental (Mil-brath 1989); feminist (Kelly 1989; Starhawk 1993); peace (Zisk 1992) new age (Satin 1979; Bookchin 1986; Spangler 1988); neopopulist (Boyte 1980; Boyte and Reissman 1986; Bellah and others 1985; Reissman 1986); and conflict resolution (Burton and Dukes 1990). Schwerin concludes that empowerment is grounded in the values of "self-sufficiency, personal competence, mass political participation, community involvement, social responsibility, human freedom and dignity, and cultural diversity,"—all nodes already described as part of the web of transformational theory. (Schwerin 1995, 165)

Steve Woolpert's examination of self-actualization theories arising out of humanistic psychology emphasizes the same themes and values of empowerment. Citing Carl Rogers' work in human growth and Abraham Maslow's theory of human development, Woolpert depicts a transformational society as one in which there is "movement away from dependency and toward the fulfillment of po-tential" (Woolpert 1984, 57). In such a "healthy" society:

> "personal well-being and political well-being go hand in hand. Such a society encourages its citizens to be open to experience, to discover and pursue their own preferences, and to join together to achieve their common goals. Authenticity, tolerance of diversity, and inter-personal understanding are highly valued." (Woolpert 1984, 57)

Conclusion

Kuhn states that new paradigms emerge for two reasons. First, the paradigm has produced achievements that are "sufficiently un-precedented to attract an enduring group of adherents *away* from competing modes of scientific study." Second, the paradigm is "suffi-ciently *open-minded to leave all sorts of problems for the redefined group of practitioners to resolve"* (Kuhn 1970, 10, emphasis mine).

Transformational political theorists are offering guides to reex-amine our study and to ask different questions as we journey on a truth quest to discover who we are, where we have been, and where we want to go. As with all paradigms, there are likely to be errors and gaps in the emerging epistemology. And clearly, there is not uni-versal consensus on the components of the theory or its methods of inquiry. Yet as this volume indicates, there is a growing consensus and synthesis arising in both the physical and social sciences that legitimize this fundamentally new way of looking at old and emerg-ing phenomena. The test remains: Can transformational theory pro-vide fresh answers, novel insights, and innovative approaches not found in theories grounded in Newtonian thought? As the next two sections of this book indicate, there are increasing numbers of polit-ical scientists testing the theory to answer this question.

2

A Theory for Transforming Political Science: The Truth Quest as a Paradigm for Politics

LOUIS HERMAN

Introduction

During the last few decades a growing number of scholars and popular writers have been integrating a vast interdisciplinary scholarship, mapping dimensions of what we could call a crisis in the ruling paradigm of political order (Ferguson 1980; Henderson 1981; Bookchin 1986; Berman 1984, Satin 1979, Capra and Spretnak 1984, W. I. Thompson 1971, 1985; Quinn 1992). Most of these writers formulate their constructive response as part of "a new paradigm of politics," and more or less explicitly apply the conceptual framework of Thomas S. Kuhn's groundbreaking historiography of science (1970). Despite a vast literature analyzing, criticizing and deconstructing virtually every sentence of Kuhn's *Structure of Scientific Revolutions*, his basic categories, loosely understood, are still enormously helpful in formulating an epistemology for transformational politics.

Kuhn's speculations on a discipline of "revolutionary" or "extraordinary" science (as opposed to the paradigm-dependent "normal science") suggest the possibility of a 'metaparadigm' for facilitating creative transformation. In the case of politics, such a discipline of paradigm critique and construction could help avoid the barbarism associated with 'paradigm paralysis'—fanaticism, the rule of tyrants, and a stupefied and submissive citizenry. It also offers the possibility of nonviolent social transformation through a process of collective creativity.

My contention is that such an extraordinary political science has always been a part of the deepest dimension of political thinking; that it is rooted in the archaic *Urreligion* of shamanism; and that crucial aspects of such a discipline are formalized in the Socratic 'method' (the search for the "Good Life"), clarified by Eric Voegelin as the "truth quest." In this chapter I argue that the contemporary reconstitution of the quest itself constitutes the core of a new paradigm for politics. The connection between the search for, and living, the Good Life is evident in many archaic and contemporary hunter gatherers, and some related horticulturalists and pastoralists. Quinn's *Ishmael* identifies such societies as "leavers," lovers of life, who struggled to live lightly, in harmony with a sacralized community of nature. I prefer the term "primal," since such societies live close to the memory of humanity's recent emergence from the natural world and exemplify a common politics based on a wisdom that remembers this origin. From this perspective the history of civilization begins with "domination at home and conquest abroad" as the anthropologist Stanley Diamond (1974) puts it. As the quest is removed from the life of the individual, and the individual removed from an experience of wilderness as sacred creation, so the history of civilization has produced a succession of reified paradigms of the Good Life—culminating in the murderous "-isms" of modernity. From this perspective the genius of the classical Greek polis appears to be less an anticipation of modernity than a struggle to hold on to a primal wisdom.

Finally I will suggest that today we see intimations of a return of the quest in some of the more visionary trends in transformational politics. The trends that I argue are rooted in a primal epistemology are: political and economic decentralization; self-sufficient, sustainable and community-based economics; minimization of the division of labor; cultivation of the whole person; participatory democracy; and a spiritual revival based on the resacralization of nature.

The Quest: Components of an Extraordinary Politics

Reflection on "The Full Amplitude of Human Experience"

By definition an extraordinary political science cannot be content to function within the ruling paradigm's intellectual division of labor. The creative revolutionary thinkers in science are often newcomers to a field, mavericks, even 'amateurs' who have a familiarity with worlds of experience beyond the pale of the ruling paradigm. The new paradigm tends to persuade by being more inclusive. It asks and answers questions at a more fundamental level than the old paradigm. This is even more apparent when the domain of inquiry is "the Good Life," since nothing relevant to "life" can in principle be excluded from consideration. Yet no one can know it all. Opening the science of politics to what Voegelin calls "the full amplitude of human experience" helps inoculate it from becoming "normal science," ideological handmaid to the ruling paradigm. An extraordinary science of politics would be democratizing, since every individual has some unique experience of life to contribute to the collective quest. The shaman's search for harmony with the community of being leads, through the shamanic figure of Socrates, to Plato's notion of the Royal Art of philosophy as ascertaining the appropriate relationship between all the other arts in order for life as a whole to be lived in balance.

The Dialectical Exploration of the Human Condition

Voegelin discovered, through his monumental cross-civilizational meditation on history, an initiating experience at the core of the quest. This is the realization of the essential paradox of the human condition: that we are capable of knowledge and choice, yet recognize that this very capacity, constitutive of our humanness, is itself a product of a larger essentially unknowable universe. We find ourselves playing a part in a drama whose beginning and end are inevitably mysterious. This experience of swimming in an ocean of mystery is fundamental to shamanism and shared by the world's mystical traditions. Voegelin uses Plato's term *metaxy* to describe this as the human condition, and then differentiates from it both the experience of the sacred and the paradoxical structure of consciousness-language-reality, the truth quest.

Very briefly, Voeglin's formulation of the paradox of living in the *metaxy* can be put as follows: subjective consciousness, which knows objective reality, is an integral part of that same reality from which it separates itself through the act of knowing.[1] Consequently all of human knowledge—each symbol representing "reality"—has a contradictory relation to experience: the symbol both is and is not the experience symbolized. In addition each symbol needs to be understood in dynamic relationship to its contradiction—"what it is not." Thus as 'hot' needs to be understood in relation to 'cold', so the sacred needs to be understood in relation to the mundane, civilization to wilderness, and all symbols in relation to the wordless experience symbolized. This is the metaphysical foundation for Socrates insisting that the Royal road to truth is through the dialectic: small group face-to-face discussion. Well intentioned disagreement heightens awareness among the discussants of the gap between experience and language. Discussants can then explore the "In-Between" through the endless give and take of thesis, antithesis and synthesis. The notion of living in the "In-Between" helps us understand 'ourselves in the world' through the movement of thought between the poles of binary oppositions. Similarly, Carl Jung's depth psychology is based on a dialectic between what is conscious and unconscious, leading to his understanding of the dynamics of the shadow (see Woolpert's chapter 15).

The Cosmic Creation Story

Knowledge claims relevant to the quest need to be formulated into the structure of a story. The birth, growth, and death of individuals, like civilizations, suns and galaxies, require the structure of storytelling. Narrative, unlike theory, describes *developmental processes over time*, and needs to be recognized as a fundamental unit of human cognition in the search for meaning. The modern cosmologist Brian Swimme (1984) points out that there are no societies without "cosmic creation stories." C. G. Jung echoed this in an interview late in his life when he remarked: "Man has always lived in the myth. And we are able to be born today and live in no myth and without history. That is a mutilation of the human being." Recent scholarship in comparative mythology and religion suggests that sacred mythic narratives of traditional societies function like Wolin's "paradigms of the good life"—symbolic representations of an ordered whole responding to the questions of ultimate concern: "Where do we come from? Who are we? Where should we go?" Quinn's novel *Ishmael*, (1992), succeeds in part because of its integration of Socratic dialogue and the persuasiveness of mythic narrative. Cosmic creation stories function like political paradigms by providing the larger context in relation to which individual action, policies, and social institution gain meaning. Voegelin emphasizes that the discovery of the "truth quest" itself establishes a 'before' and 'after' and can only be represented by the symbolism of the story. Swimme sums it up well: the story is "the fundamental unit of intelligibility for advanced hominid intelligence" (Swimme 1987, 83).

Abandoning the Quest

All paradigms tend to repress "extraordinary science" in favor of rule-guided "normal science." One of the peculiarities of modernity is the degree of precision with which it identified and categorically excommunicated various components of extraordinary politics—the quest. Liberalism as the definitively modern political philosophy, connected political authority to the demonstrable certainty of empirical science. In doing so it replaced the quest as an ongoing, self-reflective, philosophical meditation on human history, with a rationality that could predictably manipulate the regularities of nature. Thus Locke, one of the major architects of Liberalism, cast himself as a mere "under-laborer" to the "incomparable Mr. (Isaac) Newton" (Locke 1690/1964, 58). The disastrous consequences of elevating science into the exclusive model for "certain knowledge" have been extensively explored. Yet at the heart of the metaphysics of modernity is a process whose impact is still imperfectly understood—the categorical desacralization of nature (what Voegelin calls a "deformation" of the metaxic structure of human existence).

Cartesian-Newtonian metaphysics is the philosophical culmination of a process of domination that probably began about ten thousand years ago during the Neolithic revolution. It erected an absolute boundary between on the one hand, "real" mathematizable, measurable, objective experiences in the outer world and on the other hand, those emotional, subjective, confusing and therefore unknowable, experiences of the inner world. The rewards were conspicuous—attainment of what Descartes called "absolutely certain knowledge" and thus "mastery and possession of nature." However, if inner life is absolutely separated from outer, it would suggest that mind, the inner subjective principle, must be absolutely separated from body; soul from matter; the human from the animal; wilderness from civilization; and God from the world. Since this dualistic metaphysics was derived from a program of domination, it inevitably cast one partner in each binary opposition as superior. As the *metaxy* was forgotten, a complementary dialectic between humanity and nature was replaced by dualistic opposition; a sacred transaction became unremitting warfare—the domestication of wilderness.[2]

Contemporary social inquiry, like the rest of modern life, has been constructed within this dualistic, materialistic metaphysics. Analysis, the fundamental act of cutting the world into measurable entities—the act of categorizing, erecting boundaries and thus set-

ting up dualities—has become an ubiquitous methodological imperative. Even those trendy opponents of modernity, the "postmodern" deconstructionists perpetuate this Cartesian legacy by undialectically
totalizing critique. They set one pole in the binary opposition of cri-
tique-construction to rule absolutely over the other. Critical analysis
has split itself off from, and set itself to rule over, its opposite—synthesis. Wholes are dissected into parts with very little energy being
given to the task of integrating the fragments into meaningful patterns. 'Stories' have been relegated to the realm of entertainment.
Without narrative as a mode of cognition, unique developmental
processes become meaningless. In short, 'progress' in knowledge has
come to mean the proliferation of ever more precise concepts drawing
ever more refined distinctions between ever smaller fragments of the
world. For universities the metaphysics of modernity have meant the
multiplication of microspecialties and the marginalization of those
wishing to build bridges across boundaries, make connections, and
construct meaning. Although there are encouraging signs of change,
Gabriel Almond's lament is still substantially true of mainstream
political science: ". . . a loose aggregation of special interests, held together by shared avarice in maintaining or increasing the depart-
mental share of resources" (Almond 1990, 35).

Although few societies have built in rewards for questioning the
legitimacy of their foundations, I will argue that primal societies
have gone further than most in institutionalizing the quest. Despite
its current exclusion, the quest tends to persist in the fundamental
structure of human consciousness, emerging in the work of artists,
prophets, mystics, and creative political thinkers. Even Liberal
thought reproduces the spirit of the quest in its rejection of unquestioned authority and its celebration of individual freedom and unfet-
tered thought.

The Primal Art of Political Philosophy

Shamanic Exploration of the "In-Between"

The roots of the quest can be traced back to shamanism, a tradition of healing, theatrical performance and divination rooted in
the *Urreligion* of the Upper Paleolithic. The scholar of comparative
religion Mercea Eliade had demonstrated a remarkable consistency
in the shamanic practices of all cultures and all ages (Eliade 1964).
The German anthropologist Hans Peter Duerr (1985) observed that

shamanic traditions all have in common a dialectical discipline: the struggle to 'dissolve,' 'remove,' 'shatter,' 'move across,' or 'sit astride' the barriers between culture and wilderness.[3] The reason the ancients made this journey, Duerr explains, was because they recognized the fundamental tension of the human condition; that: ". . . their cultural nature was only one side of their being which by destiny was inextricably bound to their animal *fylgja* (soul), visible only to him who stepped across the dividing line, entrusting himself to his 'second sight' " (64). Thus Duerr points out that we are naive when we think of werewolves as fantastic humans who suddenly start growing carnasials and sprouting tufts of fur under their shirt cuffs. Rather they are like Hesse's Steppenwolf:

> . . . persons who are able to *dissolve* 'within themselves' the boundary between civilization and wilderness . . . These are people who can look their 'animal nature' in the eye, something usually kept under lock and key in their culture, and in this way can develop a consciousness of their 'cultural nature'. (Duerr 1985, 86)

Shamanic "boundary crossing" has a characteristically transcendent, ecstatic (*ex stasis* or "out of body") quality.[4] Mircea Eliade goes so far as to define shamanism in terms of this experience, as indicated by the title of his early work: *Shamanism: Archaic Techniques of Ecstasy*. Shamanic disciplines can be understood as psychotechnologies for dialectical shifts of consciousness. Like Voegelin's philosopher, the shaman's search takes place as a movement of awareness between the experiential poles of the metaxic duality— the "In-Between" of civilization and wilderness. Much of modern intellectual life involves "out of body" experiences, however few academics can make the journey back and forth smoothly. Too many remain stuck out of body, disconnected from their earthly roots.

Cartesian dualism confines modern necromancy to communion with our dead ancestors through imaginative exploration of library stacks. Shamanism by contrast connects the modern scholar to a tradition that includes the most exotic profusion of psychotechnologies. Voegelin's "full amplitude of human experience" is extended to include the world of animals, plants and nature.[5] Yet in psychoanalytic terms both the political philosopher and the shaman are involved in the same process: consciously assaulting (or deconstructing) the walls of everyday ego awareness (the socially constructed self or personality); an experience that as Jung pointed out can be simultaneously terrifying, humbling, and ecstatic. He noted that the encounter with the unconscious is intrinsically numinous, and helps order the life of the seeker by placing the daily projects of manipulation and control in a larger sacred context.

As one might expect, primal 'economics'—living in the lap of mother nature—softens the boundary between ego and Id, civilization and wilderness, and makes possible a more direct equivalence between the experience of wilderness within and wilderness without. Thus Ohiyesa (Charles Eastman), a traditional Santee Dakota physician, notes that the awareness of sacred creation can be spontaneous and widely accessible: "Whenever in the course of the daily hunt the red hunter comes upon a scene that is strikingly beautiful or sublime—a black thundercloud with the rainbow's glowing arch above the mountain, white waterfall in the heart of a green gorge; a vast prairie tinged with the blood-red of sunset—he pauses . . . in the attitude of worship" (Ohiyesa 1971, 36). Standing Bear, one of the first Native Americans to write in English, confirms that "no place was humble to the Lakota . . . *There was nothing between him and the Big Holy*" (Standing Bear 1978, 256, emphasis added).

Most of the world's mystical traditions cultivate a similar experience of the sacredness of creation and its power to humble ego-drive projects. Joshua Heschel, a contemporary exponent of Chassidut—Jewish Mysticism—recognizes that: "Obviously we can never sneer at the stars, mock the dawn or scoff at the totality of being. Sublime grandeur evokes unhesitating, unflinching awe" (Heschel 1984, 25). Such experiences allow us to "become aware of the throb of the cosmic subtly echoed within our own souls" (16). Echoing Socratic *Eros*, Heschel talks of "radical amazement" as the root of all knowledge. He notes the power of such experience to order individual and political life: "As civilization advances the sense of wonder almost necessarily declines and this decline is an alarming symptom of our state of mind." "Mankind will not perish through want of information; but only for want of appreciation" (37). The Lakota, Standing Bear states simply and directly how such an experience can guide the actions of an individual in society:

> The old Lakota was wise. He knew man's heart away from nature becomes hard; he knew that lack of respect for growing living things soon led to lack of respect for humans too. So he kept his youth close to its softening influence. (Standing Bear 1978, 197)

My contention is that shamanic ecstasy is part of an experiential continuum with a Socratic passion for knowledge (*Eros*). Both are constellated around a "love of life"—a sense of the sacredness of all living beings that guides both the quest and the politics of the philosopher.

The Dialectic of the Medicine Wheel

The teaching of the Medicine Wheel of the Cheyenne is a good example of how to start living this 'politics of ecstasy'. The Medicine wheel is a mandala—a cross circumscribed by a circle—the oldest known and most widely distributed sacred symbol. 'Sun wheel' petroglyphs date back to Paleolithic times and more recently appear in such diverse settings as the healing ritual of Navaho sand paintings, European alchemy, and as objects of meditation in Tibetan Buddhism. In every context the mandala suggests the metaxic condition—the paradoxical whole as balanced pairs of binary opposites: male-female, child-adult, day-night, summer-winter, human-animal, mind-body, etc. According to the contemporary Cheyenne shaman Hyemeyohsts Storm, the wheel at its most inclusive represents a paradigm of the whole of existence. Every pebble, every blade of grass, every animal, every human being and every tribe, culture and civilization has a place on the wheel. Human beings are alone among the creatures in being "determiners" yet ignorant of their limits, their part in the drama of being (Storm 1972, 1–11). The human condition is incomplete. It entails a quest—a search for the best way to live.

Storm then asks the reader to imagine the medicine wheel as a group of people sitting in a circle on the prairie trying to come to a shared understanding—the primal political-philosophical community. An object, a painted drum, is placed in the middle of the circle. As each person in the group tries to describe the object it becomes clear that the meaning of the drum will depend on one's position in the circle, powers of observation, capacity to communicate, and ultimately one's accumulated life experience. Should the object be a person or an idea, the variety and complexity of interpretations would increase exponentially. A shared understanding requires building verbal (symbolic) bridges across the boundaries separating unique worlds of experience. This constitutes a *dialectical* search—moving beyond one's starting point on the wheel towards a more inclusive awareness by encountering one's concrete "other." Rather than avoid conflict and opposition we should struggle to question our most deeply held assumptions and actively seek out those who disagree. The courage for such potentially dangerous and exhausting imagi-

native journeys comes from the shamanic Socratic passion for existence. Fascination with the diversity of nature and its creatures is
transferred to the even more startling diversity of human individuals, cultures, and races.

Socrates as Primal Philosopher

The life and teaching of Socrates helps us understand small
group face-to-face discussion as the institution that embodies both
the shamanic-philosophical quest and an emancipatory politics.
E. R. Dodds (1966) clearly places Socrates within a primal shamanic
culture. The classicist Carl A. P. Ruck (1981) goes further arguing
persuasively that Socrates participated in the Eleusinian Mysteries,
a Hellenist version of the primordial Indo-European shamanic religion which included the use of the hallucinogenic fly agaric mush-
room *Amanita muscaria* as a technique for ecstatic transcendence.
Socrates' reference to his inner *Daimon* also suggests the voices of
the shamanic spirit world. More importantly Socrates places the primal boundary crossing discipline of face-to-face discussion at the center of the search for order. Unlike Plato, Socrates had neither school
nor library, mocked the authority of lectures and books, and repeatedly distinguished his 'method' of dialectical discussion from the professionalism of the sophists. In short his "method" reproduced the
egalitarian, participatory oral culture of the primal philosophical
community.[6] The search for wisdom, so defined requires incorporation of the experience of *the ordinary citizen*.[7] Thus both the Socratic
teaching, and that of the medicine wheel have a democratic telos;
both reflect on the full amplitude of human experience; both thrive
on diversity, individuality and discussion; both are open to anyone
who experiences the calling, and both presuppose a group of discussants small enough for each individual's contribution to be recognized and incorporated. Means and ends fuse since the method both
requires and generates a democratic (liberated) community of seek-
ers (those enlightened by apprehension of the metaxic situation).[8]

Thus over two thousand years ago Socrates identified the problem that still plagues modern democracies: without some shared
commitment to the search for the Good, democracy becomes procedural and vulnerable to cynical manipulation; or else it degenerates
into the idiocy of the lowest common denominator—the notion that
every opinion is equally significant.

The Medicine Wheel helps us conceptualize how a shared vision of an ordered and meaning-filled whole requires respect for in-

dividual and cultural uniqueness. Like successful paradigms the wheel expresses how a larger truer meaning is an interpretive synthesis of as many diverse contributions as possible. Similarly the Socratic dialectic moves the awareness of the circle of discussants from the truth inherent in the experience of an individual, the thesis, through contradiction by another to its untruth, the antithesis or what it neglects. The synthesis is a symbolic incorporation and transcendence of the partial truths of both thesis and antithesis, which becomes in turn a new thesis to be contradicted and transcended. In both models synthesis has a narrative dimension (expressing at very least the development of the discussion). When the wheel represents the whole, such a synthesis could be said to have the form of a grand narrative fusing individual narratives into a shared collectively constructed cosmic creation story. The root of our current predicament is the absence of a compelling narrative that connects the human quest for the best way to live to the larger community of life.

The New Story

Perhaps one of the most astounding events in modern intellectual life has been the synthesis of a cosmic creation story from the developmental life sciences. The narrative of evolution connects us to the myriad of life forms that have preceded us and with which we now share the planet perhaps more precisely and more persuasively than any previous creation myth. Darwin laid the mechanistic foundations in the latter part of the nineteenth century. Early this century the Jesuit paleontologist-theologian, Teilhard de Chardin incorporated into the evolutionary narrative an understanding of transcendence and the sacred (the metaxic situation). His work has since been differentiated by thinkers like Rupert Sheldrake (1991) and Brian Swimme and Thomas Berry (1992) in ways that provide a planetary, and indeed, a cosmic context of meaning for the quest, and the politics of the quest.

Swimme and Berry begin their cosmic story with the primeval fireball—the big bang—and move to include the self-reflective individual. Thus we now know that the thousands of stars that can be seen in the night sky, and the billions upon billions that can only be detected with the aid of telescopes, are suns and sun-systems comparable to our sun—the energy source of all life on earth. We know our sun is an unimaginably large fusion reactor that like billions of other suns is born, grows, lives out its life and will eventually die.

We know that our planetary system crystallized out of the explosive death of one such giant sun—the supernova Tiamat. All the complex elements of the earth within which all our physics and biochemistry take place were synthesized by this incredible event. What is most significant is that we know all this with the help of that same method of reliable inference that proves itself in feats like genetic engineering and rocketing humans to the moon.

Swimme then makes that unprecedented quantum leap in reflection by recognizing our quintessentially human capacity for self-reflection. He recognizes this self-reflective consciousness as a product of that same fecund universe that we separate ourselves from in the process of objective understanding:

> Earth was a cauldron of chemicals and elemental creativity, fashioning ever more complex forms and combinations until life burst forth in the oceans and spread across the continents, covering the entire planet. This creativity advanced until flowers bloomed on every continent, then advanced further until the vision of the flowers and all beauty could be deeply felt and appreciated. We are the latest, the most recent, the youngest extravagance of this stupendously creative Earth. (Swimme 1984, 31)

Fifty years ago Chardin made the same point when he described the electron microscope as the atom's way of seeing itself. Such formulations capture the metaxic structure of language-consciousness-reality; the irreducible paradox of subjective consciousness being part of the objective reality it contemplates. Unlike traditional myths such a story is inherently dialectical and thus open ended, including the unfinished history of the self-reflective human subject. Yet taken as a whole in its largest aspect, evolution has an unmistakable direction towards what Chardin called complexity-consciousness—the amplification of complexity of form and consciousness.

Swimme returns us to the origin of the quest when he recognizes the *ecstatic* quality of experiencing a universe that "shivers with wonder in the depths of the human" (Swimme 1984, 32). As we contemplate our best empirical understanding of 'who we are' and 'where we come from' we find a radically *post*modern myth which returns shamanic ecstasy to the cutting edge of the evolution of consciousness. Construction of our contemporary cosmic creation story itself furthers the evolutionary momentum of complexity consciousness. It gives us the most self-reflective, precisely differentiated, inclusive, and thus complex account to date of the archaic creation myth: we humans are children of the stars.

Implicit in this story is a political dialectic of both individuation and connection—diversity and unity. It recognizes that a consciousness that is collectively symbolized by a diversity of individuals, cultures, and civilizations is far more complex, expanded, and vital than the ruling industrial monoculture.

Primal Politics: The Quest Beyond "Postmodernity"

When we try to construct a picture of primal politics from the archaeological evidence and anthropological studies of contemporary hunting and gathering societies, we find a remarkably stable constellation of features, most of which directly foster, and are in turn fostered by the quest. When we look at the politics of the polis from this expanded perspective, much of its creative genius can be seen as a struggle to maintain primal institutions in a "civilized" context. Finally when we examine some of the more creative political transformations informed by a revival of the quest, especially the various Green Parties (Capra and Spretnak 1984; Rensenbrink 1992; Graham chapter 5), we find echoes of the very same primal institutions. This transhistoric, multicivilizational perspective clarifies how the components of the quest and its politics are intimately interrelated; each component reinforces all the others in an integrated way of life. What I am suggesting is an archetypal politics that is rooted in the human condition. Such a formulation helps understand why echoes of this primal politics are reemerging in a postmodern paradigm during this period of crisis.

1) Decentralization. Hunting gathering societies are models of decentralization. The magic number for typical bands is thirty to fifty, although there are often seasonal gatherings into groups of several hundred or more. Where small scale was in part imposed on hunter gatherers by the carrying capacity of the ecosystem, it was actively pursued by the polis. Plato and Aristotle, insisted that the polis should number no more than a few thousand, small enough, like the primal band, for its members to know one another as unique individuals. Small size helps institutionalize a political culture of face-to-face discussion. The "Good of the Whole," instead of being some pious abstraction, becomes the good of a collection of specific, individual human beings in a unique natural ecology.

Economic decentralization makes it possible to live closer to the interface between civilization and wilderness, and thus makes shamanic boundary crossing more universally accessible. Today, this interface has been virtually obliterated by a self-fulfilling anthropocentrism that has created an environment of artifacts. Our experienced urban 'universe' has become a collection of human creations. The multiple pathologies of a mass-administered existence are driving us to decentralization. The collapse of the Soviet empire, has been a dramatic step towards regionalism. However without the moral compass of a truth quest, its demented shadow has emerged as ultranationalism and ethnic warfare. Kirkpatrick Sale's (1985) notion of "bioregionalism" is a powerful articulation of the emancipatory dimension of decentralization. As part of the Green vision, its has inspired activists like Bryan and McClaughry (1988) to suggest that states like Vermont, already having a solid tradition of local democracy, decentralize into self-governing shires along semifeudal lines.

The Israeli Kibbutz system, is an early modern example of how such intentional decentralization can be successfully integrated into a modern economy (Sprio 1958; Elon 1981; Criden and Gelb 1976; Rayman 1981). Although the kibbutzim are affiliated to national movements, each unit of around 200 to 400 adults collectively owns the means of production and governs itself through a process akin to consensus decision making. Rather than lapsing into a Marxian "idiocy of rural life" kibbutziks have been among the best educated of Israelis, and have taken leadership roles in some of the country's most progressive political movements (Elon 1981).

2) Economic Self-Sufficiency. The conventional definitions of civilization stress urban centralization, division of labor, hierarchy, a system of taxation or tribute, warfare and slavery (Stavrianos 1971). Today, political without economic decentralization (as right-wing politicians like Reagan suggested), simply intensifies the shift of decision making from governments to multinational corporations. Primal societies clarify how economic self-sufficiency and a minimal division of labor provide the material basis for liberation. It is hard to institutionalize domination in a society where the average adult could leave the band at any time and live a comfortable (even if lonely) life directly off wilderness. Group cohesion is more a product of a voluntary ethos of caring and sharing. Consequently such societies manage to balance extensive cooperation with a high tolerance for individual diversity.

When we look at the polis we find that *Autarkia*, or self-sufficiency, was, as H. D. F. Kitto puts it, the "the first law of its existence." Only by maintaining its small scale and minimizing division of labor could the polis ensure that the citizen could fulfill "the duty of taking part, at the appropriate season of life, in all the affairs of the polis." Such participation helped qualify the citizen for participation in the collective search into the Good Life (the quest) as a basis for direct participation in decision making. The increasing dependence of Athens on imported corn fueled imperial ambition, led to increased reliance on military and economic professionalism, and ultimately led to its demise.

Some creative economists are suggesting models that could reverse a four hundred-year-old trend towards economic centralization (Henderson 1981; Robertson 1990; Daly and Cobb 1994). Robertson, who is a former member of the British Cabinet Office and former research director for British Banks offers a vision of a *multilevel one-world economic system*. The principle function of each larger, higher level economic unit (nation, corporation, region, household) is defined as being to enable its component subeconomies, ultimately the individual, to be more *self-reliant* and more *conserving*" (Robertson 1990, 2). He gives examples of how international bodies like the United Nations could apply taxes to help insulate smaller economic entities (perhaps bioregions like the Hawaiian Islands) from domination by external economic forces.

In *A Green Hawaii*, Ira Rohter, chair of the local Green Party and political scientist, integrates precontact native Hawaiian wisdom with a wealth of ideas for moving the state towards economic self-sufficiency and sustainability. In part, this vision is inspired by the success of ancient Hawaii in supporting a population comparable to the present total population of the state, probably at a much higher standard of general health, using a stone age technology. The basic economic unit, the *ahupua'a*, was substantially self-sufficient, consisting of a pie-shaped segment that began from the central mountain range, included rainforest for wild gathering, the arable plain between two valleys for taro horticulture, and extended to the coastal plain, fishponds and fringing reefs where marine aquaculture and fishing complemented the diet. Sustainability of yield in fishing, and a sophisticated system of irrigation and sustainable horticulture (similar to Bill Mollison's permaculture) depended on *kapus*, a system of ritualized prohibitions and obligations based on a sacralized relationship to nature. Rohter has enriched this primal model with appropriate technologies, introduced resource and food crops, and proposals for intentional communities. He also considers integration with the global economy through ideas like ecotourism and the sort of restrained free trade Robertson suggests.

> 3) "Zen Affluence." As Sahlins and others have shown, hunter gatherers, despite their apparent poverty, enjoy more leisure than any other society, working on average two to three hours a day for necessities. Sahlins calls this disinterest in wealth "Zen affluence," a notion close to E. F. Schumacher's "Buddhist economics," where the accumulation of wealth is eschewed in favor of the higher pleasures of a rich cultural, political, and spiritual life.

Kitto suggests that the ideal of the polis involved a similar voluntary simplicity. He notes that the individual household was to a large extent self-sufficient, and that on the whole "what the polis could not produce, it did without" (Kitto 1966, 68). This noble ideal was eventually eroded by the seductions of trade and empire. It was precisely the loss of a culture of "purification of the soul" and "love of knowledge" (philosophy), and its replacement by materialism, greed, and power hunger that induced Socrates and Plato to despair of direct democracy.

> 4) Cultivation of the Whole Person. Minimal division of labor, "Zen Affluence" together with the imperative to love and live as much of life as possible, converge in the ideal of the whole person, what Kitto referred to as the *arete* (excellence) of the amateur, embodied in the Hero of the Odyssey:

> The hero of the Odyssey is a great fighter, a wily schemer, a ready speaker, a man of stout heart and broad wisdom who knows he must endure without complaining what the Gods send; and he can both build and sail a boat, drive a furrow as straight as anyone, beat a braggart at throwing the discus, challenge the Phaceian youth at boxing, wrestling or running; flay, skin, cut up and cook an ox, and be moved to tears by a song. (1966: 172)

For all its vivid contrasts, such a description is compromised by its implicit exclusion of the world of nature, the feminine, and the sacred, all of which were more readily included by primal societies. The virtual absence of a division of labor encouraged most hunters and gatherers to participate in all the archetypal roles: provider, artist, singer, dancer, politician, shaman, healer. Shamanism and the teaching of the medicine wheel further amplify a praxis of crossing social, economic, and ontological boundaries. The autobiography of the Lakota shaman, Lame Deer, makes the Greek hero look tame by comparison.[9]

This notion of the human individual as a microcosm of the macrocosm—a sort of hologram of human potential—is central Jungian shadow psychology. The heroes of Herman Hesse's novels, *Steppenwolf*, *Narcissus and Goldmund*, *Siddartha* and *Demian*, are all magnificent examples of this potential actualized spiritual growth through incorporation of the shadow. The profound political implications of failing to integrate the shadow were first explored by Erich Neumann in his groundbreaking *Depth Psychology and a New Ethic*, yet this notion is still largely unrecognized by transformational and Green politics. Woolpert's chapter 15 in this volume responds to this need by focusing on how the Greens are failing to recognize, and take responsibility for, their collective shadow. The teaching of the medicine wheel and a shamanic metaphysics provide additional (cross cultural) support for implementing the strategies Woolpert suggests. It is easier to defuse self-righteousness, bickering, and maliciousness if one takes seriously the existential struggle to move around the medicine wheel of life and live within a humbling awareness of the metaxy.

> 5) Participatory (Direct) Democracy. Primal societies fuse politics to the quest through direct participation in face-to-face discussion. Informed, responsible participation in collective decision making is quite feasible in societies where there is minimal division of labor, minimal hierarchy, and a shared culture of the truth quest. Well-rounded individuals, who have a sense of their intrinsic solidarity, not only with one another, or even all of humanity, but all of creation, have fewer ego barriers to enlightened consensus. From this perspective it is not hard to understand why representational democracy in the United States is today in a state of crisis. It is a country where the prevailing mass culture promotes competitive individualism, which holds 'experts' in awe and sanctions the unlimited accumulation of personal wealth as the highest shared goal. As E. J. Dionne (1991) and others are pointing out, a viable capitalist society depends on noncapitalist values to hold together and prosper.

What is at stake is the creation of a political culture and a civil society inspired by a vision of the quest as "the value of values." Although this notion is more or less implicit in some of the high moments of transformation this century, particularly the kibbutzim of the 1930s (Elon), it is perhaps the most neglected dimension of contemporary transformational theory.

Conclusion

The primal convergence between politics and the quest suggest that the process of teaching and learning might be the Archimedean point for transformation. As Quinn's *Ishmael* notes, people will not behave differently towards the world unless they think differently about the world. Academic political scientists could choose to model such transformation in their classes and their research.

From Plato's prolific output to Derrida's declaration that "there is nothing outside of the text," Western intellectual life has paid lip service to the Socratic dialectic while entombing its populist epistemology under a mountain of literature. Most instructors still unhappily follow the "banking model" of pedagogy (Freire) where during a typical lecture, information is transferred from the notes of the frustrated teacher to the bored student without passing through the minds of either. If we take seriously the notion that truth emerges in the process of boundary crossing, we are obliged to replace the hierarchical duality of teacher-student with a dialectic in which students also teach and teachers learn. In addition to Freire's groundbreaking study during the 60s there is a wealth of empirical evidence supporting the effectiveness of a wide range of strategies for active learning—the most fundamental being authentic Socratic discussion (See Fishel and Segal chapter 10 in this volume; Eison, Janzow, and Bonwell 1990; Paul 1990; Herman 1996).

It took me ten years of teaching to realize that most students are shamed into silence by their ignorance. The research supports my experience of the truth of the Socratic paradox—that one often teaches more effectively by biting one's tongue, listening carefully, and then learning from the inarticulate and the ignorant. The medicine wheel tells us that everything and everyone is a teacher for us. Teaching politics is unique in that the experience of the student-as-citizen is crucial 'data' for inquiry (research) into the good of all. It is also a stimulus for the instructor's personal growth in wholeness. No real teaching can take place by treating the student-as-ignoramus. Conversely research gains in political significance by incorporating the experience of the ordinary citizen. The bottom line is that effective teaching incorporates a transformational primal politics.

If projects of synthesis and integration are to regain their centrality in political inquiry, the intellectual-industrial division of labor needs to be reconsidered. Unless the walls between disciplines are bridged, funding will continue to follow the bottom line of marketable specialties, and generalists will continue to be weeded out of higher education. The abolition of conventional disciplinary boundaries in institutions like Evergreen State College in Washington need to be carefully studied as possible models for restructuring.

Promotion and tenure decisions still reward the most arcane research projects while teaching is regarded as painful duty and the search for "the meaning of existence" trashed as sophomoric. Reformulating inquiry in terms of a primal truth quest heals the split between research and teaching. The shared concern with the good of the whole and the dialectical structure of the quest can help transform the classroom, for both instructor and student into a microcosm of a primal philosophical community.

Notes

1. *"Reality is not . . . (only) an object of consciousness but . . . (also) the something in which consciousness occurs as an event of participation between partners in the community of being"* (Voegelin 1987, 15; emphasis added).

2. For a clarification of the "metaphysical barbarism of modern science" Burtt's (1954) classic is unsurpassed. For a more recent overview see Butterfield (1957). For a summary of the connection between cognition, manipulation, and profit see Berman (1984), chapter 2. For the connection between science, patriarchy and the domination of nature, see Merchant (1980).

3. Duerr's study, *Dreamtime: Concerning the Boundary between Wilderness and Civilization* (1985) considers examples from a profusion of archaic religious practices and concludes that the shaman, like the anthropologist, psychologist, and political philosopher, is concerned not with "flying, psykokinesis and talking to magical coyotes," but with the "full amplitude of human experience"—self-knowledge, knowledge of society, and knowledge of the best way to live.

4. McKenna defines "ectstatic" as "a notion that is forced on us whenever we wish to indicate an experience or state of mind that is cosmic in scale. An ecstatic experience transcends duality; it is simultaneously terrifying, hilarious, awe-inspiring, familiar and bizarre" (1992, 59).

5. Shamanic techniques range from various self-imposed ordeals like "fasting, thirsting, self-mutilation, torture, exposure to the elements, sleeplessness, incessant dancing and other means of total exhaustion, bleeding, plunging into ice cold pools, near-drowning, laceration . . ." to a variety of nonhurtful "triggers" such as "different kinds of rhythmic activity, self-hypnosis, meditation, chanting, drumming, and music"; all in addition to the near-ubiquitous use of psychoactive and sometimes highly toxic, plants and animal secretions (Furst 1976, 10).

6. Vlastos is emphatic about the distinction between Socrates and his pupil Plato on this point: "To confine as Plato does (in books iv and vii of the *Republic*) moral inquiry to a tiny elite is to obliterate the Socratic vision which opens up the philosophic life to all" (Vlastos 1991, 18).

7. One can infer a boundary crossing dialectic from the Allegory of the Cave. The philosopher who returns to enlighten the prisoners to the larger reality outside the cave is only persuasive to the degree that he demonstrates to them that he shares their experience of the cave. He has to learn from them how to adjust again to the shadows on the wall. For their part the prisoners will remain chained, ridiculing the philosopher's attempts, unless they, like Socrates, know that they do not know. The shamanic perspective suggests Socratic ignorance is not so much the ironic pose of postmodernists as a primal openness to the experience of the other.

8. We can see the turning away from the "softening" influence of nature even in a shamanic figure like Socrates. For example in the opening of *Phaedrus*, he makes clear he has nothing to learn from nature: "You must forgive me, my dear friend; I am a lover of learning, and trees and open country won't teach me anything, whereas men in the town do" (Plato's *Phaedrus* 1972, 25). With the loss of the sense of the "preciousness of all being" the polis confines "citizenship" to adult male Greeks and excluded women, metics and slaves from participating in the 'Greek medicine wheel.'

9. "I managed to both a heathen and a holy man, a fugitive and a pursuer, a lawman and an outlaw." (Lame Deer 1972, 80). He suggests an alchemy of fusing opposites as a discipline for acquiring wisdom which can heal: "A medicine man shouldn't be a saint. He should experience and feel all the ups and downs, the despair and joy, the magic and the reality, the courage and the fear, of his people. . . . Being a good medicine man means being right in the midst of the turmoil, not shielding yourself from it" (Lame Deer 1972, 79).

3

A Theory for Transforming the Self: Moving Beyond the Nation-State

---

MANFRED HALPERN

This is an invitation to take an unfamiliar journey to explore not only the nation-state but to inquire into ourselves in a new light: How can we attain a new freedom and capacity to participate in creating fundamentally new and better communities?

The Four Faces of Our Being: Personal, Political, Historical and Sacred

Who are we? We all have four interconnected concrete faces: a personal, political, historical, and sacred face of being. And our being—whatever we believe or refuse to believe—is also constituted by one of the sacred sources that patterns the living, underlying structure, dynamics, meaning, purpose, and values of the dramas through which we enact our life.

Being is both a noun and a verb: it describes the form and substance both of our constitution and our practice of life in this cosmos of continuous creation. From the perspective of transformation as the core drama of life—a perspective I will soon enlarge upon—our personal face is not simply subjective or simply our own self. It is the face of our being that has the capacity to respond and to free itself to participate creatively with the deepest source of our being (a reality also to be explored further) and thus to discover its uniqueness in the presence and process of that very connection. Such emerging being needs to augment and fulfill itself by engag-

45

ing also in creative and just participation politically and historically.

Our political face is expressed by what we can and need to do
together—together within ourselves (for none of us is only one person living within only one drama), together with others, together in
history, and together with the sacred. The political therefore does
not, as we commonly believe, refer only to competition for public
power. It includes loving, playing, meditating, learning, teaching,
producing, consuming, risking trust in testing new inspirations in
actual practice, and connecting with others in order to bring friendship, joy, beauty, and justice into being. Every relationship—every
story in which we participate—is political. The theory and practice
of transformation thus puts into question the roots and branches—
and the scarce and diminished fruits and the possessive and exclu-
sionary harvests—of politics now.

Our historical face is constituted by our personal and political,
conscious and unconscious, true and false memories, and by the living inheritance of the dramas and ways of life that arose in the past
and that continue to move us through the present into the future. If
our past no longer nourishes us and confines our vision and our capacity, we can also create turning points into a different future; historical turning points also in the personal, political, and sacred faces
of our being.

We experience and express the sacred face of our being whether
we are believers, agnostics, atheists or transformers, whether we
are conscious of it or not. We experience it as the concrete presence
of a living, underlying patterning force. We experience it most
strongly and particularly as the process of creativity, as courage, as
deep attraction and caring, as loyalty or commitment even in the
face of threats from others, as various forms of hate or love—all experiences that cannot be fully put into words. Our sacred face may
be expressed in the words or fervor of dogma—but also of deep skep-
ticism, of exclusive commitment to rationality—formulations that
by themselves alone cannot fully justify such a commitment to either dogma or rationality. Neither could deeply confirm, move or
alter our being unless it comes from such depths.

The drama of the nation-state seeks to mold our personal face
above all into conformity—one nation, under god. The only personal
contribution that is really appreciated is what makes our nation-
state, instead of the others, richer, more famous and above all more
powerful. It diminishes our political face domestically in ways we
shall soon discuss, but few indeed are the areas of life in which we

now feel ready to explore and act upon what we can and need to do together with others who are not part of our nation-state. Much of our historical face has been falsified. We are told we are one nation. But in fact no nationalism existed anywhere in the world in word or deed until the late eighteenth century. Except perhaps for Iceland, no nation in the world is in fact but one nation. All are multicultural. The sacred face of the nation-state as we shall see keeps us all partial—meaning biased and incomplete—yet ready to die for it.

Transformation: The Core Drama of Life

What are our most fundamental choices between ways of life as we seek to discover and experience the wholeness of our being in all four concrete faces and their sacred source? Our theory of transformation is built upon the discovery that its practice in fact constitutes the core drama of life. Only our journey again and again through this drama of transformation will allow us to participate with the deepest source of our being in creating the fundamentally new and better. There are indeed three, but only three, other fundamentally different choices in terms of the ultimate meaning, purpose, and values of life. (By "ultimate" I do not mean on Judgment Day but the deepest grounds we can discover within our present way of life.) But these other three ways of life are in fact only fragments of this core drama. Hence at every moment of our life, we live somewhere in one of its three Acts, in arrest or in movement.

When I speak of dramas, no mere metaphor is being used. I mean the actual reality through which the sacred sources of our being express themselves in our lives—as living, underlying patterning forces shaping the four faces of our being through the enactment of an archetypal drama. Unlike Plato, I do not see archetypes as forms that are eternal and good. As we shall explore, one of the archetypal dramas that constitute one of the four ways of life is demonic; another is dying. Archetypal dramas are born: the archetype of the state was born about five thousand years ago; the archetype of the nation-state was born about two hundred years ago. And they also die (they are born and die with our help), though they last much longer than we do. The four ways of life are expressions of the most powerful sacred sources, but they are not the only archetypal dramas. Many are the smaller dramas we enact, and can only enact, in the service of these overarching stories. But in this essay, I speak only of those four, and also of the nation-state in the service of two of them.

By "sacred" I mean nothing we must believe in, but forces that move through us as they shape the archetypal patterns of our lives and that we can therefore experience and free ourselves essentially to understand and to accept or reject. The sacred forces that arrest us in any of the three fragments of the drama of transformation I call Lords because they can command and possess us as long as we have not yet liberated ourselves with the help of what I call the deepest sacred source of our being. This source is not all-knowing or perfect, that is, it is not already complete. This source constantly seeks to renew the core drama of life through its concrete inspirations of the sacred face of our being, but it cannot command us because it needs our participation in this journey. I speak of these transpersonal forces as sacred because the living, underlying patterning forces of our life are not primarily of our making, though they remain incomplete without our concrete faces.

To free ourselves to participate with the deepest sacred source of our being in transforming the four faces of our being so that we may practice love and justice with each other means journeying through the core of life every time an unresolved problem of understanding and compassion confronts us. Here, as briefly as I may tell this story, are the three Acts of the drama of transformation:

Unless disaster strikes at the outset, all of us begin each experience of life in the first Scene of Act I, still bound within a story that gives us deep security, and which we cannot imagine (or dare) to criticize. We enact our being and all our relationships as an emanation—as the outward embodiment of a mysterious and overwhelming source of being—a sacred force also concretely embodied and enforced through relationships we practice under the order of our father, our mother, our community, their beliefs and their culture.

But in our cosmos of continuous creation, the second Scene of Act I opens again and again from the day we are born. We are inspired from the realm of the sacred by a new thought or image or feeling or intuition—by what seems like a new emanation. For we cannot understand it from the perspective of our life in the first Scene: it therefore still remains mysteriously powerful to us. In fear of opening new doors, we can repress this new inspiration with the help of our already established archetypal Lord, but at a price. Repression cannot destroy this new inspiration. It can only push it into the shadows of our life, to come forth negatively instead, hitting us and our neighbors from behind and from below, making us more anxious while not knowing why. Or else, we can champion this new inspiration and become its prophet because in its new light, we find our earlier story unbearable, untenable, or unfruitful. But that decision compels us to leave the security of the arrested—and arresting—truth of the emanational container of Act I and enter into incoherence.

In order to move through the second Act—the Act of incoherence—the new rebel prophet needs now to become a philosopher. Yes, in the first Scene of Act II, we rejoice, and experience the painful opposition of others, in our rebellion. But prophets, as al-Farabi told us in tenth century Damascus, are compelled to speak, though they do not yet know what they are talking about. We need to move on into the second Scene of Act II to discover both all the concrete manifestations and the living, underlying patterning forces of which we need to free ourselves. To say no only to particular persons, ideas, and relationships is at most to bring about incremental changes within the same archetypal drama. For example, we may overthrow the Tzar of Russia, but Stalin in fact becomes the same archetypal example of total rule as Tzar Ivan the Terrible. But to destroy opposing human beings except in unavoidable defense of our own lives is evil. Having journeyed this far through the core drama of life has opened our insight, courage, and capacity to understand not only the particular we can no longer bear. But we have also come to understand the sacred underlying force that had hitherto commanded and possessed our life, and kept us unfruitful in understanding, love, faith, hope, and justice in the constitution and practice of our being. Centuries ago, theorists of transformation said, "To know yourself is to know your Lord"—to know which source of the sacred had hitherto enthralled you and which source is now helping to free you. We become philosophers in Act II by learning to unlearn and by learning how to open ourselves and contribute to previously unfamiliar understanding.

At the end of Act II exists the only exit from the core drama of life. Here we empty ourselves both of that Lord's archetypal patterning force and of its concrete manifestations because we now know why they have become alien to our being. We do not have the power to destroy any living, underlying patterning force shaping the dramas of our lives, but without our concrete personal face, and hence also with its diminished political, historical, and sacred faces, it loses strength. If enough people reject it, it may die in the abyss beyond the exit, for no sacred source can persist without its concrete faces.

When we have thus emptied ourselves, we can count on being filled anew. This is indeed a cosmos of continuous creation. In the first Scene of Act III we now hear again, but this time in contrast to our experience of this inspiration in the second Scene of Act I, we understand what we are being inspired by. We not only feel deeply moved but we understand consciously, critically, creatively, and caringly what kind of participation with the deepest source of our being we are now risking trust in. We are now participating in continuous creation—now for the fundamentally new that is also fundamentally better—with the creator of the core drama of life who created us as creators.

But it is not enough to be inspired and to understand our task. We need now to enter the second Scene of Act III to test this new inspiration with our neighbors in order to discover in actual practice whether it is in fact fundamentally better in resolving our present problem or nourishing anew the roots of already discovered fruitful outcomes. Transformation never turns us into the great one who can solve all problems for everyone. Act III is never the final Act of salvation. What we need to complete this drama at this moment of shared history are not leaders and followers, not gurus and disciples. We need people sharing the same wounds whom we can now guide and help to transform their vision and practice of what is at stake and how healing can come about. Our best beginning is to be a living example of the experience of the journey of transformation, not simply of its conclusion at this moment. We need now to journey together. The underlying structure and dynamics of the core drama of life are always the same. The concrete outcome is always unique, depending on the actual persons and the political and historical situation at each point.

Fundamental Choices between Four Ways of Life

The obstacles along the path of the core drama of life loom larger than we have so far examined. We can also arrest or destroy ourselves along the way. The deepest sacred source of our being creates the core drama of life anew at every moment not so that we would believe in it as an eternally fixed dogma, but to risk faith, that is, to risk trust in the experience of transformation. The creator of this drama also created us with the capacity and freedom to say yes or no during our journey. We can say no to transforming ourselves and thereby seduce and be seduced by the power of an archetypal force shaping a particular Scene of this core drama. They, like us, are free to say no to being in the service of transformation. We can, through our arrest, turn these partial, that is, biased and incomplete sacred forces into Lords that come to possess and command us in our arrest in Act I or Act II or even our destruction at the end of Act II, as we shall see. We can turn what now remain only fragments of the core drama of life into three ways of life each fundamentally different from transformation.

We can arrest ourselves in the first or second Scene of Act I, for in this Act, we can hear anew not only from the deepest source of our being but also from biased and incomplete Lords. If the archetypal drama that now inspires us covers a large enough orbit, we can turn this Scene into an overarching way of life in the service of emanation. Within this way of life we experience all the other ordained dramas in its service as the outer flow of the will and revelation of a mysterious, overwhelming source of power—a web of life whose ultimate meaning and purpose has been decreed by that source once and forever. Many thousands of different concrete manifestations of this archetypal way of life have existed throughout history among the peoples of this world. Yet almost every community has held its own form of this web of life to be the only true one in existence.

Emanation as a way of life is dying in our time because in all its concrete manifestations—wherever it is being practiced in this world—we are not ever allowed to ask fundamentally new questions or experiment with fundamentally new answers. And in our rapidly changing world of ever new challenges, this closure prevents us from facing and dealing with the problems of our time.

Hence for the first time in human history, people all over the world are rebelling and thereby enter the first Scene of the second Act of the core drama of life. The great majority are also arresting themselves there and turning it into a way of life of incoherence. We proclaim that we are now free to pursue our self-interest. But since we have not yet completed our journey, we cannot truly know our self or our interest. Hence in all the dramas in the service of the overarching way of life—for example, within the story of capitalism or of democratic or authoritarian liberalism—we rebel again and again. We seek bigger fragments of life and hence try to oust or at least diminish the power of those who now control these fragments so that we may attain the power to get hold of them or to create new fragments. Yet in the service of incoherence we ourselves remain only fragments of being, unable truly and fully to understand and to connect to ourselves and to the rest of humanity. At best we can agree on procedures that limit the violence of this kind of perennial rebellion within this way of life. But since power counts more than anything else, such procedures limit suffering and destruction far more for the powerful than for less powerful and the powerless.

The Nation-State Exemplifies the Costs of Incoherence as a Way of Life

By "nation" I do not simply mean citizens of a sovereign political state. That definition would give us no clue as to what kind of community exists, what holds it together, what moves its actions. Since the late eighteenth century, the "nation" has for the first time in history been experienced as born out of "nationalism," and the nation-state has striven to be the most powerful manifestation of the political face of our being.

From its beginning, the nation-state has acted in perennial rebellion against other nation-states—to preserve and enlarge its own power, and hence also the power of those who control it. The state may be able to claim a legitimate monopoly of coercion. But to rely solely on the threat of naked force to extract taxes and enforce laws in a way of life within which we cannot know the ultimate meaning, purpose, and value of anything is not a very reassuring basis of power. While organizing and reorganizing our insecurity of living in competition for fragments of life, the closest substitute we can find for the overarching security of emanation as a whole way of life is an emanational relationship to an archetypal drama—nationalism— which inspires a seemingly similar devotion, security, commitment, conformity for us to this hopefully most unifying fragment—in contrast to them, the alien outside our sacred container.

If we have uncritically accepted incoherence as a way of life, we say that we have only two choices: either order or else anarchy. We need order to prevent institutionalized rebellion from leading to the war of all against all. Within this way of life, we need the state to mobilize resources and manpower, to organize public institutions, to prevent private and gang vengeance, to protect property, to enforce laws and contracts, to organize help in emergencies, and to defend us against other aggressive nation-states. Why not accept the nation-state as the empowered unit to improve our community?

What is the community within a nation-state? Even welfare activity by the state for the poor is usually motivated less by compassion than by calculations for preserving order. We must give them enough so that they will not rebel against the nation-state. Amnesty International tells us that among the 167 sovereign states of this world, torture by the state is "normal" in 60 states and "frequent" in 36 more. Even in the democratic United States, most of the homeless are simply removed from the better neighborhoods and certainly from all suburbs to become invisible. People on welfare who cannot find a job after two years are also rendered invisible. The majority of people are turned into lesser human beings: they are treated only as tools (if not yet unnecessary tools) of capitalist enterprises. Bureaucracy is organized to process human beings impersonally according to impersonal rules. If the case of a particular human being does not fit under any existing rubric, then that person (unless one of the powerful) becomes not only a lesser being but indeed invisible and may die of it. The invisibility or at best, the lesser role of "the weaker sex" is just beginning to change. Our suffering remains "private" and "subjective" and does not become political until we gain enough power to be considered an "interest group"—still far from what we can and need to do together.

The nation-state has not brought community into being. In fact, there exists hardly any true nation-state in the world. If you ask where on earth is there a state that governs a people who have shared the same history for centuries, with the same religion, language, values, and ethnic roots, the only answer is: Iceland. Certainly the United States does not qualify, and in various disproportions, neither does any other "nation-state." Is the "nation-state" a mere fabrication? Then why, in the face of about 8,000 different languages spoken on this earth, in the face of so many different cultures alive within most nations, is the nation-state nonetheless so powerful an experience for so many people? All nation-states originally came into being by conquest—and still have no room for feminine archetypal forces except as defined by men. But if even its monopoly of coercive force cannot inspire devotion toward the nation-state, even unto death, what keeps it alive?

The nation-state is indeed one of the most powerful archetypal dramas in sustaining incoherence as a way of life and preventing us from getting out of incoherence. Incoherence cannot bring community into being. Hence the nation-state in the face of constant self-interested competition is the only available archetypal drama to substitute for the absence of community. Self-interested power, including the power of the nation-state, thus substitutes power and loyalty for our capacity and freedom to become whole human beings together with our neighbors.

Over 100 million people died in the twentieth century in wars to become nation-states, in wars between nation-states, or thanks to the intervention by other nation-states in internal wars within nation-states. Thus incoherence allied itself with deformation to attain its goals as a way of life.

Beyond Incoherence into Deformation or Transformation

People have begun to question the nation-state from two major directions. Fascist and fundamentalist forces of deformation do not intend to be confined within present borders or act primarily on the basis of the "state" or the presently established "nation." Others realize that nation-states split the people of the earth into pseudo-species, a splintering that endangers the human species and our ecology and prevents us from solving our problems. These critics are potentially attracted to transformation.

If in our despair that the existing nation-state no longer unites us, we attach ourselves totally to one remaining fragment of life and rely on it to restore us to glory, we exit into deformation—the third possible way of life—a way that constitutes the road to destructive death. Many are the fragments of life in our time that are in danger and that we may seek to clutch into deformation. Some groups attempt desperately to hold on to—or win—a nation-state as their biggest fortress in a hostile world. Current examples in Yugoslavia and the former Soviet Union are not the first or last cases of nationalism in the service of deformation.

Increasingly more pervasive in the world is what is often called "fundamentalism," although in no instances does such a movement accurately remember the past or offer new foundations except for an alleged fragment of the past to be imposed by force upon those who cannot devoutly believe it. This road into deformation is empowered by a deep, double sense of loss: the dissolution of emanation as a way of life and the failure of our relationship to the nation-state (or to capitalism) to create a real community. It is therefore a movement inspired in the first instance by a sense of betrayal and suicide. Most of these movements of deformation turn to charismatic heroes who will lead them to the restoration of glory through revengeful terror.

We spoke earlier of the only exit from the core drama of life as an exit that allows us to expel from our being the Lord and his or her archetypal drama and its concrete manifestations that we have come to understand and that we have found unbearable or at least unfruitful. We have another choice at this exit: If in our despair that the archetypal drama of the nation-state, and indeed our present way of life, no longer unites us or champions the ideas and values we cherish, we can merge our very being to a fragment that inspires us, and thus enter the road to the destructive death of others and of ourselves, this time by fragmenting ourselves concretely into the abyss.

If instead we mean to begin a transformational journey beyond the nation-state, we cannot rely upon those whose power is based upon a way of life that has arrested our development. We cannot free ourselves of the nation-state unless we also free ourselves of arresting our being in the service of incoherence. We need to organize political movement not from the already prevailing top down but among people who have personally freed themselves to deal with political problems that are at one and the same time, local and global: peace, ecology, hunger, exploitation, the equality of men and women and of different ethnic groups, indeed the very quality of daily life.

We start with whatever issue we know best and care most about, but what distinguishes us from present interest groups, what unites us with people now strangers to us, are two essential and necessary facts of life: We each move through the core drama of life again and again to free ourselves to express fully all four faces and the deepest source of our being. And we form local and global confederations not only of political movements but also of new communities whose memberships overlap, in part because we share the experience of transformation and in part because we are concerned with more than one issue at a time, for we understand that a whole way of life is at stake. Our task is not to overthrow the nation-state, but here and now to begin creating interconnected communities of transforming human beings. Forming such new communities, so that we may be understanding, loving and just with ourselves and each other is the heart of the politics of transformation.[1]

Note

1. This essay reflects two works-in-progress, *Transformation: Its Theory and Practice in Our Personal, Political, Historical and Sacred Being* and *Practicing Transformation: Obstacles and Opportunities*.

4

A Theory for Transforming Political Community: Applying Chaos and Feminist Theory

BARBARA KNIGHT

Introduction

Our conventional political institutions and values were derived from the worldview provided by Newtonian science. This approach led to linear reasoning and dualistic thinking, separating observer from observed, mind from matter, fact from value. Scientific metaphors portrayed individuals as material, separate, self-contained particles. No longer members of a whole body politic, we seemed to be self-interested, isolated atoms colliding with one another like tiny billiard balls (Hayward 1990). "Society" could be created only with external connections mediated by outside force; Newtonian atoms do not relate internally. Governments attempted to maintain control while adversaries engaged in politics to balance conflicting demands and interests of groups and individuals. Conventional politics today takes place in institutions designed from Newtonian images.

Scientific findings in studies of complex systems provide a holistic perspective with potential for the "politics of integrity" in the basic meaning of that term: a condition of wholeness or completion achieved by bringing parts together. The politics of integrity stands in relation to conventional politics as chaos and complexity theory are to Newtonian science. Each transforms its predecessor by means of an "alchemical"[1] synthesis of what Carl Jung termed Eros (Feminine) and Logos (Masculine) archetypal principles. When we reenvision political communities as complex, dynamic systems, holistic

57

Eros qualities inherent within the new science combine with Logos characteristics of differentiation and separation to form a new blend. We are far more complex and multifaceted than the linear, quantitative, mechanistic approach alone conveys. We pay lip service to this scientific method, but our interior experiences lead us to sense a deep recognition and resonance with findings in the new science. "It is almost as if nature, in its playfulness, was attempting to piece through the barriers of logic with its synchronicities and moments of illumination" (Peat 1991, 35). Conceptualized through the metaphorical lens of complex dynamic systems revealed by new scientific findings, the politics of integrity engages us in the process of transforming ourselves and our social and political relationships. Approaching political thinking and acting as more nearly whole persons, we can transform our political community.

Properties of Complex Dynamic Systems

Based in the interconnectedness that **chaos** and **complexity theory** find at deep levels of the universe, the politics of integrity is a holistic, transformational politics. When we see ourselves and our relationships from the perspective of complex systems and take part in communities patterned in line with their qualities, we engage in inner and outer transformation.

From varied scientific disciplines Bohr, Prigogine, Bohm, and Sheldrake envision an "emerging science of wholeness" (Peat 1991). With the advent of chaos theory, we see that dynamic systems do not operate in isolation. These complex systems manifest holism; everything potentially influences everything else. All things are in some sense constantly interacting. "Complex" means to weave together; the image of a web portrays the holism of complex systems. These systems are webbed with feedback so that a small twitch anywhere, the flap of butterfly wings, may be amplified, transforming the whole system. Key features of complex systems shaping the new politics are **nonlinearity**; **scaling** and **self-similarity**; and **strange attractors** and **self-organization**. (See the glossary at the conclusion of this chapter for explanations of terms in this section.)

Nonlinearity

All components of nonlinear systems affect each other, and small changes in one variable can have disproportional impacts on other variables. A simple example of this is a sound system with a microphone close to a loudspeaker and enough amplification in the system so that the feedback becomes positive. Then the slightest disturbance, auditory or electronic, results in the an ear-splitting squeal. The extreme sensitivity of chaotic systems sets strict limits on prediction and control of nature and explains the internal interdependence of natural systems (Peat 1991, 198–9).

Machines show Newtonian linearity; nonlinear systems are best portrayed by the metaphor of a waterfall—turbulent, irregular, unpredictable, and taking on forms of infinite variety. Hayles (1991) suggests that the broad implications of chaos studies derive from a change in vision, not from supposed changes in how the world actually is. As we view the world through the icon of a waterfall, complexity, scaling, self-similarity, and turbulence of chaotic systems appear.

Scaling and Self-Similarity

Fractals, computer-generated images of complex systems' spatial movement, seem to depict much of nature: tree branches, waterfalls, clouds, coastlines, lungs, and blood vessels. Fractal geometry's qualitative measurements show the shape of a whole system's movement and the nature of relationships throughout.

Fractals reveal properties of scaling and self-similarity within complex systems. Similar details at different scales indicate that a system's whole movement takes place continuously at every scale. Self-similarity at all scales means that all important details are repeated at each scale. Each part of a fractal is an image of the whole, with self-similar repetition of the basic shape of the whole at different scales. Holistic self-similar images occur in ferns, broccoli, cauliflower, and ocean waves. Fingers appear self-similar to hummingbird wings and dolphin fins, evidence of our evolution within the same holistic dynamic system called life (Briggs 1992, 19).

Strange Attractors and Self-Organization

Fractals also show the presence of strange attractors that come into play when complex systems move toward chaos. They form a "basin of attraction, an area displayed in computer-generated phase space that the system is magnetically drawn into, pulling the system into a visible shape" (Wheatley 1992, 122–3). Systems wander and experiment in multidimensional phase space. They are never in the same place twice, but their movements respect certain finite boundaries. Systems show unpredictability and inherent orderliness as they stay bounded within shapes recognizable as strange attractors (20–21). Boundedness reinforces the self-organizing capacity of systems.

According to Prigogine and Stengers (1984) self-organization occurs when a complex system, open to new information from both within and without, reaches a far-from-equilibrium stage. At bifurcation points, the system undergoes transformation; new order emerges out of chaos. These structures maintain basic identity by staying open to the environment; from the complex coupling of feedback continually reiterated, they are spontaneously reordered. A key property of complex dynamic systems, chaos is a "... new order so rich and subtle that it lies beyond any pattern or periodicity. Chaos is an order of infinite complexity" (Peat 1991, 196). Whether chaos contains deeply encoded order, as Feigenbaum, Mandelbrot, and Shaw think, or gives rise to emergent order, posited by Prigogine and Stengers' concept of self-organizing systems (Hayles 1991, 12–13), chaos studies clarify and validate new understandings of relationships between order and disorder. They are dialectically related, connected at deep levels.

Fractal images evoke deep recognition, similar to mazes and labyrinths in mythology, the iterative language games of children everywhere, patterns in chanting, ancient Celtic interlacing and Hokusai waves. "Confronting the orders of chaos, of growth and stability, it appears we are now coming face to face with something that is buried at the foundations of human existence" (Briggs and Peat 1989, 110). Fractals resonate with scientific discoveries, religion, psychology, literature, art, and music. This intuitive sense of congruence suggests connections between the new science and values linked to what Jung named the Eros, or Feminine, principle.

Integrity and the Feminine Principle

Conventional politics is grounded in the Logos principle's linearity, abstract analysis, and differentiation. The politics of integrity includes the Feminine principle as well. Instead of splitting apart and segmenting our private and public selves, thinking and feeling functions, theory and practice, we overcome their seeming opposition when we approach our lives and work from a new synthesis. Psychologist Carl Jung recognized archetypal patterns of human behavior not intrinsically connected with anatomical gender, the Logos and Eros principles. He associated qualities of abstract reasoning, differentiation, and valuing through analytical objectivity with the Logos principle. Our culture views these qualities as masculine. Intuition, flexibility, relatedness, interiority, and value through the feeling function, linked with the Eros principle, are attributed mainly to women. (Singer 1990, 13–20).

There is some Eros in men and Logos in women to be cultivated and integrated in the second half of life for health and wholeness. Jung advocated that each person develop both qualities. The Feminine in men's psyches enables them to connect with their feeling function and to develop the capacity to relate and connect. In women the Masculine brings relationship with their analytical and logical thinking capacity. With this integration, human fullness is enhanced.

The Absence of Eros from Mainstream Science

The Feminine has been absent from mainstream Western science. Science defines itself with Masculine characteristics and is then identified as the male intellect at work. Active, knowing subjects investigate passive, separate nature, equated mainly with the Feminine. "The presumption is that science, by its nature, is inherently masculine and that women can apprehend it only by an extreme effort of overcoming their own nature, which is inherently contradictory to science" (Bleier 1988, 196). Science epitomizes and represents the male-female dichotomies that it then discovers and measures. Polarized object-subject, active-passive, thought-feeling are symbolic and descriptive of the fundamental male-female dualism, as well as the associated relationship of dominance and subservience.

Kellert (1993, 152) investigated the repression of chaos findings by many scientists. Drawing from the feminist philosophy of science, he constructed a model analyzing interaction between the scientific sphere and the rest of society and culture. He examined a social explanation that focuses on scientists' and society's interest in dominating nature. This suggests that "chaotic behavior was screened off from study by a procrustean form of attention paid only to elements of the world that could be reduced to objects for human use." The overall goal guiding scientific work was manipulation and control. This analysis may overstate links between quantitative prediction and domination of nature, but the notion that solutions to physics problems must be simple, exact formulae providing predictability took hold partly because of a specific social interest (156–7). Nature was once feared to be full of turbulence and chaos, disorderly, needing control. Machiavelli's political leadership writings illustrate this view. He substituted fortune for the concept of nature and compared it to a violent, turbulent river, advising that fortune is like a fickle, capricious woman to be conquered by force. Men of "virtu" (masculine noun), more rational and orderly than women, analogous to "fortuna" (feminine noun), must subdue the disorderly and potentially destructive feminine. Humans, more purposive than natural processes, must take control of nature (Pitkin 1984).

New Science and the Threat of the Feminine

Hayles (1990) notes that to many scientists profiled by Gleick, chaos represents an opening of the self to the messiness of life, the "noisy," unpredictable phenomena of nonlinear dynamics that their orderly, linear models taught them to ignore. Characteristics that chaos theorists find fascinating and beautiful represent aspects of life usually labeled Feminine. Despite this, Gleick related the story of chaos science's development in exclusively masculine terms. He referred to few women and portrayed men living in environments from which anything feminine is remarkably absent. Women are depicted as distractions from the important work at hand. Including this detail let Gleick maintain an image of the scientific world as genderless or "one-gendered," inhabited by disconnected, solitary individuals.

Gleick and scientists he profiled may have unconsciously expunged Eros qualities from their world in order to validate chaos as a scientific concept. This exclusion depotentiates threats from the seeming "otherness" of chaos. Gleick's study indicates that opening themselves to the presence of chaos is fruitful for scientists' work and personal lives. Yet fascination with its wildness and otherness may arouse a need to control or even ". . . to subsume it within the known boundaries of the self . . . annihilating the very foreignness that makes it dangerously attractive" (Hayles 1990, 170).

The mere fact of studying chaos and complexity does not free scientists from the trap of old paradigm thinking. Until one recognizes and embraces the Feminine principle in science and in political theorizing, no transformation takes place. Gleick dismissed the work of Ilya Prigogine and Isabel Stengers (one of the few women scientist-authors or coauthors in complexity or chaos theory) with a brief mention. Chaos scientists whom he highlights hypothesize that within chaos there are embedded structures of order. By contrast, Prigogine and Stengers set forth the concept of emergent order, order not hidden within apparent chaos, but emerging from it. Their view permits chaos to function in its "liberating role as a representation of the other" (Hayles 1990, 170). This explanation retains a residue of the untamable and nonrational in understanding chaos. These scientists are far more transformational than Gleick and others who remain attached to old paradigms even as they explore new areas.

The Feminine Principle in Chaos and Complexity

Archetypally Feminine images abound in chaos and complexity studies despite efforts to ignore or to erect boundaries against them, as "noise" was dismissed from Newtonian science. New findings in science are strikingly similar to qualities ascribed to the Feminine, including nonlinearity, unpredictability, relatedness of parts to the whole and the importance of context. Feminine valuing is a qualitative, feeling function, similar to the nature of complexity theory. As Zisk explains in chapter 8, qualitative, subjective approaches, such as participant observation, enhance our knowledge and understanding of our subjects.

Shepherd (1993, 153) explored the presence in the new science of such Feminine qualities as receptivity, multiplicity, cooperation, intuition, and relatedness. Women tend to think contextually, discuss collaboratively and view life as a web of interconnections. The Eros function leads to awareness of the whole network of relationships impacted by a situation. Women approach nature receptively, in dialogue with it rather than as inquisition. ". . . (T)he Feminine process of circumambulation looks at a problem from all sides and at many levels, circling around it and seeing all of the relationships . . . giving us an appreciation for the complexity. . . ." Harrison's chapter 9 in this volume reveals how this approach is utilized by the professor in the university classroom. Multiplicity, complexity, interdependence, and cyclic processes in dynamic systems resemble the Feminine principle of relatedness. The key contribution the Feminine principle makes to scientific study is a vision of wholeness, seeing relationships and interconnections, stepping back to see the big picture (156). Thus, we discover that the whole gives meaning to the parts in ways before unseen. Chaos studies show order and pattern in the richness of diversity where once we observed only the erratic and random. Scaling, self-similarity, sensitivity to initial conditions, and emergent order manifest underlying webs of relationship.

Scientists use language of "hearth and home" to describe the findings of chaos and complexity studies because the linear language of Newton's universe is inadequate. Wheatley (1992) points out that there are no familiar ways to view levels of interconnections which characterize the universe that the new science reveals. Space is filled with connections, similar to webs and weaving. "In contrast to the starkly abstract and efficient language of mathematics, concepts in chaos science are described as dust, webs, cups, foam, . . . curds and whey" (Shepherd 1993, 90). The world of complexity science is the everyday, homely world, messy, fecund, with chaotic areas, rich in detail, traditionally relegated to the Feminine. Discoveries come from studying objects previously ignored as trivial: static, dripping faucets, clouds, waterfalls, boiling water, and smoke drifting upward from a hearth. "Like women, nonlinear systems were put aside, as women were relegated to attic offices, so as not to disturb the order of rational discourse" (Shepherd 1993, 93).

When we view chaos as richly complex information rather than absence of order, Feminine ways of knowing and valuing become vital to understanding the world. Nonlinearity and sensitivity to initial conditions show nature's underlying connectedness. Uncertainty and unpredictability offer freedom, flexibility, and creativity. These chaotic qualities, long identified with Mother Nature and women in general, are essential to continuing life. Chaos science shifts our world view and ". . . as a voice of the Feminine, chaos theory is changing science at its roots by changing its language. . . ." (Keller 1993, 35). Including the Feminine principle, the politics of integrity can transform political discourse and political community.

The Politics of Integrity

Efforts to transform social and political institutions will fail unless the deepest informing assumptions are examined. "Only if the powerful dynamics and historical tenacity of the core values are understood can the depth of the transformative task be embraced" (Spretnak 1991, 133). Chaos and complexity studies provide insights for thinking creatively about ways in which scientific findings shape values, institutions, leadership, participation, and policy-making processes in community life, and about political community and citizenship marked by integrity.

New scientific findings yield a perspective that integrates the whole and the interactions and relationships within it. Released from a talismanic focus on institutions, rules and procedures, we return to original values and meanings that serve as strange attractors and give our institutions and processes coherence, flexibility and boundedness (Wheatley 1992, 133–4). Sensitivity to context, emergent properties and indeterminacy inherent in nature elicit an evolutionary outlook, focused on where things are going and what they may become, beyond merely seeing things as they are (Zohar and Marshall 1994, 46).

Integrity of Self and Polity

New understandings of ourselves and our world begin internal personal transformation that can result in external changes to our polity. Block (1993, 77) writes that "If there is no transformation inside each of us, all the structural change in the world will have no impact on our institutions." Aligning our understanding of political community with what we know about complex dynamic systems promises to bring greater integrity and congruence into our lives.

Jung's metaphor of the alchemical process in psychology gives insights into the transformational effect that metaphors from the new science and the Feminine principle may have on us and on our political thinking. An "alchemical model calls for a breakdown of the present structures so that the opposites can unite to form something totally new . . ." (Shepherd 1993, 29–30). At the heart of the alchemical process is transformation in which more and more opposites are encompassed and integrated, leading to increasing wholeness, like the holism in chaos theory. Personal transformation leads toward inclusion of all aspects of our selves and our lives, worldly and spiritual, Masculine and Feminine, and private and public. For other aspects of the politics of integrity, see Halpern's discussion in chapter 3 of moving from partial selves to whole persons and Woolpert's chapter 15 on including the shadow side of the self in political life.

True to the Eros principle, the complementarity of Eros and Logos provides a broad perspective, richer than either alone can give. The two perspectives show aspects of a situation's deep underlying reality, like quantum physics' vast sea of potential and chaos theory's emergent order. Joining Feminine and Masculine principles shows us individual parts and their relationship to context and to the nature of the total system. The evaluative function can work with the logical function. From issue to issue, one perspective may be emphasized over the other; neither is neglected. Viewing issues from both perspectives provides more balanced information.

New scientific findings transform our views of human nature and society. From this, everything else follows. We transcend polarities of organic or collectivist views of polity which tended to submerge individuals into the whole community, and of atomistic approaches that elevated the individual, diminishing community. With an act of will inspired by creative imagination we can shift to new science metaphors and see ourselves as individuals in an inclusive commonwealth. (McCullough 1991, 104–5). This broad, flexible and balanced image of the self fits what we know we are: separate, independent persons (our "particle" aspect) and social creatures (our "wave" aspect). We see public lives and private selves interwoven, mutually enriching, with boundaries between public and private fluid and responsive to context.

From the viewpoint of integrity and holism, we and our relationships are webs of interactions, linked in complex, spiral or circular ways. Modern communications systems join all people and places in a vast information network. Small changes at a distance create large system changes as they share in the unbroken wholeness beneath apparent separation. Scaling and self-similarity suggest that it is impossible to divide issue areas automatically into local and national. The global impact of a drop in stock prices in New York and the effects of small numbers of consumers on the direction of whole industries (Arthur 1990, 92–9) demonstrate Lorenz's butterfly-wings principle. Working with flows of simultaneous small events in one subsystem can instigate large system change (Wheatley 1992, 42).

Integrity in Institutions and Processes

Seeing political processes and institutions as complex dynamic systems highlights the importance of the "edge of chaos." The balance point at which ". . . the components of a system never quite lock into place, and yet never quite dissolve into turbulence, either" (Waldrop, 192, 12) is central to complexity theory. Here energy and stability meet to provide spontaneity, adaptation, and system transformation. Life in complex systems is made possible in the balance of forces of order and disorder. At the edge of chaos, systems are stable enough to store information and evanescent enough to transmit it. In human organizations, this shifts the focus from systems' construction to their behavior. When some members are free to march to different drummers, the system becomes more fluid, aggregate fitness goes up and agents together move closer to the edge of chaos (312).

Fear of chaos as dangerous and destructive leads to hardened boundaries and controls, to preserve structures that seem threatened by externally induced change. Studying organizational complexity, Wheatley (1992) found that a system's self-organizing dynamic preserves its identity if it is open to information flowing in from outside. Freedom and order, once thought antithetical, are partners generating well-ordered, viable, autonomous systems. Permeable systems stay healthy and resilient and contain rich areas of information at the edge of chaos. Their strength is at the center, so the periphery does not need the protection of rigid boundaries.

In political institutions and processes we turn attention to the whole, to points of intersection and overlap, and to shared values, interests and capabilities, with less concern for parts, boundaries and exclusivity. Natural systems model the process of unfolding, whereas we struggle to construct layers; they openly participate and produce emergent complex structures while we labor to hold things together; in short, nature is an interweaving of process at a deep level from which are created whole organizations that are harmonious and orderly (Wheatley 1992, 118). Complexity theory suggests the need for a variety of information and viewpoints for healthy balance. Our task is to develop ways to balance openness and flexibility in institutions with stability, and balance concern for individuals and groups with attention to the public good.

Applied to political community, concepts of webbed connectedness, emergent order, scaling, and self-similarity show that all players and all parts of a system are vital. In webbed fields, no points are insignificant points; everyone contributes energy and information. According to the property of emergent order, a whole system is shaped by participation at all points in the web. This occurs in the public realm when dialogue becomes central. In ordinary conversation people hold and register points of view which they often feel compelled to defend, but in dialogue participants give serious consideration to others' views which may differ substantially from their own (Keepin 1994, 16). Dialogue requires openness to many varied positions and possibilities. Listening is as central to the process as speaking; we stand in the tension of opposites, of not yet knowing, which leads to creative breakthrough. Public spaces become arenas in which to consider together res publica, tables at which we take seats around issues concerning our community lives. Arendt believed that plurality allows us to come together and act in concert, seeing ourselves within a "web of relationships" (Dietz 1991; Kemmis 1990). People must be willing to hold many conflicting possibilities in their minds simultaneously. In dialogue about public matters, citizens create possibilities for insights and creativity to emerge, beyond what they might think on their own (Keepin 1994, 16).

Values are key subjects for dialogue, the strange attractors that give order to political systems. They shape constitutions and institutions that serve as their carriers. Joining the dialogue about the values important to us and what they mean and require of us, we retrieve them from submersion in institutions, processes, and rules. We balance creatively between commitment to values and recognition that they always express only partial truth. Choosing together among partial truths, we seek richer, more complex patterns that embrace essential elements of simpler truths (Zohar and Marshall 1994).

Partnership in Community

The alchemical process symbolizes political community's transformation to a partnership model congruent with the new science. Eisler developed "partnership" to describe the normative ideal of the culture of Minoan Crete. With insights from scientists studying chaos and complexity, Riane Eisler (1987) reassessed formation, persistence and change in complex social systems. After a stable period, social organizations experience disequilibrium and reach the edge of chaos. At a critical bifurcation point, a new and different social system emerges. She finds signs of approaching transformation, a shift from the patriarchal dominator society to a more advanced version of partnership society, based on "actualization power," not domination power. Partnership society transcends polarities, including those between right and left, capitalism and communism and Masculine and Feminine. The dominator model views power as the capacity to control and destroy; the partnership model views power as empowerment.

With self-similarity and symmetry across scale, complexity theory presents an alternative model for power in which hierarchical control and domination have no place. Neither "top down" nor "bottom up" concepts of power apply absolutely. Instead, in light of the presence of self-organization around attractors, power becomes "power with" not power over, shared as well as concentrated at points. This includes the Feminine capacity to nurture and support life and gives new metaphors for organization, leadership, and participation. Waldrop (1992, 295) analyzes complexity at the edge of chaos. He contrasts an overly rigid, centralized, controlled USSR and a laissez-faire England during the industrial revolution with a view of healthy societies that keep order and chaos in balance: "Not a wishy-washy, average . . . balance; like living cells . . . regulating themselves with a dense web of feedback . . . [with] room for creativity, change and response to new conditions." Systems move toward greater health and complexity when bottom-up organization fosters flexibility and top-down organization channels information and preserves the organization.

Community members are empowered to create the institutional culture, to be accountable and to own their actions. They bestow power upon leaders who seek emerging patterns, free from futile efforts to maintain external control and direction. Each citizen has a stake in civil community and the community has a stake in each citizen. Voices receive respect, not just equal votes (McCullough 1991). Redesigning governance includes commitment to act in the interest of the whole community. "Freedom and commitment in every case are joined at the hip" (Block 1993, 75). Sharing in power, "power with," leads to decision making based on discussion and search for consensus. Partnership permits openness to information and processes to channel its inflow. Self-organizing systems resemble whirlpools with information entering from the surrounding environment and forming into dynamic patterns. As more information enters, the mix is richer; more choices are available. Valuing diversity and including multiple points of view add to the chaos of a decision-making process. Openness and flexibility take us to the edge of chaos and revitalize the process of self government.

Institutions aligned with a partnership model replace old-style leadership with stewardship, and self-interest with service. In chaos theory terms, faith in ourselves and our world lets us remove control from the center of our transactions. "To surrender is to accept that there is a waxing and waning rhythm to events and to trust that good things can happen without our needing to control them. . . . Stewardship is the choice to unravel the connection between control, safety and success . . . essential to discovering what is possible for us" (Block 1993, 75; Zimmerman and Hurst 1993). In partnership organizations stewardship and service add meaning and integrity to our lives.

Conclusion

The politics of integrity is based on a partnership model of holistic community, with self-organizing properties, attracted to naturally flowing organizational states. Power through experience of life replaces power over life. Whyte (1994, 243) asks of corporate America: "What would it be like to grow organizations whose complexity arises from the cross-pollinating visions and imaginations of their constituent members?" Strong vision and purpose act as strange attractors; a cohesive group with a set of ethics, values and tasks has room to develop its own approach. The presence of potent strange attractors assures us that apparently disorderly systems are made up of orderly behaviors. Complex systems are multifaceted and flexible, allowing them to switch and adapt among different behaviors.

Politics can be structured ". . . to enhance the great unfolding [of the universe], drawing forth the creativity and deep interiority of the individual as well as the bonds of communion in many directions." (Spretnak 1991, 217). This entails evocative relationships and cultivation of wisdom and compassion. Entering ongoing political discussion as individuals and groups with diverse interests and as relational selves, citizens search for what is good for themselves and their community. The public interest is the process of deliberating about public values. Barber (1984, 137) views politics in "strong democracy" in alchemical terms: a group of citizens around a cafeteria table inventing new menus and recipes, experimenting with new diets to create a public task, and reconstructing their values as public norms.

Evolution continually creates more complicated, richer, more structured things. ". . . slowly, haltingly, but inexorably, learning and evolution move agents along the edge of chaos in the direction of greater and greater complexity" (Waldrop 1992, 296). A universal evolutionary process with new patterns draws chaos into order, simple patterns into more complex ones. Like all of nature we evolve when we are poised at the edge, both holding to tradition and letting go as new possibilities emerge. Open to widening possibilities, we move toward integration and complexity and realize ourselves more fully as individuals, groups, and societies.

When significant numbers of strategically located political actors operate from the new scientific worldview, they generate strange attractors within whose boundaries a holistic politics of integrity can form from the chaos of current politics. Groups at the edge of our political process, such as those Brettschneider (chapter 7 in this volume) studied, seek politics of dialogue and empowerment. They may be joined by liberals discarding outmoded categories of individualism and collectivism, ecologists, and advocates of a spiritual or prophetic approach to politics, all sharing a holistic worldview consistent with the new science. As such groups and individuals work together, they can become transformation agents, transforming themselves and their communities (Knight 1995; see Lerner 1996, 285–6).

Drawn from the perspective of the new science, the politics of integrity leads us to understand our natures as both separate individuals and social persons and to include our mundane and spiritual aspects and Logos and Eros qualities when we enter dialogue as participatory citizens. We approach political thinking as increasingly whole persons, bringing the Feminine principle's evaluative function into public life. Political values of freedom, equality and justice gain fresh meaning and vitality when brought into thoughtful community conversation (Roelofs 1994). Today's issues require ethical judgment based on commitment to public values that transcend narrow self-interest. Accountability to others for what we know and say and do creates the public (McCullough 1991). Thus we create and transform ourselves as partners in community.

Chaos and Complexity
Brief Glossary of Selected Terms

chaos.   The property of a complex, nonlinear system that causes the system's behavior to be unpredictable and seemingly random.

Chaos Science/Theory.   Research areas that deal with complex, nonlinear systems that cannot be fully explained by the conventional Newtonian science. Disciplines have adopted different names, such as adaptive systems, complex systems, nonlinear dynamic systems, etc.

complexity.   The property of a system deriving from the interconnectedness of its components. The degree of complexity of a system is a function of the number of parts, the linearity or nonlinearity of their relationship, and the tightness or looseness of their coupling. "Complexity science" is the study of these systems.

edge of chaos. The region where systems exhibit behavior in which components never quite lock into place, but never quite dissolve into random turbulence.

fractal. A computer-generated geometrical object of infinite complexity, often seen as a visual paradigm for a complex, chaotic system, because it is generated by solving a simple, nonlinear equation many times and plotting the solutions on a plane. Fractals are characterized by self-similarity, scaling, and the presence of a strange attractor that gives the system its boundedness. Each part of a fractal contains an image of the whole.

nonlinearity. The characteristic of a system in which each of its components affects all the others as information feeds back on itself. Nonlinear, complex systems are so webbed with feedback that changes in one variable can have disproportionate impacts on all other variables.

self-organization. The ability of a complex system that has moved far from equilibrium to reorganize itself into a new structure, which occurs spontaneously from the emergent behavior of the whole system.

self-similarity. The characteristic of fractal images where all important details are repeated at each scale. Scaling refers to the recurrence of symmetries across levels of scale, with different levels interconnected through nonlinear loops.

strange attractor. A graphic portrayal of a system's tendency to cluster its behavior around a set of values so that no one value or sequence of values is repeated. Its behavior is bounded, that is, stays within a shape recognizable as its strange attractor.

Note

1. Carl Jung used the concept of the alchemical process to illuminate the transformational process by which substances undergo fundamental change and opposites unite to form something altogether new.

5

The Theory of a Transformational Political Movement: Green Political Theory

DANIEL NEAL GRAHAM

Introduction

There are many similarities between Democratic Left and Green politics. Yet the philosophical underpinnings of traditional Democratic Left politics remains boxed in an old paradigm that Greens have transcended in favor of an emerging ecocentric alternative. This novel paradigm provides Greens a "new" (renewed) framework to evaluate the role of economics, science, technology, culture, epistemology, ideology, and spirituality in political/social transformation. My chapter will explore how the paradigm encompassing Green philosophy can transform the politics of the Democratic Left and offers a synthesis that can bridge the gap between those concerned primarily with environmental issues and those concerned primarily with economic and equity issues.

Although both Democratic Left politics and Green politics have attempted to transform modern industrial polities, ecocentrism differentiates Green politics from the Democratic Left in many ways. The Green philosophy itself has ten major points. Green politics was founded on four basic pillars: 1) Ecology: understanding nature's interconnected webs that lead to holistic, network-thinking, and acting; 2) Social Responsibility: social justice incorporated within national and international class concerns; 3) Grass Roots Democracy: decentralized, nonhierarchical, participatory blends of direct and representative democracy; and 4) Nonviolence: rejection of personal and structural violence; occasional civil disobedience (Capra and Spretnak 1984). These were expanded by American Greens to form the "Ten Key Values", adding: 5) Diversity, 6) Future Focus, 7) Feminism, 8) Social Justice, 9) Decentralization, and 10) Community Economics. Together they form a social/ecocentric framework for radical systemic and cognitive transformation. (Coleman 1994, 97–119; Rensenbrink 1992, 110, 153)

There are three major philosophical differences between Greens and the Democratic Left that this chapter will explore. These differences are attributable to different paradigmatic views. The Democratic Left operates within an old, anthropocentric paradigm, and the Greens embrace a new, ecocentric paradigm.

First, Green philosophy poses a paradigmatic critique to models that embrace Cartesian instrumental rationality and modern scientific reductionism. Greens incorporate a holistic relational epistemology that rejects dualism in favor of "and/and" integrative thinking. This holistic science challenges *how* as well as *what* we think and rejects the pretense to "value-free" science.

Second, ecofeminism has influenced Green thinking and transformed feminist concerns for equality by linking ecology and feminism. Ecofeminist insights have expanded traditional feminist attention from gender, class, and race, to species and planetary considerations.

Third, Green philosophy offers a synthesis of ecology and equality that challenges anthropocentric assumptions and offers an ecocentric alternative. Ecocentrism is a life-centered, dialectically interdisciplinary world view that transcends the limits of humanism by incorporating social concerns within the biospheric whole.

While these paradigmatic differences will be the major focus of this chapter, it is important to note that there are several ideological, strategic and tactical differences that demonstrate a contrast between Greens and the Democratic Left.

> 1. Greens have shown greater attention to movement/party balance. Although labor unions and social justice groups remain important components of contemporary Left politics, there is much less concern with party activities gaining dominance over the movement wing. Green social movement roots (peace, feminism, human rights, environmentalism) provide them with more potential auxiliary support than the Left.
>
> 2. With their explicit goal of keeping means and ends congruent, Green parties have taken numerous steps to prevent the creation of internal hierarchy through rules that keep elected officials more beholden to members than they are in traditional parties, resulting in gender balance requirements for electoral slates, limited policy-

making power for elected officials, and a preference for consensus decision making whenever possible.

3. Greens have moved beyond materialist values while at the same time embracing some preindustrial values derived from indigenous non-European cultures. These value shifts have been tied to specific issues that are salient for the Greens but often ignored by the Democratic Left.

4. Green approaches to spirituality also distinguish them from most of the modern Left, although both support the formal separation of church and state. Secular humanism appeals to people's civic ethics. Greens go further by addressing important spiritual estrangement from the rest of nature. Ecotheology's inclusion of nonhuman life and the planet itself for moral consideration expands modernity's spiritual realm.

5. Greens' promotion of common values within a diversity of settings is significantly different from Enlightenment Humanism's assumption of linear progress toward future social harmony. Political disagreements and diversity are natural in a world of constant change. Green bioregionalist sensibilities oppose the misplaced promise of one world government, without embracing ultranationalism.

6. The call for more decentralized political and economic democracy also differentiates the Greens from traditional social democracy. Greens oppose the paternalism, centralization, bureaucratization, and increased dependency associated with modern industrial statism. Their goal of increased local and regional self-reliance and control over the basic necessities of life overlaps with several traditional conservative values (self-initiative, entrepreneurship, prudence, pay as you go, efficiency, conservation, individualism, and community). Greens temper their decentralist goals with national and global standards for environmental protection, human rights, equality, and diversity.

It is also important to point out that while Green transformationalists have worked towards unity on these key values, there has been significant diversity of interpretation, emphasis, and application based on global geopolitical distinctions, the social movement background of various currents, and the explicit attempt to balance unity and diversity within Green parties/movements. United States Greens include: deep ecologists, (left) social ecologists, ecofeminists, ecosocialists, bioregionalists, spiritual lifestyle groups, left/liberal environmental populists, and radical conservative libertarian types. These overlapping currents may be flowing in the same general direction, but not always in one smooth river. Debates have often been turbulent, leading some to branch off into tributaries, chaotic white-water, and harmful whirlpools. Divisions continue over party/move-ment balance, the role and scale of electoral politics, and relative issue saliency. In spite of such diversity, Green politics has evolved over the last ten years to the point where it has become a distinctly transformational alternative to traditional Left politics (Bahro 1984; Coleman 1994; Graham 1995a; Rensenbrink 1992). The stamina of the Greens as a political movement and growth in its party organi-zation is due in large part to the viability of the ecocentric philoso-phy that supports the Green movement-party.

Green Philosophy as Holistic Science

Greens reject the modern scientific reductionism that can be traced to Newton, Bacon, and Descartes (Milbrath 1989). That method of study analyzed materials and problems by reducing them to their building blocks, an approach now prominent in social science attempts to become "value free." No whole can be reduced to the mere sum of its parts; far more important are the relationships among the different parts of the whole and to its environment. Greens see the earth as an interactive biotic system, rather than the dead mechanical entity es-poused by the founding fathers of modern science.

Capra's alternative scientific paradigm highlights the intercon-nections between ecology, economy, technology, science, society, polity, culture, and perceptions (Capra 1982). His five criteria of holistic "systems thinking" emphasizes the relationships among variables by shifting: 1) from parts to the whole as the focus of analysis; 2) from structure to process as the underlying basis for reality; 3) from objec-tive to "epistemic" science; 4) from foundation building to networks as the metaphor for knowledge; and 5) from claims of truth to one of approximate description, sometimes described as "intersubjective truth" (Capra 1992–1993, 9–10; Milbrath, 1989, 61–62).

Green epistemology is transscientific, not antiscience (Graham 1995b). Science can only approximate the discovery of "objective truth" since the observed is always impacted by the observer and her scientific models—including reliance upon the visible light spectrum itself (Heisenberg's "Uncertainty Principle"). All human models are approximations, not duplications of reality. Flat road maps are useful guides for some distances, but not for transatlantic flights. As Knight and Zisk's chapters in this volume make clear, quantitative analyses are informative but limited. Capra's approach is more inclusive.

"Science, in my view, need not be restricted to . . . quantitative analyses. I am prepared to call my approach to knowledge scientific that satisfies two conditions: all knowledge must be based on systematic observation, and must be expressed in terms of self-consistent but limited and approximate models. These requirements—the empirical basis and the process of model-making represent . . . the two essential elements of the scientific method." (Capra 1982)

As a human project, science is always a subset of the biosphere. My diagram, "Overlaps: Biosphere, Social, and Science Realms" (Figure 5.1), illustrates the following:

Figure 5.1
Overlaps: Biosphere, Social, and Science Realms

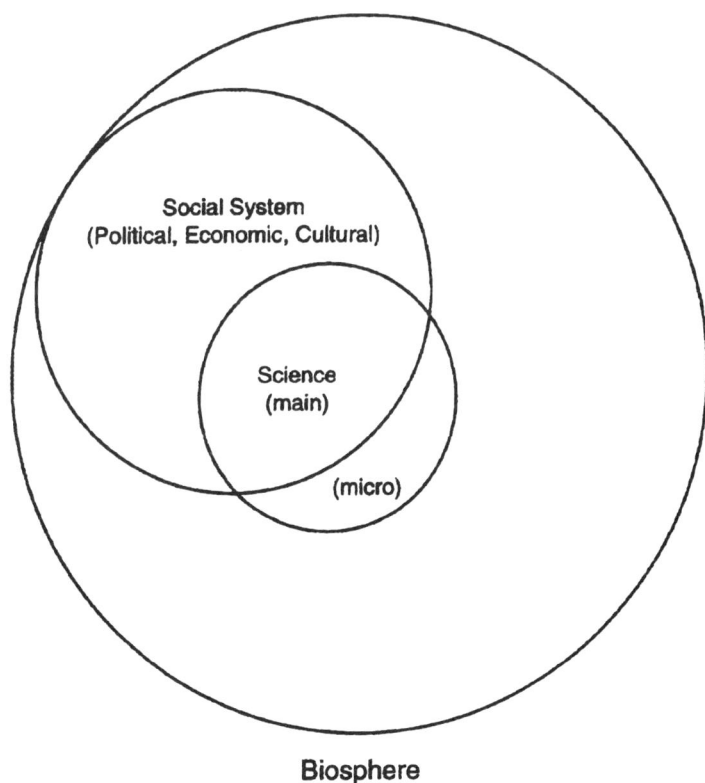

Social System
(Political, Economic, Cultural)

Science
(main)

(micro)

Biosphere

Social (Human) System:	Subset of Biosphere
Science:	Subset of Social System, with "semi-autonomous" overlap with Biosphere

1. Observers can never be completely detached from what they are studying because all social systems are subsets of the biosphere.

2. The scientific realm is one subset of the social realm, influenced by political, economic, cultural, and philosophical value factors at the macro level.

3. The scientific realm has a particular overlap with the biosphere not usually occupied by the general public. However, even basic research is constrained in its search for objective truth by the microlevel limitations of scientific methodology itself.

Modern science continues to make important contributions to monitoring and mitigating environmental problems, but informed decision making must also be supplemented by social considerations.

Overlaps: Biosphere, Social, and Science Realms

How we interpret the world directly affects whether and how we might try to change it (Hughes 1985; Thompson 1987; Winner 1986). Green transformational politics uses observations of Nature's lessons as guidelines (not pronouncements) for how to organize human societies in a sustainable manner. Henderson's "Social Implication of Six Emerging (Post-Cartesian) Principles" applies insights from her paradigmatic principles to social organization (Henderson 1991, 99).

Overreliance on quantifiable analysis is a primary example of scientific reductionism and social science positivism. In Henderson's view, "economics is not a substitute for thought, computation cannot substitute for conceptualization, nor do correlations necessarily imply

Table 5.1
Social Implications of Six Emerging (Post-Cartesian) Principles

Interconnectedness	Planetary cooperation of human societies, living systems policy models.
Redistribution	Justice, equality, balance, reciprocity, sharing.
Change	Redesign of institutions, perfecting means of production, changing paradigms and values.
Complementarity	Unity and diversity, from "either/or" to "both/and" logics.
Heterarchy	Distributed networks and intelligence, no rigid organizations or hierarchies.
Indeterminacy	Many models, viewpoints, compromise, humility, openness, evolution, "learning societies."

causality" (Henderson 1991, 333). Henderson maintains: "What is required . . . is not so much micro-rigor and more data collection, but paradigmatic rigor, in which we unravel the models and deeply imbedded assumptions." (350)

Important to these differences is the contrast between "knowledge" (the accumulation and cataloging of facts) and "wisdom" (which incorporates intuition, empathy, compassion, and emotion as complements to rational, logical, and analytical thinking)—a distinction explored in detail by Herman in chapter 2. Green transformational epistemology is multivariable, relational, integrative, and holistic (Kelley 1991). "Ecosophy" critically revises our modern industrial values of domination, growthism, controlism, competitionism, rationalism, instrumentalism, materialism, reductionist scientism, and techno-fixism (Drengson 1991).

Green political philosophy incorporates physical, mental and physiological forms of understanding, based on the recognition that mind/body dualism is a misleading concept. Greens reject reductionist "either/or" thinking in all fields including the debates over "political correctness" (PC), which trivializes the historical record by turning substantive discussions into differences of opinions. As Cummings demonstrates in chapter 14, transformational thinking should transcend the constraints of PC thinking, not as a rejection of ideology per se, but to emphasize how all classifications are artificial replications of reality.

> I am not denouncing ideology itself or hoping to see its end . . . As Marx said, the point is not only to understand the world but to change it, and change requires the action-oriented commitment of ideology. But a danger . . . is the temptation to distort reality in ways that are politically convenient and psychologically gratifying but ultimately false and self-defeating . . . (Cummings 1995, 17–18)

Reflecting their sensitivity to the interrelationships among parts of the political whole, Greens also advocate a more diverse and decentralized approach to the dissemination of information, and democratic decision making. They reject the notion that elites have an expertise that qualifies them to set agendas and establish policies and priorities without consultation and deliberation with those affected by their decisions. Greens embrace the democratization of the work as well as political environment.

In chapter 3, Halpern demonstrates how transformational politics challenges the capitalist and statist norms that maintain elitism, bureaucracy, and social alienation. Advocacy of more personalized social relationships should not be seen as an attempt to turn back the clock to some idealized "good old days." It more closely resembles the classical socialist goal of freely associating workers/citizens, based on new modes of ecocentrically informed political and productive organizations (Luke 1983).

Green Philosophy as a Synthesis of Ecology and Feminism

One of the most vital aspects of Green transformational politics is the synthesis between ecology and feminism. Ecofeminists see the domination of women by men historically connected to men's domination of nature. This patriarchal kernel of objectification laid the basis for the exploitation of humans by race and class, as well as the exploitation of other life forms (Merchant 1980; Yeich 1991). Ecofeminists also address issues of power, truth, spirituality, scientific objectivity, modes of interpreting the human condition, and the inequalities of formal/informal economic systems (Caldecott and Leland 1983; Plant 1989; Mies and Shiva 1993). Greens try to balance traditionally "feminine qualities" (cooperation, empathy, intuitive thinking, nurturing, spirituality) with traditionally "masculine qualities " (competition, assertiveness, analytical thinking, rationality).

Green politics extends the concerns important to democratic left politics from class, race, and gender, to species and planet, and paradigmatically challenges the limitations of enlightenment-based instrumental rationality. This paradigm shift has also prodded debates within established religious traditions, redefining the role of humans from dominators to stewards (Hart 1984; Spretnak 1986; Berry 1989; Skolimowski 1985). Ecotheology is clearly not an other-worldly form of escapism. As the best known Western Saint of Secularity declared, "the point is to change the world."[1] Green transformationalists concur: ". . . we have an obligation to contribute human talents . . . to the success of Earth and Universe, and to find our fulfillment . . . in activities which make the Earth and Universe successful . . ." (Berry 1993).

Green Philosophy as a Synthesis of Ecology, Equality and Ecocentrism

As discussed earlier, Green Transformational Politics is more holistic than modern Left approaches. Greens' insistence that humans must remember their biological status highlights the degree of Western thought's estrangement from the rest of nature. Living in climate-controlled cubicles has squeezed our range of perception to the point where people talk about "being into the outdoors" as a lifestyle choice. Human societies are biological and social. Any political philosophy that ignores this reality is incomplete and unrealistic.

Environmental protection policies have been accepted by most Left parties as necessary for human health and as aesthetically desirable, but still counter to the growth economics deemed necessary for job creation and other equity goals. The editor's introduction to my 1985 article in the *Socialist International Journal* was indicative of the established Social Democratic attitudes towards emerging Greens—a grudging acceptance of the incremental importance of environmental issues for public health reasons. More than ten years later most socialists acknowledge (if not accept) the transformational content of the Green critique. As I indicated in 1985:

> Above all, I believe, greens, democratic socialists, feminists and other progressives need to develop a much more ecumenical spirit towards each other's motivational character. We all have an increasingly clear idea of who our political adversaries are. It is now time we gained a better understanding of who our potential allies are.

All Greens, most environmentalists, and many on the democratic left now accept the interactive links between ecology and equality goals (i.e., poverty and the low economic, political, and cultural status of women are now seen as major factors underlying overpopulation). On the whole, Greens have been quicker to embrace equality concerns than socialists have to accept ecological imperatives (Graham 1986; 1989). Although some ecosocialists have moved closer to Green politics in recent years, they still see ecological concerns as a subset of modern radical humanism. Green transformational philosophy incorporates human concerns within a wider life-centered perspective.[2]

Robyn Eckersley sees theoretical bridges being built from both sides. Whether they join together in the middle or end up as parallel linkages may not be as important as whether people from each side make the crossing to see the other side's view:

> Indeed, there is already a strong resonance between ecocentric social goals and key ecosocialist goals such as the new internationalism, democratic participation, and ecologically sustainable production for human need . . . both ecocentrism and ecosocialism reject an atomistic model of reality in favor of a reciprocal model of internal relations . . . The upshot for ecosocialism would be a widening of its field of moral concern considerably so that it

reaches beyond the human community to include all of the myriad life-forms in the biotic community . . . The upshot for ecocentrism would be a strengthening and broadening of its political and economic analysis . . . to determine the kinds of institutional changes and redistributive measures . . . required to ensure an equitable transition toward a sustainable and more cooperative society. (Eckersley 1992,)

Green Philosophy as a Basis for Transformational Policies

Greens have forced modern social democrats to redefine their ideological positions, which often fall short of the classical goals of socialism concerning peace, participatory democracy, equality, ending work alienation, and creating a humane and harmonious society. By promoting "post materialist values," Greens have also helped revive debates over some important perennial themes in western political philosophy—human/nature relationships, power, morality, technology and modernity, alienation, ends/means relationships, spirituality and truth, within a new ecocentric paradigm (Inglehart 1977; Milbrath 1984; Inglehart and Abramson 1994).

Balancing Economic and Ecological Concerns

The most common conflict between Greens and organized labor has concerned job-dependent economic growth, ecological concerns over finite resources, pollution, and unsafe energy technologies like nuclear power. Corporate-capitalist interests have long used the threat of layoffs to pit labor against environmentalists. Kazis and Grossman (1982) have challenged the myth that sound environmental policies destroy job opportunities, noting how job blackmail has historically been used to control workers efforts to unionize, create safe working conditions, and control the work process. They also show how pollution control in the early 1980s actually created a net increase in jobs through new occupations, and the protection of fishing, forestry, and tourism (Kazis and Grossman 1982, 24–28). A 1994 Massachusetts Institute of Technology (M.I.T.) study based on twenty years of economic and environmental data indicated that environmental regulations have improved overall economic performance in the United States. A corroborating study by the Institute of Southern Studies revealed a significant correlation between positive environmental and economic rankings by state (Springston, 1995).

Economic growth measured in GNP or GDP terms has not succeeded in evening out the maldistribution of wealth and income (Kazis and Grossman 1982, 17–35). GDP quantifies the aggregate output of goods and services without distinguishing between socially/environmentally useful and destructive production. Guiding an economy using GDP alone is like flying an airplane with no altitude indicator, no compass, and a finicky fuel gauge. GDP growth is no longer the means to economic ends—it has been reified into the end goal itself. As Marx noted a century ago, making money becomes the goal and the exchange of goods and services merely the means (see, e.g., McLellan 1977, 109–11). Misguided economic debates between Greens and labor unions will continue as long as capitalist rationale remains unchallenged, especially in the areas of economic growth, environmental impacts, and investment decision criteria (Aronowitz and DiFazio 1994).

Divisions between Green and Left economic positions continue, although there have been efforts to link jobs and environmental protection. In 1980, close to 1,000 unionists attended the first U.S. National Labor Conference for Safe energy and Full Employment. Fifty-five unions from thirty-three states met to call for an end to further dependence on nuclear power, guaranteed jobs for displaced workers, and a rapid switch to policies for safe energy and full employment (Labor Committee for Safe Energy and Full Employment 1980). Four years later, the AFL-CIO industrial unions department helped form the OSHA/Environment Network which linked unions and environmentalists on right-to-know laws, revitalizations of the EPA, and policies to protect the environment without sacrificing jobs (OSHA/Environmental Network 1984). Throughout the 1980s some elements of the peace movement worked with environmentalists and labor activists on economic conversion campaigns (Renner 1990), redefining "security" from a nationalistic military basis to one of global environmental and economic interdependency (Henderson 1987). Conversion campaigns help counter the charge that Green politics is made up of selfish middle class nature lovers who care little about how lower income groups are affected by environmental protection.

During the 1980s, United States environmentalism became more of a mass movement extending across class, race and gender lines (O'Brien 1983). Campaigns dealing with toxic waste emerged in working class neighborhoods where many women became personally involved in environmental activism for the first time (Geiser 1983). An "Environmental Justice Movement" evolved, targeting corporate responsibility for unhealthy homes and communities. "Environmental racism"—the tendency for incinerators, landfills, and other pollution sources to disproportionately affect nonwhite, lower class communities—has now become an issue for many established environmental groups, especially those on the left like Greenpeace, the Student Environmental Action Coalition (SEAC), and Friends of the Earth. These equity concerns have also received increased attention from more moderate groups like the National Wildlife Federation (NWF), Audubon Society, National Resources Defense Council (NRDC), and the Sierra Club (Bullurd and Wright 1992; Cable and Cable 1995). In conjunction with the increased political participation and sense of efficacy by many working class women in antitoxic waste campaigns, these developments have helped synthesize the issues of class, gender, and nature conflicts, strengthening the transformational link between equality and ecology within left, Green, and feminist groups during the 1980 to 90s.

Economic policy debates still divide Greens and the contemporary Left. Greens reject unlimited economic growth policies because all economic systems are subsets of the biosphere. Ecological realities challenge the inherent logic of modern growth economics, which assumes capital substitutability for nature, and technofix solutions to environmental problems (Haenke 1989; Eleff 1985). Diminishing returns (in employment and "socially useful" productivity) from increased capital, energy, and resource investment fly in the face of GNP growth promises. (Henderson 1981; 1991) Overconsumption in the first world, entrenched poverty in the third world, and global environmental damage are all direct results of an economic system that demands consumption of goods and services beyond the saturation point (Trainer 1985). Economic equity and sustainability are interdependent with ecological sustainability (Kassiola 1991; Stretton 1976; Schnaiberg, 1980; Schnaiberg and Gould 1994; Ophuls 1992).

Emphasizing Planetary Sustainability

Underlying this debate over economic growth is the philosophical question of how humans relate to the rest of the natural world. Instrumental materialism is interwoven with capitalist industrialism, as well as patriarchy, which feminists see as the precursor to other forms of objectification. Although most Left models embrace a manipulative approach to nature, some social democratic parties and unions have promoted the idea that only environmentally sustainable economics can fulfill traditional socialist goals of job and income security (McClure 1985; Schohl 1985). Green transformationalists oppose the instrumentalist thinking historically common to both state-socialist (communist) and capitalist industrial models, opting to work with Nature rather than trying to dominate and control (Kothar 1981; Schroyer 1983).

A major distinction between the dominant industrial paradigm and transformational Green thinking is the contrast between (social-centered) "anthropocentrism" and (life-centered) "biocentrism." Greens see the earth ("Gaia") as a complex living entity—the holistic product of all its life-forms in dynamic harmony with the planet's maintenance systems and ecologies. All life has subjectivity and a degree of intrinsic value—an expansion of the "natural rights" claims of enlightened humanism (Devall and Sessions 1985; Tobias 1985; Thompson 1987; Bunyard and Goldsmith 1988). Ecocentrism transcends the anthropocentric/biocentric debate by recognizing the codependency of humans and other species for ecosystem integrity (Eckersley 1992, 49–71; Skolimowski 1981).

Having the distinct technological ability to destroy ecosystems places a uniquely powerful responsibility on humans. It signals a culmination of scientific hubris towards nature, which has been used to justify the objectification, exploitation, and commodification of other species, other people (by class, race, gender), and the planet (Merchant 1980). While (left) social ecologists emphasize exploitation within human societies, and deep ecologists focus more on the-exploitation of nature by humans, Transformationalists' main concern is how these objectifications are mutually reinforcing. Both currents seek earth-based ethics to insure social and planetary integrity (Bookchin 1990; Leopold 1949).

Green Philosophy as a Basis for Political Action

Modern Western political theory, including the Marxist tradition, see human freedom and security as inversely related to the necessities of nature. Freedom *from* nature has been pursued through a plethora of technological inventions and applications, beneficial and destructive alike. Floods, famines, fires, earthquakes, droughts, hurricanes, and mudslides highlight the brittleness of industrial infrastructures. Human impact may be increasing the probability of these "natural disasters." In any case, it is clearly impossible to totally dominate nature (Tenner 1996).

For Greens, freedom is found in learning how to work *with* nature, rather than trying to dominate and control it. A surfer catching a wave illustrates freedom within nature. Riding a rocket ship to escape earth's gravity reflects the Cartesian/Industrial version, which can never completely escape nature's pull. Surfers find freedom through respect and balance rather than in attempts to overcome or escape.

Social democrats, environmentalists, feminists, native peoples, and environmental justice populists, continue to be Greens' most likely allies. Philosophical affinity with some classical conservative values (libertarianism, decentralism, self-reliance, prudence, conservation) provide even wider ideological overlap possibilities (Rensenbrink 1992, 157). Like plant stems that bend but don't break during a storm, being flexible can be a source of strength rather than a sign of weakness. Finding points of common ground while maintaining key principles should aid transformational change more readily than the sectarian "lines of demarcation" that have haunted radical movements of the past.

An accompanying source of strength for Green transformationalists is their ecumenical approach to political motivation and activism. Some people are activated by secular ethical considerations, others by more spiritual/religious concerns, many by scientific insights, and still others by self-interest responses to exploitation. Striving for unity/diversity balance is a difficult but necessary goal (see Woolpert, chapter 15 in this volume). Orthodox notions of ideological consensus ("workers of the world unite") overstate potential class solidarity, and under-appreciate national, cultural, religious, ethnic, and individual differences. By accepting diversity as natural, Greens may have a better opportunity to remain true to their principles, finding alliances based on coalition efforts where possible, rather than trying to be all things to all people. Green parties should continue to be the radical conscience of their respective political systems, competing and working with other parties, especially those on the democratic left. Successful protest campaigns, alternative institution-building, and principled electoral contests cannot guarantee systemic reforms, but there is little chance without them.

If Greens are serious about making transformational change, their philosophical and paradigmatic understandings will have to be formulated into salient political-economic program alternatives to a much greater degree. Creative work in this area continues (Brown 1990; Korten 1994; Wachtel 1993; Sears 1993; "Business on a Small Planet [special issue]," *In Context,* No. 41, Summer 1995; Miller

1993; Renner 1992; Durning 1993). Sustainable and equitable political economies will require the use of full-cost environmental accounting, like the "Green GNP" introduced in Germany and Holland (Brown 1990, 5). Additional policy tools could include: baseline data of natural capital; environmental impact statements; new economic instruments; environmental audits; full cost accounting (for extracting and production); environmental reporting, and regulatory enforcement that incorporates positive and negative incentives.

Although Green transformation requires personal and cultural changes, individualist/lifestyle solutions alone cannot succeed without systemic reforms.

> Making such a vision a reality will require . . . vigorous political education, workplace and community organizing, building alternative institutions, independent electoral work outside of either of the capitalist parties, coalition building, and aggressive nonviolent direct action campaigns. As Frederick Douglas pointed out so long ago, 'Power concedes nothing without a struggle.' (Chase 1995, 9)

Conclusion

The Greens' most lasting contribution has been the restoration of Ecology ("Earth Wisdom") to the social marquee, joining the three concepts that have become permanent elements of the modern political lexicon. *Freedom, equality, democracy,* and *ecology* have become as integral to the modern era as the "Four Basic Elements" of the ancient world: *Air, water, fire* and *earth*, with which they also share some symbolic affinity.

1) Air   Symbolizes *freedom* to live and express.

2) Water   Symbolizes *equality* in that it is a mixing medium, and an equal necessity for all life.

3) Fire   Symbolizes *democracy* in its ability to create light, warmth, and community; being produced by friction it can also burn and divide.

4) Earth   Symbolizes *ecology* with its interconnected wholeness, unity/diversity balance, and provisions for life.

Transformational political movements are the social equivalent of individual human survival traits like doubt, anger (not hate), reflection, flexibility, intuition, instinct, empathy, and adaptability.

Greens have revitalized the biological basis of political philosophy through their ecocentric sensibilities and holistic paradigm thinking. Seeing ourselves as guests rather than owners of this living planet might seem *radical* in the modern age. It is *axiomatic* when we step outside of our physical and mental edifices.

Notes

1. "Marx as an empiricist would have been just another learned man. As an apocalyptic dogmatist, he became the founder of a new religion, whose writings would be quoted as part of a new sacred canon. The most interesting portion of this transformation of an empirical observer into a religious prophet . . . was that from the beginning the common humanism was subordinated in Marx's vision to the purposes of a revolutionist who wanted not so much to understand the world, as to remake it." (Niebuhr 1964, xii).

2. Eckersley (1992, 126): "The major thematic innovations of ecosocialism—the rejection of the economic growth consensus, the emphasis on ecologically benign production for human need, the attempt to widen the productivist outlook of the labor movement and new social movements, and the new internationalism—together represent a major overhaul of socialist thought. Moreover, these theoretical revisions place ecosocialism squarely within the spectrum of Green or emancipatory political thought."

II

The Study of Transformational Politics

6

Transformational Research and Teaching:
An Overview

ED SCHWERIN

"The real voyage of discovery consists not in finding new lands but in seeing with new eyes."

—Marcel Proust

Introduction

Research and teaching are the major ways that we study, and help our students to study politics. Along with service to the academy and the community, these interrelated activities comprise the multiple mission of most scholars. However, many conventional approaches to research and teaching are inconsistent with the theories of transformational politics discussed in Part I. Therefore, in this introductory essay I will explore innovative approaches to political pedagogy and inquiry that are more consistent with transformational values and principles. After a discussion of the relationship between research and teaching, I will consider critiques of conventional approaches and then discuss alternatives that are more congruent with transformational theory. Although the effort to transform teaching and research is not without some risk and difficulty, those who advocate transformational values could benefit from experimenting with the models considered here.

From the holistic perspective which typifies transformational politics, research and teaching are not conflicting activities. Although time and energy are limited resources, and research is generally more highly rewarded professionally than teaching, they are complementary and synergistic activities in many ways. For example, an active research scholar can share the latest theories and methods with students. Teaching and dialogue with students can provide insights and pose provocative questions that may stimulate interesting research projects. The classroom can serve as a laboratory for designing and testing new experiments in teaching. Students from the same class or another class may benefit from helping to develop the research design, collect the data, perform the analysis, and collaborate with the teacher in writing up the results.

Transformational scholars also see a synergistic relationship between *what* is researched and *how* it is researched, and between *what* is taught and *how* it is taught. For example, a scholar studying democratic grass roots movements might use participatory action research techniques which are based on collaborative teamwork. Someone teaching democratic theory might model democracy by employing nonauthoritarian teaching techniques such as dialogue, and collaborative teaching techniques to build community (Becker and Couto 1997). A scholar researching the connection between mediation as a form of conflict resolution and empowerment of the participants might collaborate with the mediators in designing the research and interpreting the findings. A class in environmental politics could spend time in nature, not only to see how the local bioregion illustrates the issues involved, but also to develop an experiential appreciation for the ecological web of life. From a transformational perspective, research and teaching, process and content, enrich and enhance each other.

This chapter is divided into two major sections. First, after considering some of major critiques of conventional social science research I will suggest how a transformational approach would differ in terms of both subject matter and methodology. The second section of the paper will similarly consider the critique of conventional teaching methods and then discuss how transformational teaching would differ in both what is taught and how it is taught.

Transformational Research

The Critique of Conventional Research.

BEHAVIORAL POLITICAL SCIENCE. Modern political science research has largely focused on the political behavior of individuals and groups, as part of the larger behavioral movement spanning the social sciences. (Knorr and Rosenau 1969). A number of assumptions and analytic prescriptions are at the core of the behavioral approach. Behavioralism seeks statements about regularities that hold across time and place. Science, the behavioralists claim, is primarily a generalizing activity, the purpose of which is to discover recurrent patterns of behavior and their causes. A theory is built up from hypotheses about the relationships between two or more variables. Theories are uncovered and tested by systematically collecting and statistically analyzing empirical data (Isaak 1985). As the eminent political scientist David Easton (1969, 11–13) points out, this approach makes a number of epistemological and methodological assumptions, such as, "There are discoverable uniformities in political behavior. These can be expressed in generalizations or theories with explanatory and predictive value . . . Precision in the recording of data and the statement of findings requires measurement and quantification. Ethical evaluation and empirical explanation involve two different kinds of propositions that, for the sake of clarity, should be kept analytically distinct . . ."

What made behavioralism innovative was not so much its reliance on data collection and quantitative analysis as its attitude toward inquiry. Behavioralists sought greater rigor and precision in analysis. They advocated replacing subjective knowledge with verifiable knowledge, supplanting intuition with testable evidence, and substituting data and reproducible information for mere opinion (Hall 1993). They aspired to conduct objective (value-free) research. They strove to replace verbal definitions of concepts with operational ones—indicators on which empirical tests could be conducted and replicated by others.

POSTBEHAVIORAL CRITIQUE. But generalized explanations of political phenomena have proved to be elusive. Early enthusiasm and optimism began to wane as the effort invested failed to produce significant results. Critics began to ask hard questions about the approach and its suitability. First, they pointed to the trivial nature of some of the applications of scientific methods to the study of politics. The quest for scientific knowledge often led to a focus on topics that were quantifiable and easy to verify empirically but that were not related to significant, enduring, and relevant social concerns. Second, not only was behavioral research not really conducted in an objective value-free scientific fashion, but the values and philosophical questions to which the research could be related were seldom considered. Behavioralism was criticized for neglecting ethical questions about poverty, violence, and other forms of powerlessness and oppression. Third, the implications of research findings for important public policy choices were rarely addressed. This critical reaction led to the "postbehavioral revolution" which brought about renewed interest in normative political philosophy, the policy-making process, and policy analysis. (Easton 1969; Haas 1970; Ricci 1984).

POSTMODERN AND PHENOMENOLOGICAL CRITIQUES. A more recent critique of behavioralism, postmodernism is an approach that emphasizes the meaning of texts and discourses. Postmodernist political scholars are post-positivistic in that they call for a reexamination of the philosophical basis for making truth claims in political theory, as part of a broader movement known as "critical social theory," "poststructuralism," or "deconstructionism." Critical theories take the inherently subjective nature of images of politics and the "social construction of reality" as their point of departure. Postmodernists believe that there is no objective reality that we can discover—it is inherently intangible, and what we assume to be true masks the values on which we base our analysis. The purpose of inquiry therefore, is to expose the fallacy of those who contend that they understand reality (Onuf 1989; Der Derian 1995).

Polkinghorne (1983) and Lincoln and Guba (1985) have challenged positivism from a humanistic/phenomenological perspective. According to the "naturalist paradigm" developed by the latter, realities are multiple and holistic; knower and known are interactive; only value-, time-, and context-bound (idiographic) hypotheses are possible; and the mutual, simultaneous shaping of political phenomena rules out the possibility of distinguishing causes from effects. The methodology that follows from these axioms employs emergent rather than *a priori* research designs, tacit as well as propositional knowledge, qualitative over quantitative methods, purposive rather than random sampling, natural versus artificial settings, and inductive rather than deductive data analysis (37–43).

FEMINIST CRITIQUE. New concerns and challenges emerged from feminist social scientists. As Sandra Harding (1991, viii) notes,

> "In the last five years there has been an outpouring of critical examinations of Western science, technology, and epistemology from the peace and ecology movements, the left, philosophers, historians, and sociologists of science, and Third World critics, as well as from Western feminists. Consequently, the feminist critiques are not isolated voices crying in the wilderness . . . but are linked thematically and historically to a rising tide of critical analysis of the mental life and social relations of the modern, androcentric, imperial, bourgeois West, including its sciences and notions of knowledge."

Harding outlines three approaches that feminists use in changing science. First, "feminist empiricism" argues for empirical science that is free from existing biases and exclusions. Second, the "feminist standpoint" epistemology argues for constructing knowledge from the perspectives of women. Indeed standpoint theory suggests that there are many perspectives to consider (women, people of color, low income, gay, etc.), and that science must be conducted with those perspectives in mind. Researchers need to start from where they are in asking questions, developing concepts, designing research, collecting data, and interpreting findings. The third approach, "feminist postmodernism" provides a deconstructive critique of normal social science but does not really provide viable alternatives.

Feminists point out that, just as in the political arena, the scope of political research has been defined in ways that exclude women as women. Therefore it is necessary to develop a new vocabulary of politics that expresses the different ways in which women wield power and practice citizenship. The major themes of feminist criticism include the importance of "reflexivity" (examining critically, and exploring analytically the nature of the research process), of an "action and praxis" orientation, of the affective component of research, and of the use of the "situation at hand" or women's everyday lives as a necessary subject of feminist scholarship. Placing women and the construct of gender at the center of research analysis is a hallmark of feminist research. These themes are derived from multidisciplinary and cross-cultural perspectives. Feminist perspectives also stress the importance of a more collaborative approach to research in order to empower both the researcher and the researched (Lather 1991).

TRANSFORMATIONAL CRITIQUE. Much of the transformationalist critique is congruent with feminist positions, especially regarding the importance of constructing knowledge from multiple perspectives, and the emphasis on reflexivity, praxis, and collaboration. And like the phenomenological critics, some transformationalists argue that conventional political science has been based on outmoded and reductionistic assumptions of Newtonian physics, which views the world as a mechanical entity and is based on concepts of certainty, order, structure, and determinism (Landau 1961). Transformational scholars such as Slaton in chapter 1 and Knight in chapter 4 challenge the viability of the Newtonian paradigm and suggest that the principles of quantum physics and chaos theory may be applied to developing alternative political theories that transcend some of the limitations of logical positivism.

But transformational scholars would concur there is no one right way to do transformational research, and there is no one transformational epistemology or methodology. As Herman points out in chapter 2, transformational politics is an interdisciplinary field of inquiry, with many contributors from fields such as physics, psychology, economics, history, and literature. Therefore it is a diverse and dynamic field of inquiry with regard to topics, theoretical foci, and methodologies.

Transformational Research: Topics, Themes and Theories

TOPICS AND THEMES. Transformational researchers are interested in a variety of topics and phenomena: peace and other social movements (Brettschneider chapter 7; Zisk chapter 8), Green politics (Graham chapter 5; Woolpert chapter 15; Rensenbrink 1992), democratic movements (Diamond 1994), new models of strong or mass participatory democracy (Barber 1984; Mansbridge 1980), developing tools for enhancing democratic participation, such as teledemocracy (Slaton 1992; Becker chapter 12), transforming leadership (Gilbert chapter 13; Burns 1978; Fishel 1992; Couto 1993), environmental politics and sustainable development (Milbrath 1989; Coleman 1994; Conley 1997), spiritual politics (Lerner 1996; McLaughlin and Davidson 1994; Spretnak 1986; Wallis 1994), neopopulist and progressive politics (Boyte 1980; Boyte and Reissman 1986; Bellah et al., 1985), transformational policy prescriptions (Cummings chapter14; Woolpert 1980, 1988), and the impact of multinational corporations and economic globalization on domestic and international politics (Dolbeare and Hubbell 1996; Korten 1994; Holm and Sorenson 1995; Lopez, Smith, and Pagnucco 1995; Mander and Goldsmith 1996).

Transformational researchers draw theoretical insights from each of the four themes set forth in the introduction to this volume. The first theme, the obsolescence of the prevailing paradigm and the emergence of a new paradigm, was discussed above with regard to the transformational critique of conventional behavioral research. Some transformationalists are conducting "thought experiments" to apply the principles of quantum and chaos theory in order to transcend the limitations of the Newtonian model underlying conventional political theory (Becker 1991; Dator 1984; Slaton chapter 1; and Knight chapter 4). Others are exploring psychological and narrative analysis to provide a more humanistic perspective on political life (Abalos 1993; Harman 1984; Herman chapter 2). But all recognize that thinking about politics in new ways is essential to our political well-being. As Slaton argues in chapter 1, a "theory of transformational politics is a web of theories, ranging from ancient to novel . . ." (5). She argues that the emerging transformational paradigm should draw from many sources, "including quantum theory, chaos theory, ecofeminist theory, archetypal theory, empowerment theory, self-actualization theory, participatory democratic theory, and new theories of spirituality . . ." (12).

The second theme, ecological focus and systems thinking, is pervasive in the transformational research agenda. The ecological principles which need to be understood in order to transform our understanding of political communities are the interdependence of all members of an ecological community; the pervasiveness of partnership, cooperation, symbiosis, and permeable boundaries in ecological communities; the flexibility of ecological cycles; the advantages of diversity in complex communities; and the primary value of sustainability (Introduction, xx–xxii). In this regard transformationalists are researching the creation of a political process in which communities, institutions, and policies are constructed according to ecological design principles and integrated into the natural systems that sustain them.

Many transformational scholars have been active in Green Politics (Affigne 1995; Rensenbrink 1988; Rohter 1992; Slaton and Becker 1990), or are sympathetic to Green philosophy and values (Graham chapter 5). Each of the Greens' ten key values including ecological wisdom, social justice, grassroots democracy, personal and global responsibility, nonviolence, decentralization, community-based economics, and economic justice, gender equity and cooperation, respect for diversity, and future focus and sustainability, generate research questions for transformational scholars. For example, research questions related the value of nonviolence might include the following: How can nonviolent methods be used most effectively to reduce the atmosphere of polarization and selfishness that is itself a source of violence? What are the alternatives to current patterns of violence at all levels, from the family and the street to nations and the world? Are some types of conflict resolution such as mediation, more empowering for participants than formal legal alternatives (Schwerin 1995)? How is it possible to foster community, to create responsive governance, and to develop peaceful and productive ways of solving problems and resolving public conflict (Dukes 1996)?

Ecological thinking is closely related to systems thinking which focuses on interdependence and emphasizes a holistic perspective. As pointed out in our Introduction, "systems thinking emphasizes

context over content, form over substance, and process over structure. It avoids reducing the operation of complex wholes to one-way,
cause-effect explanations and linear relationships. It encourages
cross-disciplinary study and an awareness of politics' global reach"
(xxii). By taking a systems view of educational communities, for example, research and teaching are seen in a larger context, with feedback loops connecting them, as contrasted with the conventional
view which treats them as isolated, compartmentalized activities.
Other principles of complex systems could also be applied to educational communities to tie together approaches to teaching with
praxis and political activism. For example the principle of "self-
similarity" discussed by Knight in chapter 4 is exemplified by seeing
the classroom as a microcosm of the larger political community.

The third theme is the linkage of personal and political. Like
feminist scholarship, transformational research expands the domain
of political life to include how we live our lives in the broader sense:
at home, in the workplace, and in the natural world. It resists the
behaviorist tendency to reduce political affairs to the external and
the material, and takes seriously the view of politics as a search for
purpose and meaning. It redefines the core concept of politics from
"power over" to "power with," and looks at the intrapersonal and interpersonal aspects of political inquiry. Epistemologically, transformational study accepts the inseparability of the observer and the
observed, and designs research accordingly, as evidenced by both
Brettschnieder in chapter 7 and Zisk in chapter 8. The "politics of
transcendence" discussed in Part III continues this theme of the
complementary relationship of inner and outer domains.

The fourth theme is the inclusion of the spiritual and sacred. All
of the theory chapters mention the spiritual dimensions of life; it is
particularly germane to the chapters by Herman and Halpern.
Louis Herman discusses the insights derived from the "primal truth
quest" and a primal epistemology associated with the transformational visionary trends, and Manfred Halpern delineates a new theory of personal transformation constituted by the "four faces of our
being: personal, political, historical and sacred. While there is broad
consensus among transformationalists on the importance of spirituality and the "reenchantment of the world" (Berman 1984), there is
less consensus on the role it plays in teaching or doing transformational politics. Some see a theoretical convergence between new developments in science and the perennial philosophy (Abram 1990;
Capra 1982; 1991); deep ecologists, ecofeminists and others see it as
having practical application for studying political action from a

planetary perspective (Bunyard and Goldsmith 1988; Diamond and Ornstein 1990; Lerner, 1996; McLaughlin and Davidson 1994).

EMPOWERMENT THEORY. While all these themes are important strands in the fabric of transformational research, developing a theory of empowerment to inform both personal and political transformation is also an important goal of the transformational research agenda. Empowerment is central to the theoretical and ideological concerns of most transformational groups and movements including green politics, feminist politics, participatory democracy, and communitarianism. It is a multidimensional concept with relevance for individuals, groups, organizations, communities, and larger social and political systems. Personal empowerment can be defined as "the process of gaining mastery over one's self and one's environment in order to fulfill human needs" (Schwerin 1995, 81).

The components of individual empowerment most relevant to transformational study are self-esteem, self-efficacy, knowledge and skills, political awareness, and rights and responsibilities. These components are discussed more fully below in the section on transformational teaching. But at this point I will focus on the implications of political awareness for a transformational research agenda. The development of a more robust political awareness is essential for those studying personal and political transformation. Political awareness is closely linked to Paulo Friere's (1970) concept of "critical consciousness" and his ideas about "liberation education." Underlying my conception of political awareness are four interrelated questions: Where are we now? Where are we headed? Where should we be headed? And how do we get there from here? These difficult questions provide four vital foci for transformational researchers (Schwerin 1995, 63–65).

The first type of political analysis requires the theories, analytical skills, political experience, and political intuition to determine **what is.** Understanding how the political game is played is essential for scholars and political activists who seek to critique the existing political process in order to transform it. For example, a transformational researcher might focus on the causes and consequences of the growing economic disparities in the United States and other areas of the world (Rifkin 1995; Thurow 1996; Henderson 1996), or seek to discover "Why Americans Hate Politics" (Dionne 1991), or map out the environmental consequences of economic globalization (Mander and Goldsmith 1996).

The second type of political analysis asks **where are we headed, or what will be?** In other words, given our understanding of apparent trends, changes and continuities, what will the future look like? Anticipating alternative futures is even more difficult than understanding the present, but it is essential for planning and developing effective policies. Forecasting "what will be" is crucial for transformationalists who believe that the long run consequences of present trends will be disastrous, and that consequently major preventive efforts are needed to avoid the possible environmental and political calamities looming in the third millennium (Ehrlich and Ehrlich 1990; Henderson 1991; Ward 1966).

The third aspect of political awareness is prescriptive analysis, or the study of **what should be.** Transformational "visions" of a better future are based on theories such as ecofeminism, nonviolence, and empowerment, or on ideologies such as the Green's ten key values (Lerner, 1996; Graham chapter 5).

The fourth aspect of political awareness is the study of viable transition strategies, or determining **how to get there from here.** If one believes that the present economic-political structures are oppressive, dysfunctional, and disempowering, or that these structures are seriously deteriorating, then the task is how to achieve major structural transformation (Kim and Dator 1994). Under these circumstances, the ability "to get there from here" involves capabilities such as the analysis of the root causes of alienation and other barriers to transformation, developing transformative leadership skills, and developing competencies in conflict-resolution and community organizing. Political awareness as I have described it is the core component of developing political competencies, or of "political empowerment" (Schwerin 1995).

The discussion above provides an overview of the topics, themes, and theories relevant to transformational research. It is now time to consider methods particularly suited to transformational research. In addition to accomplishing more conventional research objectives, many of these approaches seek to empower individuals and transform structures.

Approaches to Transformational Research

Transformational researchers use a broad array of conventional and unconventional methodological approaches including content analysis and empirical data analysis (Bond 1993), quasi experimental design and qualitative analysis (Schwerin 1995), interviews (Brettschneider chapter 7), the use of dramatic narrative, storytelling, myths and symbols to interpret the meaning and significance of political phenomenon (Halpern and Herman in this volume; Abalos 1993), analysis of the world view of indigenous peoples (Sachs 1993), Jungian symbolic analysis (Woolpert chapter 15), and the narrative analysis of literature, music and art (Zisk 1993). The approaches that deserve special attention here are those that synthesize sound research with transformational values and empowering political action. Three approaches exemplify the transformational emphasis on political activism, praxis, and empowerment of participants; the use of participant observation by scholar-activists, action research, and participatory action research.

SCHOLAR ACTIVISTS. Many of the transformational research projects are done by "scholar-activists" who are involved with social movement organizations as active members, and with conducting research on the same or similar organizations. For example, both John Rensenbrink (1992) and Christa Slaton (1994) were early members of the American Greens and produced significant research based on their roles as participant observers of Green politics. Brettschneider's participant-observer research in chapter 7 grew out of her political activism in the American Jewish community, revealing the inadequacy of conventional measures of group effectiveness. In chapter 8, Betty Zisk explains how she used participant observation techniques to do a comparative study of a large number of "transformational" and "incrementalist" peace movement groups. A long-time member of peace and environmental groups including the Quakers, Greens, and the Sierra Club, Zisk discusses her methodology in detail and provides an insightful analysis of the costs and benefits of using participant observation in political research.

There are numerous advantages of being a scholar-activist. Many social movement members are reluctant to talk candidly to "outsiders." Scholar-activists who have been involved in social movements will generally have greater access, understanding and empathy than academics who have little experience in "grass-roots" political activism. For example, having inside knowledge is useful in identifying the key players and in knowing what questions they should be asked. Familiarity with the history of groups and individuals also helps to put the analysis in a fuller perspective.

But there are corresponding difficulties and disadvantages, such as the difficulty of gaining access to some groups and developing sufficient trust to get reliable information. There may also be some risk in researching groups that practice civil disobedience or other forms of illegal activity, such as "Earth First" (Lee 1995). Third, the scholar-activist must always be aware that developing close relationships with group members, or being very sympathetic with their mission, carries the danger of developing a strong bias that can taint the research process. This may not be entirely avoidable, but the researcher should be aware of any possible bias, and be completely honest about his or her values when communicating research outcomes. Finally, Zisk points out that some of the difficulties of being a "scholar-activist" include both the reluctance of "mainstream" scholars to accept the validity of nontraditional research, as well as, the common view of many community activists that scholarly research has little relevance to problems in the real world.

ACTION RESEARCH (AR) AND PARTICIPATORY ACTION RESEARCH (PAR). Traditionally, political science research has been conducted by professional academic or think-tank researchers. They generally choose their topics and publish their work in order to contribute to their academic discipline, thereby advancing their professional careers. In much of "normal science" the scientific method is used to accumulate knowledge *within* the scientific community. Methodological rigor is of primary importance, not the relevance of the research to the problems of the larger community. Indeed, doing "applied research" is usually regarded as less important and less prestigious than doing "pure" scientific research, especially in most of the top ranked research universities.

But decades ago, the pioneering psychologist Kurt Lewin (1946) called for a new kind of research in the social sciences that would simultaneously solve social problems and generate new knowledge. Like many transformationalists today, Lewin was concerned with positive social change. He suggested that social research should lead to social action. His Action Research (AR) model combined research and social action to increase understanding and generate social improvement. Lewin emphasized that the introduction of action into the scientific model "by no means implies that the research needed is in any respect less scientific than would be required for pure science" (35). He saw action research as a means to both assist practitioners and to facilitate social change. AR links theory and practice: the researcher acts as a consultant to people engaged in real-life problems by providing them with methods of diagnosis, action, and evaluation. AR is a cyclical inquiry process that involves diagnosing a problem situation, planning action steps, and then implementing and evaluating outcomes. The main idea of this approach is that action research uses a scientific approach to study important organizational or social problems together with the people who experience them. Whereas conventional social science focuses on producing new knowledge by solving scientific problems, action research focuses on solving practical problems to create new general knowledge.

Newer models of Participatory Action Research (PAR) extend the empowering benefits of action research for both the community and the researchers by stressing *research collaboration*. Whereas in most "normal" scientific research and even in the classical action research models, the academic researcher is the expert who makes all of the important decisions about what will be researched and how, in PAR all concerned parties exercise strong influence, amounting to *codetermination*, in all phases of the inquiry, most particularly in the critical phases of designing the inquiry and in making sense out of the data (Park 1993). Its goal is to enable the participants to "learn how to learn," thereby enhancing the capacity of the system being studied to study and change itself. Thus, knowledge, skills, and resources are transferred from the scholar to the community empowering all participants. PAR is change oriented and seeks to bring about change that has positive social values such as healthy communities and responsible organizations. PAR has been defined as "an integrated activity that combines social investigation, educational work, and action, with the ultimate goal of structural transformation and improvement of the lives of those involved" (Hall 1981, 7).

AR and PAR approaches have been used in a wide variety of situations including grass roots settings in Appalachia (Gaventa 1993), economically depressed communities in West Philadelphia (Harkavy and Puchett 1991), with migrant farm workers (Kieffer 1984), and in organizations such as factories (Israel, Schurman, and Hugentobler 1992) and corporations (Whyte et al. 1989). While these approaches are congruent with transformational theory they also have a number of difficulties and limitations. First, many community members are suspicious or hostile to academic researchers, either because they have been previously exploited by academics who treated them as research "subjects" and had no sincere interest in helping them, or because they regard academics as "ivory-tower" intellectuals who have little knowledge of the problems of oppressed groups from different races and classes. Second, it may be difficult to deal with the delays and frustrations that are part of doing research in natural settings. Third, for those attempting to do participatory action research, it may be hard to give up control of research decision making and to share research outcomes with community members.

Finally, in many universities AR and PAR are regarded as less important and less prestigious than doing "pure" scientific research. There are fewer journals to publish this kind of research and in some cases it is viewed with suspicion by tenure and promotion committees. Transformational thought's emphasis on the interweaving of subject and object, facts and values, theory and practice, therefore plays an important role in providing an epistemological context which validates these ways of knowing. AR and PAR models are also powerful as transformational teaching methods when combined with service learning. This pedagogical approach is described below after a discussion of the limitations associated with conventional teaching approaches, and consideration of transformational teaching objectives.

Transformational Teaching

The Critique of Conventional Education

The traditional or conventional approach to education includes some or all of the following elements: the lecture presentation of substantive content, the teacher as authority and knowledge expert, a hierarchical power structure in the classroom, students as mostly passive recipients of knowledge who regurgitate back their understanding of content for exams, and students who compete with each other in a zero-sum game to get good grades. Despite the convenience and familiarity of this approach, its critics argue that it fosters dysfunctional behavior (see Becker and Couto 1997; Boyer 1987; Friere 1970, 1973; Giroux 1981, 1983, 1994; Kriesberg 1992; Shor 1980; Schor and Friere 1987). First, it is argued that the traditional classroom pits students against each other in the struggle to succeed and get the best grades. Some students must lose in order for others to win. Such competition does not foster a sense of community. Instead, it promotes inequitable social divisions and impedes attempts to build a more peaceful and just social order in which people live cooperatively with each other in supportive and mutually responsible communities.

Second, the conventional approach fosters passivity towards teachers and other authority figures. As the influential Brazilian educator, Paulo Friere (1970) has pointed out, education can either domesticate or liberate. The traditional teacher-centered classroom is hierarchically structured and students are taught in an unquestioning way to digest information offered to them in a lecture format. Traditional educators acting as authoritarian experts often behave as if they are the sole possessors of "truth." In teacher-centered classrooms their function is to impart their knowledge to students whose minds are like blank slates. Concentrating on what is right or expected, stymies creative thought. This type of teaching, called "banking education" by Friere, involves a one-way exchange between teachers and students in which information and skills are deposited in a student's brain to be used at some later time (Harrison chapter 9). Students in traditional classes become authority-dependent, and therefore are unlikely to value their own insights.

Third, traditional classrooms are characterized by the use of "power-over" instead of by the more empowering use of "power-with." There may be a distinct difference between the overt curriculum, such as democratic theory, and the "hidden curriculum," i.e., what students learn from the way a class is structured. Teachers not only transmit certain kinds of knowledge but also establish norms for acceptable behaviors by the *way* they teach (Becker and Couto 1997). As John Dewey (1966) has argued, we learn the things we do. In traditional classes students have little power over how the class is run. They learn from the hidden curriculum to acquiesce to authorities, not to become more efficacious.

Fourth, when teachers use their positions as authorities to control students, they reinforce the dominant social order. Traditional educational practices may socialize students to value the authority of the state, preparing students to defend the status quo. Students who sit quietly as passive receivers of "truth" from an authority figure will have learned how to function well in a hierarchical consumer society. In short, schools are not merely instructional sites, they are also cultural and political sites and powerful agencies of social, economic, and cultural reproduction. Traditional education is thus a political instrument that perpetuates the privileges of the power elite and justifies a conservative continuation of the economic and political status quo.

These criticisms are squarely addressed by a transformational approach to education. Developing such an approach encourages teachers to examine their teaching style and consider its consequences. For example, does the pedagogy promote democratic concepts of peace and social justice, or does it reinforce patterns of domination and violence? Is it reductionistic or holistic? Does the curriculum prepare students for active and environmentally responsible citizenship? While there is no one ideal approach to transformational teaching, there are values, principles, and theories that may serve as guidelines to teaching in transformational ways.

Transformational Education: Goals and Objectives

Teaching the whole person is the *sine qua non* of transformational education. Students cannot be prepared for responsible citizenship in a transformational era without developing virtue, wisdom, and imagination, as well as cognitive skills. The transformational perspective challenges the prevailing culture of selfishness, cynicism, and alienation which is too often perpetuated by the academy. It does not seek to socialize students to fit into the status quo, nor to deconstruct it *ad infinitum*, but to wake them up to a richer political perspective (Moffett 1994). Transformational education focuses on facilitating the personal empowerment of students and teachers as well as enabling political transformation to a more just and sustainable democratic society.

In order to accomplish these objectives, transformational educators would benefit from a theoretical framework that could inform both pedagogy and curriculum. Just as empowerment theory constitutes an important part of the transformational research agenda, I suggest that empowerment theory also provides a theoretical foundation for much of transformational education. The components of individual empowerment most relevant to transformational teaching are self-esteem, self-efficacy, knowledge and skills, political awareness, and rights and responsibilities (Schwerin 1995, 81).

Self-esteem is the evaluative function of the self-concept. High self-esteem indicates a positive attitude toward oneself and one's behavior. Educators emphasize that self-esteem is essential to learning, and research has linked high self-esteem to higher levels of democratic political participation (Mecca, Smelser, and Vasconcellos 1989; Sniderman 1975). Perhaps even more important is the related concept of **self-efficacy,** which refers to the experience of one's self as a cause agent. High self-efficacy implies a positive attitude toward one's control over the social or political environment. Albert Bandura contends that both self-esteem and self-efficacy "contribute in their own way to the quality of human life" (1986, 410). In addition, both contribute significantly to the formation of an individual's psychological empowerment. Students operating out of increased self-esteem and self-competence are more likely to take risks and face challenges that have disempowered them.

The inculcation of general **knowledge and skills** is a fundamental objective of most forms of pedagogy, but transformationalists are concerned with types of knowledge and skills that are not usually included in the college curriculum. First, the most important type of knowledge relevant to personal empowerment is, of course, basic literacy (Friere 1970). Second are the kinds of knowledge that enable individuals to survive in a recalcitrant environment and facilitate personal and social competence, such as knowledge about conflict dynamics and conflict resolution processes. Third, awareness of one's goals, values, limitations, and strengths is fundamental to empowerment. The skills not normally taught in traditional education that contribute to political empowerment include systems thinking, stress management, negotiation, and conflict resolution skills (Moore 1996). In addition there are skills directly relevant to political action and social transformation, such as critical reflection, community organizing, and developing grass roots transforming leadership. Most recently, computer literacy is becoming essential for those who desire to be effective citizens, scholars, and political activists.

As mentioned above, the development of **political awareness** is essential for those concerned with personal and political transformation. While the questions linked to political awareness are integral to the transformational research agenda, they also provide relevant foci for transformational teaching. Combined with high levels of self-esteem, self-efficacy, and knowledge and skills, political awareness enables a citizen to function effectively in normal politics, reform politics, revolutionary politics, or transformational politics.

The last two components of personal empowerment theory directly relevant to transforming education are **rights and responsibilities**. Political rights include the traditional values of democratic societies: freedom of thought and political movement; free speech and assembly; the rights to organize politically, to run for office, to vote, to have a fair trial, and to be treated equally before the law. Democratic responsibilities include voting, political participation beyond voting, payment of taxes, service to the common good, accepting majority decisions, respecting the rights of others, and living in an environmentally sound way. In an unjust political system, political responsibilities may also include political mobilization and civil disobedience intended to transform the system.

Until recently most political science curricula focused on rights and entitlements. A citizen's responsibilities were rarely discussed.

Now empowerment theorists generally acknowledge that meaningful empowerment also means taking control of your own life and making your own decisions. This requires accepting responsibility both for yourself and for others, both in your community and in the larger world, especially the powerless and oppressed. This is a major emphasis in models of service learning, Green politics, and the new "communitarian" movement (see Barber 1992b; Etzioni 1993; Graham chapter 5).

In short, transformational approaches should be designed to enhance self-esteem and self-efficacy, to develop the knowledge, skills, and political awareness essential for democratic citizenship, to teach students how to teach themselves and others, to respect the rights of students and encourage them to take responsibility for their own education, and to accept greater responsibility for their communities and their world. A guiding question or compass for transformational teachers might be, *What can I do to make my approach to teaching more empowering?*

A model transformational curriculum would emphasize ecological literacy by challenging the conventional faith in unlimited economic expansion and technological fixes, and by integrating direct experience of the natural world and ecological design principles into the curriculum (Orr 1994). It would also include ethical training, in which both the coherence and universality of values as well as pluralism and diversity are recognized (Sandin 1992). Multidisciplinary peace and conflict resolution studies are central to students' understanding of nonviolent approaches to security issues (Cancian and Gibson 1990; Galtung 1996; Klare 1994). Normative and empirical futures studies are needed to develop proficiencies in forecasting and trend analysis, envisioning and evaluating alternative futures, and to provide tools for working towards a desirable future (Masini 1993; Beare and Slaughter 1993; Kim and Dator 1994). Students should learn about a variety of transformational theoretical perspectives such as feminist theory, quantum and chaos theory, and deep ecology. They should be encouraged to be politically active citizens through the study of social movements and participatory democracy.

Transformational Teaching: Models and Approaches

Transformational teaching should be a symbiotic process in which the teacher is transformed in the process of empowering students. The role of the empowering teacher is to create settings that enable students to develop their potential to the fullest by clarifying learning objectives, motivating and inspiring students, and serving them as a guide, mentor, and resource person. The teacher encourages, leads, and creates opportunities for otherwise passive students to be active partners in the learning process. He/she creates a self-help/mutual help environment in which students are treated as intelligent adults capable of quality work, and as valuable learning resources. The role of the student is to be an active partner in learning and disseminating knowledge. Students must strive to achieve clarity about their personal and collective objectives. They must commit to collaborating with peers, working persistently, doing quality work, taking risks to grow, seeking and giving help when needed.

Compared to traditional approaches, transformational learning represents a *shift* of power, control and responsibility. Teachers move from using power *over* students to power *with* students to achieve mutual learning objectives, as the chapters by Fishell and Segal, and Harrison in this volume demonstrate. The lines of authority are reshaped and control is shared as students become more active partners in the learning enterprise. In the following, I discuss four approaches that exemplify transformational teaching methods: (1) Using dialogue to promote the development of critical consciousness and problem-solving skills, (2) Using cooperative/collaborative techniques to develop a democratic learning community in the classroom based on mutual respect and shared responsibility, (3) Involving students in the larger community through experiential education methods, such as service learning, action research projects, and political activism, and (4) Using the Internet to break classroom boundaries, promote critical reflection, and spur activism.

THE CRITICAL CONSCIOUSNESS/CRITICAL THINKING APPROACH. Transformational education is furthered by a dialogic teaching style that encourages students to question the subject matter being taught and to develop "critical consciousness." In a classroom structured upon the principles of a dialogue, teachers and pupils together share information, respond to a common experience (such as an assigned reading), and seek answers to difficult questions. Everybody contributes their perspectives in the search for truth. The key to this type of education is an open exchange of ideas in which each learner respects the opinions of others.

In a dialogic classroom a teacher does not abrogate responsibility for student learning, but shifts from being the expert to being a facilitator who keeps the class moving, provides resources, and chooses appropriate topics to study. Thus, the teacher maintains the cohesiveness of the learning group. She or he asks leading questions, encourages those reticent to speak, and discourages verbal domination. Paulo Friere's widely known writings on the dialogic approach have been a major influence on the development of this pedagogy, covered more fully in Harrison, chapter 9.

The development of critical/creative thinking skills that assist in problem solving is also central to transformational teaching. These skills can be taught through a process of inquiry that involves the following steps: (1) present and clarify a complex problem, (2) develop hypotheses from which to explore the problem, (3) define the hypotheses, (4) explore the assumptions, implications, and logical validity of the hypotheses, (5) gather qualitative and/or quantitative evidence to test hypotheses, and (6) generate viable solutions. In this model, the teacher helps to move the students from stage to stage by sharpening discussion, focusing student questions and interests, and providing information. Teachers provide resources and access to expertise while students investigate social problems and reach conclusions. By developing hypotheses and supporting them with reasoned arguments, students test the consequences of their own judgments. Using these critical thinking skills to solve complex problems can help students improve their self-esteem and political efficacy. A related process called "critical reflection" is inherent in the service learning model described in the following.

THE DEMOCRATIC LEARNING COMMUNITY APPROACH. Democratic learning communities can be created in the classroom by modeling democracy and by using cooperative/collaborative approaches. Many studies of learning settings have demonstrated that cooperation and collaboration provide the basis of good teaching (Abrami et al. 1993; Astin 1987; Bruffee 1993; Cooper 1994; Cuseo 1992; Davidson 1994; Johnson and Johnson 1989, 1991; Sharon 1994; Slavin 1990; Wiener 1986).

A "cooperative goal structure" exists when students realize that they can obtain their learning objectives if and only if the other students obtain their goals. In a cooperative lesson students work together to master the subject matter. They help each other diagnose and solve problems, as described by Fishel and Segal in chapter 10. In contrast, most conventional classes are structured competitively. In a competitive classroom there are a limited number of rewards; therefore a large proportion of students experience failure, which discourages them from taking on challenges. Students in competitive classrooms learn that winning is the major goal in life. Learning thus becomes another means toward the goal of winning. This view is incompatible with the transformational objective of rooting out behaviors such as ruthless competition that may lead to social violence. The development of a just, sustainable, and peaceful democratic society involves respecting the rights of all people, valuing the intrinsic worth of all beings, and taking the needs of the whole system into account when making decisions.

In a cooperative classroom informal groups can be used in the midst of a lecture to help students process what they have learned. Focus groups of two or three students can generate questions before a presentation and help students master information at the end of a presentation. Such informal groupings allow students to process actively what they have been learning and allow the teacher to gather information about how concepts are being received. More formal groups can be used in laboratory settings to review homework or to work through problems together. Cooperative/collaborative learning is also facilitated by using a variety of role-playing and simulation exercises (Macy 1991; Fishel and Segal, chapter 10).

Research demonstrates that cooperative learning environments promote higher achievement levels and greater peer support among students. Students acquire important emotive gains and social skills from cooperative classrooms. They tend to know and like their peers better, which increases their motivation to learn. They acquire valuable communication skills when they incorporate diverse viewpoints into their understanding of the subject matter. In small group settings, students learn to work together regardless of individual differences. Cooperative learning situations teach individuals to care about other group members and provide them with empowering skills that foster good working relationships throughout their lives.

Transformational teachers are also experimenting with democracy in the classroom—teaching democracy by modeling democracy (Becker and Couto 1997). This approach does not imply an abrogation of authority, eliminating evaluations, or permitting anarchy to reign in the classroom. There must be norms to govern behavior in classroom settings. In a traditional classroom, teachers set rules authoritatively. In democratic classrooms teachers invite students into the rule-making process by explaining to them the necessity of setting boundaries for acceptable behavior and encouraging them to participate in their creation (Caspary 1997; Herman 1997). By involving students in setting the rules needed for the class to reach its goals, this procedure gives students some control over their learning environment and allows teachers to make explicit the norms for acceptable behavior.

Transforming educators using these principles can build in their classes a sense of community wherein students begin to trust the instructor and one another, value each other's opinions, and achieve a sense of unity from working through complex problems together. The transforming educator attempts to create a supportive, respectful, and nonjudgmental classroom that affirms each student, reinforces their accomplishments, promotes self-esteem and self-competence, and helps students to feel both liked and appreciated.

THE COMMUNITY AND THE CLASSROOM: THE EXPERIENTIAL/SERVICE LEARNING APPROACH. In addition to developing a democratic learning community *within* the classroom, transforming educators utilize the larger community *outside* the classroom as a setting for empowering learning experiences. The pedagogic possibilities include community service, internships, social activism, and action research projects. These diverse activities can be located on a continuum according to their potential for personal empowerment and political transformation. For example, some community service activities involving volunteering with community agencies may provide humanitarian assistance to those in need but they may also help to support a fundamentally inequitable political status quo, whereas students involved in political activism may be learning to be social change agents, working to expose the root causes of social violence and radically restructuring inequitable power relationships. Let us consider briefly the potential of these activities for personal and political transformation.

Experiential learning as a pedagogic method is not new (Kolb, 1984), and there are lively debates about what constitutes "good practice." Recently, a type of experiential learning based on community service called "service learning" has come to dominate the discussion and has spread rapidly throughout many American universities and colleges. Its proponents argue that it offers unique educational rewards for students, benefits to the community, and great potential for personal and political transformation. Some argue that service learning can revitalize civic education and promote "strong" democracy. Barber (1992a, 1992b) and Couto (1993a, 1997) argue that civic education can only be effective when it encompasses community involvement combined with reflection and discussion in an academic setting. The ideal learning unit here is not the individual but the small group or team, working and learning together. The point of service learning is to remedy the disaffection and alienation of the young, not through philanthropy, but by teaching citizenship and rebuilding civic community.

The civic approach to service learning also encourages an educational partnership between college and community, with the community actively involved in defining its own needs and the role service will play in the education of students (Barber and Battistoni 1993). For example, service learning courses have been designed to connect students with communities suffering from the strains of deindustrialization (Guarasci and Rimmerman 1997), to involve students in a community mediation service in order to teach democracy and conflict resolution (Slaton 1997), and to use "televote" polling experiments as a form of experiential education in modern democracy (Becker 1997). At the University of Richmond, the Learning in Community Settings (LINCS) Program offers several credit-bearing service learning models including: (1) community service, (2) school-based instruction, (3) a community problem-solving seminar, and (4) action research (Couto 1997).

The action research component of service learning at the University of Richmond is of particular interest here because it provides a linkage between the two primary foci of this chapter, transforming models of teaching and transforming models of research. Action research can play an important role both in the classroom (as Fishel and Segal show in chapter 10) as well as *outside* the classroom in many models of service learning. According to Couto, when students participate in action research there are several distinguishing features of a successful service learning project, "First, it involves independent research by students. Second, that research is requested by a community group or agency and conducted under their supervision. Third, the community agency has a use for the research that it can specify clearly. Fourth, the research is turned over to the community agency for its use" (1997, 96). This kind of action research empowers students by developing research skills, knowledge of community needs, and critical insights into social injustice, and also empowers communities by enabling them to document their concerns and take effective political action to solve their problems. As Couto points out, "Action research imparts several democratic lessons. It instructs students in the limits and possibility of addressing political problems efficaciously. If done in the manner of participatory research, this form of service learning also requires students to listen to one another, to deliberate critically about common problems and issues, to arrive at solutions to mutual problems creatively in a community setting, and perhaps to work together to implement solutions" (1997, 97). Thus, the use of participatory action research in the context of service learning, links research teaching, praxis, and political activism into a powerful pedagogic model. It also links university students and faculty into a partnership with community groups and private non-profit agencies.

THE INTERNET CLASSROOM: TECHNOLOGY AND TRANSFORMATION. A significant aspect of the present transformational period is the emergence of the "information age" and the telecommunications revolution that is exemplified by the Internet and the World Wide Web. But there is little agreement about the impact this technology will have on our lives. Some contend that computers allow centralized political authorities to collect extensive data on citizens and may enable transnational corporations to create a destructive global economy (Mander and Goldsmith 1996). Others argue that computers will lead to decentralization of power and provide greater opportunities for mass political participation (Naisbitt 1995). Given the power and potential impacts of this technology on individuals, society, economic, and political systems, it is essential that students and other informed citizens must develop computer knowledge and skills, and seek to understand the implications of this technology for personal and political transformation. Therefore, many transformational teachers are developing new classes on the Internet and other computer applications, that provide students with opportunities for personal empowerment, collaboration and community building, political activism, critical reflection, and policy analysis.

Internet and other computer skills can empower students to be more efficient and effective researchers, communicators, and political activists. Students can significantly improve research skills by learning about the potentialities and pitfalls of using the Internet as a research tool. The Net provides access to valuable resources for researchers such as, e-mail, Usenet, Free-net, library catalogs for many of the great libraries of the world, FTP sites, free software, electronic newsletters and journals, Internet relay Chat (IRC) and many kinds of data banks. Students can learn to use search engines, and meta-search strategies to quickly and accurately access large amounts of information, and they can learn to evaluate the reliability and validity of the information obtained. They can also download large data bases directly from the Internet and easily perform statistical analyses with SPSS or other statistical programs.

Communications skills can be expanded by learning how to use email to continue the dialogue with other students and teachers between classes, and to communicate with others almost anywhere in the world conveniently and at relatively little expense. By learning simple HTML language and using text editors to design and develop their own web pages students can also publish their views on the Internet. Unlike traditional media where reporters broadcast what they decide is news, the Internet allows any individual to broadcast information in any way they choose. There are no editors, no censors, no bureaucracies.

An Internet class provides ample opportunities for collaboration and community building within class and outside of class. For example, students can work in teams on research projects and students with little computer experience can be encouraged to seek assistance from their computer literate classmates rather than automatically turning to the professor as the only expert in the class. Students can interact with the local community in several ways. For example, using a service learning approach students can take their new Internet skills out to the community to do participatory action research, and to create web pages for community groups and non-profit agencies. This transfer of computer training, resources, and skills to the community is empowering for both students as well as the community groups.

An Internet course can encourage political activism by focusing on the potential of the Internet for citizen empowerment. American citizens are increasingly alienated from the political process and on the local, state, and national level, professional politicians and special interest groups appear to dominate and control the democratic process. But many political activists believe that the Internet has the potential to return political power to the grassroots. Activists can marshal their forces, broadcast their views, and build alliances on the Internet. In these ways citizens can use the Internet to level the playing field with the political power brokers.

Students can be given assignments relevant to citizen activism such as joining and participating in political activist electronic mailing lists, finding activist web sites for such as community sites like Charlotte's Web, environmental sites like Environlink, democracy sites like the Global Democracy Network, and TAN+N, and political party, interest group, or state and national government sites. Finally, students can develop case studies demonstrating how the Internet could be used by citizen activists for political organizing, advocacy, or influencing policy. As a result of these exercises students may decide to become citizen activists and benefit their communities and themselves.

As with all powerful new technologies, the Internet confers benefits on some and costs on others. An Internet class provides the opportunity for critical reflection on important questions such as, What is the relationship between technology and transformation?

and more specifically, What are the positive and negative impacts of the telecommunications revolutions and the Internet on individuals, society, economics and politics? Who gains and who loses in the telecommunications revolution? How will the Internet impact the future of work? Who will benefit most and how will the productivity gains of the Information Age be shared? How will power be distributed in the new order? Will it centralize or decentralize power? How will this technology affect our concepts of self, community, and nation? Will existing sources of injustice be reduced or amplified? How will these technologies affect and shape politics—locally, nationally, and internationally? Are these technologies neutral in nature or do they advantage some individuals and groups more than others?

Some of the problems cited by critics of the Internet include, the problem of gaining equitable access to the Internet and the growing gaps between Internet haves and have-nots, the availability of pornography of all kinds, the increasing presence of the Ku Klux Klan and other hate groups, and the rapid growth in economic globalization and the growing power of transnational corporations which has been facilitated by the Internet.

The Internet is a powerful technology that is already revolutionizing the way we do many things and it will become even more important in the future. This tool can be used to either help shape a better world in the future that reflects democratic transformational values, or it can be used to subvert these values and promote authoritarianism, unbridled corporate globalization, ethnic strife and other forms of extremism. Empowering teachers can help their students to master the possibilities of this technology and use it to promote an agenda of personal empowerment, strong democracy, and true political transformation as we enter the new Millennium.

Conclusions

Transformationalists agree that existing social, economic, and political systems are seriously flawed and dysfunctional, and that major structural transformations are necessary to obtain greater social justice, more participatory democracy, environmentally sustainable economic development, peace, and prosperity. This in turn calls for a reexamination of how we study and what we study as political scholars. Transformational teaching seeks to establish dynamic, nonhierarchical classroom environments where teachers and students encourage each other to question the nature of the political world. Each of these components of political study promotes learning which strengthens participatory communities. Where there is no sense of community and no sense of belonging, people will not develop a sense of responsibility for others or for the natural world. Without this sense of responsibility there will be no lasting peace, justice, or environmental well-being. But research and teaching that foster community, also foster a politics of hope.

While models of transforming research and teaching have multiple benefits for all participants, these initiatives may be hampered by a variety of personal, political, professional, and institutional barriers. First is the human problem of overcoming inertia and the force of habit. Most of us have developed approaches to research and teaching that are comfortable and require relatively little thought or effort to carry out. Students also are reluctant to change. Even if they are bored with the lecture method they often resist teaching innovations such as working collaboratively in groups or taking full responsibility for their educational outcomes (Caspary 1997).

Resistance to change also comes from our educational institutions. Transforming education and research will challenge existing social and political systems, structures, and institutions. Courses and research programs that support the status quo are so firmly established in most Political Science departments that they are often mistakenly regarded as neutral and objective, and therefore rarely challenged. "Speaking truth to power" carries risks, since the academic incentive structure rewards publishing "normal" science and not making waves. Despite these very real obstacles, the benefits to all participants of developing and implementing transformational approaches to teaching and research justifies significant effort and at least some risk-taking. This is especially true for those of us who espouse the need for personal empowerment and political transformation.

7

Transformational Research: A Groups Approach

MARLA BRETTSCHNEIDER

Introduction

Political scientists and democratic theorists tend to have a difficult time telling if groups engaged in the political process actually have any effect in their worlds of political experience.[1] The attempts made by liberal democratic theorists to answer this question exemplify what, from a perspective of transformational politics,[2] could be called a thin theory of change: refined assessments are rare, and often success is measured in quantitative rather than qualitative terms. The political process gets reduced to the arena of government,[3] and thus scholars often measure the effectiveness of groups in terms of legislative victories. Much of the real life of politics gets lost in the reduction and leaves no room for a serious exploration of the concept of social and communal transformation.

How might we begin to analyze and evaluate political transformation? In this article I discuss the standards most often used to evaluate whether groups are successful in their attempts to affect the world, because even transformational groups are effected by the pressure to conform to these standards.[4] The critique comes by way of rooting these measurements explicitly in the traditional liberal theory from which they are generated. Most political scientists who study groups seeking to affect the political world are relying on Hobbesian premises, which translate into three major quantitative criteria for success in contemporary research: longevity, membership numbers, and budget size.

This approach can only go so far toward assessing the actual strength and success of political groups when politics is understood

119

not in this limited liberal sense, but in the broader sense of politics as "figuring it out." Here politics is understood as the struggle for dignity and fulfillment through intersecting communal reinterpretation, meeting and ongoing valuation. As the theoretical chapters in Part I make clear, we must understand politics as a deep process whereby individual and communities, on their own and with others, wrestle with their identity, heighten awareness of their historical experiences and reframe their aspirations within their present worlds of political experience. When our understanding of politics remains connected to the loss, anxiety, celebration and concrete needs of our very lives, counting roll call votes in Congress is a minute, and often misleading measure of success.

In this chapter I then discuss how groups seeking transformation *define success for themselves.* Listening to groups who are explicitly struggling with ways to challenge liberal norms articulate their own guidelines can give us much deeper, qualitative measurements. My insights here are gleaned from a long-term project on communal and group-based democratic theory exploring the multiplicity and contradictions of our American subcommunal identities as they play themselves out in politics. With a feminist/multiculturalist orientation and a background in Marxist dialectical methodology I undertook a study of the groups involved in the changing pro-Israel identity of the American Jewish community. This is a group cluster and issue domain I had long been involved with as a member of the Jewish community and as a political activist.

I utilized an activist-research, or participant/observer, method and developed my research plan and interview questions with the participation of activists themselves (to ensure that the work would be relevant to the concerns of real people). I built the research design in order that the process might allow liberal characteristics of groups to show themselves, while also enabling other characteristics to expose themselves, to the extent that either were there.

In addition, I sought to be attentive to the potential political influence of the research process itself. I interviewed people involved with the organizations individually and in groups, as thought processes and insights work differently in these settings, and was attentive to internal diversity issues (such as gender, age, geography, religious observance, status in the organizations, movement background). Using this methodology, I conducted formal detailed interviews with a range of staff/leadership/rank and file individual members of four organizations, less structured in-depth interviews with individual leaders from over twenty organizations, four group interviews run on the model of activist workshops, and shorter interviews with key individual players in close to thirty other organizations.[5] I attended many of their in-house meetings and public events and followed their exposure in the press.

Longevity

There is the expectation that groups will absolutely seek to avoid disbanding so that longevity is an unquestioned organizational goal.[6] As Wilson writes, "organizations tend to persist. That is the most important thing to know about them" (1973, 30). This focus on longevity as a measure of success bypasses more qualitative considerations about groups, politics, and needs. If groups honestly begin with process-oriented intent concerned with assessing needs, it is assumed that they, like individual men, are subject to Hobbesian laws of nature. Groups, despite their intentions, will succumb to the iron law of self-perpetuation. It is assumed that groups will seek to exist and to expand at all costs.

Is this the reality of all groups? My research has shown some evidence that corroborates this assumption. However, this is by no means a total picture and, in fact, listening to groups articulate their own manner of evaluation we may even find something fundamentally different. An interesting case is that of Americans for Peace Now (APN). APN was formed in the early 1980s as an attempt to support the massive mainstream peace movement in Israel, Shalom Achshav (Peace Now). On the one hand, APN has claimed that its goal is to "go out of business." When Israel has achieved peace with its neighbors, the organization will shut its doors. Granted, this just may be public relations rhetoric and it would not be easy for an organization to disband. What is interesting, however, is that APN is not the only dovish organization which has risen to power that describes its goal in direct contrast to the expectation of longevity. Another example is a group called Project Nishma.

Formed in the later 1980s, Project Nishma works within the establishment of the American Jewish community, combining unequivocable support for the peace process with a strong concern for Israel's security needs. Although Project Nishma has an organizational infrastructure, which develops as the organization gains recognition and takes on more complicated projects, its founders use the term "project" in the title intentionally to indicate the organization's semi-*ad hoc* nature. Even after the first few years of its existence, its leaders remained consciously committed to its temporary nature.

I do not wish to suggest here that groups will not become entrenched. My research suggests that groups feel keenly pressured by
this expectation of success. However, interviews reveal a substantial
level of group commitment to the cause. When group members were
asked to evaluate other groups, their responses affirmed respect
for other groups' commitment to ideological goals rather than self-
perpetuation. Furthermore, nowhere did members of these organizations offer longevity as an example or self-measure of their own
success. Research on actual groups compels us to look deeper, to pay
attention to the criteria that groups use for their own assessments.

Numbers

Such a pursuit is not that simple. My research has shown that
groups feel additionally pressured to succeed in other quantitative
ways, assumed by legislators and political scientists, which do not
necessarily express their own standards of success. For example,
unless a group explicitly aims to be exclusive, many scholars assume membership size to connote success.[7] It is important, however,
to examine how actual groups respond to this pressure.

When asked what they would consider success for their group,
some interviewees did answer in terms of membership size. One or
two people even led me to believe that numbers, in a narrowly quantitative sense, is a significant measure. They say that congresspeo-
ple want to hear that an organization has many members. Numbers
often impress funding sources, the press, and other centers of power.
As they exist in this kind of political world, numbers are definitely
a consideration for these groups.

However, it would be incorrect to say that such quantitative
measures are the only standards by which these organizations perceive their own strength. Actually, there is much evidence which
shows that growing numbers are often a cause for concern. There is
a perception in some groups that smaller numbers would increase
effectiveness (not because they seek more exclusive memberships to
build prestige). Several reasons were suggested that reflect qualitative considerations for "effectiveness": increased ability to communicate across geographical boundaries, increased intimacy among
members, greater benefits enabling activists to do more solid work
in the local organizations, and facilitating the consensus method
which allows for a stronger decision-making process.

I do not intend to say that everyone wants a small group. Although some activists believe that more emphasis on outreach

would force the group to clarify its positions, others work from a contradictory view that having fewer members enables their groups to make clearer policy statements. It is true, however, that many feel the pressure to prove their strength in terms of their numbers and that a large membership could indicate a broad base of ideological support. When a group's goal has more to do with deeper conceptions of politics, however, the issue of membership size becomes a topic of strategic and ideological discussion, rather than just accepted as a simple measurement of success. An interesting point to note here is that many of these groups were much smaller some years ago, and activists then said similar things. Such a phenomenon reminds us that the perception of optimal group size is thus a relative measure in itself.

There are also other indications that suggest that mere numbers are not a standard by which those involved in these groups measure their success. For example, members do not perceive that their groups are more concerned with expanding the number of members when compared to consciousness raising and developing relationships between the members. Their feeling is that by developing a stronger membership, the organizations will be more solid. Even when asked about involvement in the Hobbesian world of pressuring United States political actors, members expressed their own standards of strength in other than numerical terms.

With respect to the goal to expand, activists said that developing the character of the organization and its members is necessary for expanding in what they characterize as a more important way. While expanding the number of members is a goal, there is concern with the qualitative aspects of membership. They are interested in expanding in ways that promote the quality of the organization (including building infrastructure and developing membership skills). This decision to expand with care, which was expressed by activists across the board, demonstrates that quantity ranks well below quality in the groups' own perception of success.

Money

Another example of gross measurements is found in the expectation that money is power.[8] The case study groups feel the pressure of this standard of success keenly as well. I will not argue that my case study groups are not concerned with money, and do not seek larger budgets. In a capitalist world money often *is* power. However, much of the transformational approach reminds us to look locally, to specific sites of political engagement and social interaction in order to acknowledge and examine alternative practices and nodes of resistance. Liberal and capitalist expectations have not been simply and uncritically absorbed by the whole of society. Many individuals and groups such as those discussed here are struggling to live out and further develop alternative standards. Not only does their difference from the perceived norm affect the internal life within the groups, it also affects the way that these groups interact in the larger, capitalist sphere as well. The issue of money as power, when probed, demonstrates that there are groups struggling to find innovative ways to interact with the dominant paradigm itself.

The Progressive Zionist Caucus (PZC) provides an interesting example. PZC is a grassroots organization working with a miniscule budget. It constantly faces debt and the threat of dissolution based on financial problems. However, not one of the members of PZC mentioned money when asked how they measure their own success, nor did they suggest monetary considerations when questioned about their standards of success for other similar groups. It is interesting that all of the activists I interviewed have financial responsibilities and pressures and must deal with the financial requirements of their part of the organization on a constant basis. Although money seems a fact of life that they must contend with, budget size itself is not a standard of success.

For the most part, activists did comment on the benefits that a larger budget could have for PZC. It is essential to note, however, that this was expressed directly in qualitative terms. In addition, despite the desperate need for funds, the organization has committed not to fundraise at the expense of solid programming, a qualitative measure. Such a decision has been upheld numerous times in the face of intense pressure to fundraise. Some respondents also noted that there have been years when the organization ran on larger budgets and was less effective than other years when it ran on smaller budgets. It is also helpful to remember that the relatively large budget Breira managed to achieve did not help avert its rapid demise. Thus, research shows that despite intense concern over funds, members still do not consider budget size to be a dominant measure of success.

The case of APN is more complicated. In direct responses I found much more usage of Hobbesian terminology. More references were made to quantitative measures of success than in some of the other organizations. When questioned on this issue, one APN woman said that she "does not really care about the members, [she] just wants their bodies." Another woman said, "If I believed that there were a way to make governments move without members, I would dispense with the membership. But, it is a democratic tendency . . . to rely on numbers . . . We are not trying to develop our membership for the sake of the members, but for political reasons. We are trying to develop clout."

It is clear from some of the APN responses, therefore, that liberal expectations have definitely effected the organization. However, my research also shows significant evidence of qualitative, non-alienated thinking. On this issue, APN is an excellent example of a group struggling between the vision that many members joined with and that the organization proposes to pursue, and a largely alienated legislative arena in which only quantitative evidence of success tends to be taken into account. In this case, it is possible that more APN members use liberal language because they are more influenced, due to their closer involvement, by that part of the political universe than are some other groups' members. However, this is not a sufficient explanation for the different levels of alienation.

First, it is important to note that these same people used qualitative language at different points in the interviews. For example, the man who said, when asked directly, that success will be measured in terms of money and numbers, talked of moral imperatives elsewhere on this issue. In his response to a different question, he talked of the role of the organization in terms of teaching and mobilizing people. The person who "just wants their bodies" also talked about the need for creative involvement, and the need for more emphasis on education in the Jewish community than on fundraising. She talked about members' needs to become "broader, deeper, smarter, and wiser." The respondent who would "dispense with the membership" if she could said that she finds in her concrete, daily political activity, the way for activists to change and to create environments where people will be able to develop. She stressed the importance of day-to-day work with the people involved in the organization on issues that are both political and emotional and that affect real political change. Another activist who also used quantitative language when responding to certain direct questions, talked of the need for the younger generation of Jews to reconnect with the community. She said that the most important thing APN can do as an American Jewish organization is to provide a home for these people. The research design allowed the respondents room for a fuller reflection on these issues. In each case, in their more detailed responses, these visions of a "deeper, broader, smarter, and wiser" community emerged. Connections between the role of quantitative and qualitative factors made here demonstrate a wider range of ways to understand group success.

Second, other groups whose focus is legislative influence did not use the same degree of quantitative language as APN, and instead expressed themselves in more qualitative terms. Leaders talked of mobilizing, encouraging and empowering members. They also mentioned the need to feel in touch with the community, to listen and to engage. A group does not need to be a membership organization to have influence. Some of the alienated language used by APN members was related to their suggestion that a membership organization was the only legitimate pathway to power in Washington, D.C., and thus they felt pressured to build membership size. An important contrast to such expectations is the alternative path chosen by Project Nishma, which also works in Washington, D.C. Project Nishma also has achieved quite a measure of success, but does not operate on the principle of a large membership organization. The Jewish Peace Lobby is another example. Although the organization seeks to expand its membership, district representation and activist commitment and resources are essential. Thus, the standards by which these groups measure themselves, and the language that they use, demonstrate that lobbying does not necessitate wholly acquiescing to alienated expectations of success standards.

Another example of how groups have been able to function in their relatively nonalienated way within the current political expectations of groups has been through their use of coalitions and mutual support. Relying on cooperation, rather than on competition, groups have been able to—and further seek to—work with the size and wealth they feel comfortable with so that they will not feel forced to abandon their longer-term goals. Small groups staying more responsible to their organizational aspirations can still act in an alienated political environment through pooling resources. For example, during the Gulf War, a coalition of small groups were able to lobby in Congress claiming strength in their joint numbers. The groups did not have to abandon the particular characteristics and platforms which make them unique, but bolstered their effectiveness by joining forces when appropriate.

Redefining Politics, the Political Sphere and Group Success

It is possible that examining only groups who are primarily lobby groups will generate a certain perception of success. The standards assumed in the groups literature may be applicable, but only to a subset of political groups. Yet, the fact that most traditional studies look at "lobby" groups cannot entirely explain why they have such narrow expectations of group behavior and success. Particularly in light of the tendency to reduce politics to government, it is important to remember that the world of government is but a slice of the political universe. Among the groups I have studied who focus on legislative influence in Washington, D.C., however, such narrow expectations do not adequately reflect even their standards of themselves.

Like the interest groups usually studied by group scholars, the political groups of my case studies also want to have an impact on government policy. However, the case study groups tend to perceive the political world with which they are engaged as broader than relationship with governments. Their political world is also the world of the community. For these groups, given their issue area of focus and the communal-historical moment in which they are active, a most significant aspect of community that they hope to bring about is an arena in which heated dialogue and debate can occur. These groups are working towards a community where dissent will not be silenced and core issues of the self can be explored, challenged as well as shifted if necessary. To these groups which also understand their existence as in the realm of communities, politics involves consciousness and identity, reinterpretations of history and reenvisioning the future. Politics is a process of empowerment of individual members and of the collective. What we see is that the way a group defines its political world and the political process affects its standards of success.

The groups organized in Washington, D.C. are aware of, concerned with, and motivated by their relationship to their community. They are concerned with their standing among other Jews. They are also concerned with foundational questions of identity and the need for a more affirming political process. Some of those interviewed discussed how their role is to listen to the community, respond to its needs, and help shape its future. Thus, even among lobby and advocacy groups these considerations of what politics is ultimately about suggest that measures of success must be based on standards that go far beyond traditional group theory's base in legislative victories.

Those groups not primarily focused in the legislative arena definitely see their relationship to the community as essential to their *raison d'être*. They define success in terms of the community being able to hear their voice and recognize them.[9] They talk about promoting dialogue and more authentic relationships within the community. These people have refused to be marginal and care deeply about the content of Jewish life in the United States (and globally, although that was not the focus of my research).

Respondents across the spectrum of case study groups talked about success in terms broader than their influence in government or counting legislative victories. In response to questions concerning how activists measure the success of their organizations, respondents frequently spoke in terms of their relationship with individuals and other groups within the community. People active in the groups discussed the quality of their programming, and whether they are being heard by the organized mainstream and by nonaffiliated Jews. They talked about educating and empowering individuals, and reinvigorating the community as a whole. The responses from those involved in these political groups suggest that, scholars who measure group success must take into account the groups' relationships with society as a whole, and not just with government, qualitative considerations and not only quantitative ones. Thus, the empirical research demonstrates that success for political groups involves making progress in the more basic effort to create a public sphere in which conversation and empowering struggle are possible.

Conclusion

In sum, group scholars and liberal democratic theorists tend to reduce the political world to the governmental arena. They follow a common paradigm, utilized by Hobbes and Madison before them, which seeks solutions to societal problems, identified as based in a common angst, only in the public legal realm. With this focus, much of the qualitative nature of group goals are lost. Group scholars discuss success in distinctly nonqualitative terms such as longevity, membership numbers, and budget size. Such standards share their roots in Hobbesian assumptions of the quest for mere survival.[10]

The groups I have studied, on the other hand, demonstrate that the world of politics is much broader and reaches deep into the very consciousness of community life. Even with their goals of affecting policy, those active in these groups talk more about qualitative engagement with a living, diverse community than they did about influence in government. They discussed success in terms of being sensitive to the various needs of the community and discussed vitality more than numbers. Also, more than gross budget size, they talked of the need to be creative and effective. Those involved in these groups, on the whole, seek a politics of dialogue, stimulating and empowering people, and promoting qualitative connection to Jewish life. The groups feel tremendously pressured to prove their success in certain superficial, quantitative ways: government policy, larger budgets, increased memberships. Despite these external expectations, however, it is also a web of more qualitative standards by which the groups evaluate themselves and other groups. Their responses point to a theory of democratic politics defined by such process-oriented engagement. For those working to build a new democratic theory that includes a commitment to social transformation, such standards will be more fully expressive of our successes and failures to bring about such transformation.

Notes

1. I would like to thank Manfred Halpern and the editors of this volume for their thoughtful comments.

2. See the work of Manfred Halpern, for example chapter 3 in this volume.

3. Some studies focus on the city (Dahl 1961; Crenson 1978), state (Malecki and Mahood 1972; Brown 1985), or national (Denzau and Munger 1986) levels of government. Further variations are found in the study of the legislative (Smith 1984), executive (Heclo 1978; McGlennon and Rapoport 1983), or judicial (Epstein and Rowland in Cigler and Loomis 1986; Stewart 1987) branches or in the bureaucracy (Aberbach and Rockman 1978; Gormley, et al. 1983; Romzek and Hendricks 1982; Berry 1981).The most popular evaluation of success, however, is legislative influence at the national level in the United States Congress (Pool 1981, Herndon 1982). This level of influence gets measured in various ways. For example, some scholars have commented on the structure of influence in terms of the provision or exchange of information (Matthews 1960, 178; Hinckley 1978, 51–4), or "access" to legislators (Truman 1951, 264–70). By far the most common evaluation is in terms of legislative victories. These are either examined in terms of single issues at one point in time (Ornstein and Elder 1978), or in quantitative terms according to "roll call" votes (Fowler and Shaiko 1987).

4. See Zisk (1992), Abalos (1996), and in this volume Graham, Woolpert and Knight for a transformationalist analysis of some of these movements.

5. See Ollman (1993), Reinharz (1979), Harding (1986), and Zisk (1992). Formal reflections on my methodology, as praxis, were presented as a paper to the Midwest Women's Studies Conference (1993). See also Brettschneider (1996).

6. See for example, Olson (1971, 6); Clark and Wilson (1961); Wilson (1973).

7. See for example, Smith (1984); Clark and Wilson (1961); Wilson (1973, 262).

8. For example: Wilson (1973, 266); Smith (1984).

9. For discussions of this level of politics see Young's "Five Faces of Oppression," (1990) and Taylor (1992).

10. See Daly (1978) for the way she distinguishes between a quantitative survival and a qualitative revolutional survival.

8

The Study of Transformational Politics: Participant Observation and Objectivity

BETTY ZISK

Introduction

Participant observation—the study of groups, individuals, or institutions with whom the researcher is involved as a guest, an observer, or a member—has long been respectable among sociologists and anthropologists. Political scientists have been more cautious: note the summary treatment of the topic in most methods texts, and our infrequent use of the technique.

Most arguments against participant observation stem from its nonquantitative nature and its subjectivity, in comparison with methods like the use of surveys and structured interviews, mathematical modeling, and the like. How can data derived from personal observations be verified or falsified, replicated or built upon in a cumulative way by other researchers?

At the same time, the argument can be made that participant observation is one of the few tools available for studying some of the most interesting but intransigent political problems and populations. For example, those seeking to change political, social, and economic institutions in basic ways—sometimes by nontraditional means (civil disobedience, demonstrations)—and those who seek to build alternative lifestyles and institutions—often mistrust scholarly research. Similarly, oppressed and alienated people (the homeless and jobless, new immigrants, and prisoners, among others) are not easily available to traditional research teams. And if they are, they may embrace values or employ language and other symbols in

ways foreign to the models, typologies, and standard right-left ideological continuum that social scientists currently employ. In short,
the ideas and activities with which the student of transformational
politics is most concerned (developing nonhierarchical and nonop-
pressive institutions; building new theories; eliminating behavior
and processes that harm humans or the planet) may be virtually im-
penetrable by traditional techniques.

This essay is divided into three sections: first, an overview of
different types of participant observation, along with some noteworthy examples of the genre; second, some concrete examples of the
problems and rewards I have encountered as an activist-observer, as
a means of highlighting the arguments outlined above, as well as
additional questions about the role of research subjects and the use
of research findings; and finally, a few conclusions about the utility
of participant observation for the study and nurturance of transformational politics.

A Definitional Overview with Historical Examples

Most classical participant observers (e.g., Whyte 1981; Liebow
1967) were avowed outsiders who moved temporarily into a community to form "a close attachment to an alien or exotic group [they
wished] to study" (Nachmias and Nachmias 1976, 90). They could
never be an integral part of the groups they observed—white ethnic
"streetcorner boys" in one case, young African-American men in the
other—but they "hung out," occasionally questioned, and patiently
watched their subjects openly, in much the way that Chicago sociologists had studied prostitutes and professional thieves some years
earlier. In many ways, Richard Fenno's (1978) work on representatives in their home districts, while of shorter duration, is similar to
Whyte and Liebow's approach.

In contrast, the early works of David Mayhew (1974) and Jeffrey Berry (1977) are based on a closer relationship between observer and subject: both scholars were Fellows or Interns who
worked for the organizations they studied (Congress; public interest
groups). Sensitive, admittedly qualitative essays came out of these
observations.[1] Finally, moving one step further in closing the distance between observers and observed, many of the authors in Freeman's (1983) collection on political movements were advocates for
the causes they described. Similarly, John Rensenbrink (1992) wrote
as both an active Green and as a scholar. That indeed was my own

position as well, in regard to peace and environmental groups (Zisk 1992) and, more recently, on social justice groups working with the oppressed in Massachusetts (1994).

Patricia and Peter Adler (1987) describe these varying degrees of scholarly participation as fitting on a continuum from "peripheral" through "active" to "complete" membership. In their terms, White, Liebow, and Fenno would be peripheral members, Mayhew and Berry active members, and Freeman's authors, Rensenbrink, and I complete members. (I was a committed participant in the work of several of the 154 groups I observed in 1987, and a mailing list member of others. In addition, I took on an advisory or full participant role in several more groups as a result of my initial research on those groups.[2])

To avoid the cumbersome terminology used by the Adlers (1987), I prefer the term "activist observer." An activist observer is well characterized by Hayano (cited in Adler and Adler 1987, 68): "[I]n each case, the researchers possess the qualities of often permanent self-identification with a group and full internal membership, as recognized both by themselves and the people of whom they are a part." It should be noted that the activist observer internalizes most of the values and shares much of the lifestyle of the groups observed. He or she is likely to socialize, as well as identify, with fellow members, to share their language and symbols, and of course to participate in their goal-oriented activities. There is no question that this identification with the observed group(s) can sometimes create a conflict of interest with the scholarly identity—even for a scholar committed to the study and teaching of transformational politics. This is because, with rare exceptions, the tenets and priorities of academia, *particularly* in regard to scholarly "objectivity," do not always coincide with those of transformational politics. I shall return to this point in the sections that follow.

Travels of an Activist Observer: Scylla, Charybdis,
and the Long Way Home

The major costs of participant observation (especially of activist observation) are (1) loss of objectivity; (2) effects of the observer on the events observed; (3) difficulty in quantifying (and attempting to falsify) subjective data. Some benefits that might be denied to (or missed by) an outsider are (1) access to key people, and information about what is happening; (2) prior knowledge of the history and problems of the phenomena studied (and information about key players); and (3) an ability to empathize with those who are being observed (in part through introspection) in a way that is not often possible for outsiders. Some problems are unavoidable; in other cases, researchers may be forced to make a conscious choice, on the spot, about their appropriate role in the field.

The question of scholarly objectivity rears its head most notably at two different points in the research process. First, there is the problem of interpreting and classifying data (can activist observers be objective about groups in which they have a personal stake?) Second, there is the interactional question: does activist status significantly change the way in which interviewing takes place, or informants act, in comparison with the way they would respond to neutral or hostile observers?

It is clear that activist status affects all of these processes, and that this fact is both a strength and potential weakness of participant observation. But the corollary is that an aloof or hostile observer will interpret or interact as an outsider, and may misunderstand or antagonize the subject. The outsider may also miss crucial parts of the action or behavior observed, if he/she comes too late to the process, is mistrusted, or misunderstands what is going on.

Participant status can be problematic, but if the purpose of the observation is to explain an act or event *from the perspective of the actor*, then the odds are that the "insider" will capture that meaning in a way not always possible for the "outsider." This *empathy* is especially valuable in studying the perceptions or motives of political actors (topics very difficult to pin down, or even to verify, by more traditional research techniques).

Three examples from my fieldwork illustrate the subjectivity-objectivity problem at different stages of the research process. The first concerns the research instrument: in this case, the informal set of questions posed in interviews with 164 peace and environmental activists (Zisk 1992). Very late in the fieldwork, one activist-respondent complained about the omission of a crucial aspect of "success," in a series of questions I asked about the impact of group efforts—namely, fundraising. He was right. I had based the questions on group success on my reading of the scholarly literature: concrete impact via lobbying, litigation, or other strategies; media coverage; coalition formation; stability or growth in membership. Here my observer/researcher role had taken priority over my activist role—i.e., I had tried so hard to be "objective" in formulating research questions that I overlooked part of my own experience as treasurer of two of the groups in question, and on a fundraising committee for a third. (Thus there is little discussion of fundraising in the study; the idea came too late to be included in all of the interviews.)

On classification of responses to interview data, and later interpretation, a very different problem arose. All leaders interviewed were asked to describe what their group did to advance their cause. (No checklist was used, because it might bias the answers.) A predictable range of answers followed: lobbying, litigation, educational work, and in some cases, civil disobedience, demonstrations, marches on Washington. A few respondents mentioned individual members' civil disobedience, making a careful distinction between group and individual acts. Others did not volunteer this information, confining their responses to officially endorsed activities. When writing the chapter on civil disobedience, I realized that I knew (from prior reading and/or interaction with the people concerned) that some interviewees had indeed participated *as individuals* in civil disobedience (resistance to federal war taxes, nuclear arms production and testing, and/or in providing sanctuary to Central American refugees). What to do? Several groups had already been classified as participating in civil disobedience, as individuals only; now several more could fit into that category, if the respondents had mentioned this activity in the interview. But they had not. My decision was to use the interview data literally, but to report in a footnote that several respondents were involved in civil disobedience as individuals. But note—an outsider would not have known and would not have gone through the internal doubts about classification of data, on this question.

My third example concerns the truth or accuracy of responses to interview questions. This is a problem that plagues all survey research. We learn to be wary; we all dutifully check the boxes at the end, on honesty, openness, and sophistication of respondents. But what of the people (in this case, about ten respondents, or 6% of the sample) who either overestimate or downplay their success? These are not liars; these are optimists and pessimists. Again, since this study focused on the activist perspective, and since there was no outside confirmation of many claims, I took activists at their word, even when responses seemed colored by modesty or braggadocio. I tried to err (if there was error) on the side of the actor. It was worrisome, however, to record a response that seemed, for whatever reason, to miss the mark.

Finally, what of possible bias in the interactions between researcher and subject, given that subjects knew of the sympathy and shared values of the researcher? One eloquent statement has been made by sociologist Gordon Zahn (1969, 20) in response to the criticism that his status as a Catholic pacifist might have endangered his "objectivity" in studying military chaplains.

Any issue as grave as war, and especially war in this nuclear age, demands concern and some measure of direct engagement on the part of all people, not only Christian and certainly not only pacifists. To require, as the criticism would seem to, that only those who are somehow able to detach themselves so completely from the affairs of man that they have no commitment one way or the other would be to limit the scholarly virtue of objectivity to those individuals (assuming such can be found!) for whom these questions related to human survival hold no measure of saliency at all.

Zahn goes on to argue that this narrow requirement would also call into question the value of work by former chaplains (who support the military effort), because they too are not disinterested. Finally, such a requirement would extend as well to other topics—for example, rendering "competent social researchers who happen to be Negro or Jewish ineligible for research into problems associated with racial or religious prejudice and discrimination" (1969, 20). Zahn ultimately agrees with Myrdal's classic assertion that the only way to handle such biases—given the fact that they cannot be fully eliminated—is "to face the valuations and to introduce them as explicitly stated, specific, and sufficiently concretized value premises" (1969, 1043).

I agree with Myrdal's position. And the point can be buttressed by the argument that nonobjectivity (or empathy) is an advantage in two ways: for concrete access to people and data, and for understanding what is studied. But first, we must face another problem. This concerns observer effects on data, in addition to the interactional problems already mentioned.

Concern about observer effects often focuses on interviewer-interviewee relations—the point just addressed. This is only the tip of the iceberg. What about the effect of an activist observer on the behavior of the group itself? In a small group, this is no idle question. If the observer abstains from the decision making process, that abstention may affect the decision; if the observer participates, and a decision hinges in part on his/her actions, that too is part of the result. I decided, early in my work, that the only answer to this dilemma was to try to behave as I would if I were not conducting a study. In a few groups, I thus became a part of my own data. I attempted to wear two hats, in a very self-conscious way. There was no other choice: my withdrawal (even temporarily) into "academic objectivity" would have removed my "normal" input, however small, into the group, thus creating a different form of bias.[3]

But there is another element in the problem of biasing the data—namely, movement networking. I promised anonymity to all those I interviewed, in the sense of a commitment not to identify specific responses. On several occasions, however, I found that a group was working on problems that had been tackled earlier by activists in other regions, and that the group might benefit from the experience of their counterparts. What was my responsibility in this case, given my sympathy and participation in their cause? Should I remain silent, on grounds of scholarly distance, or should I tell them of potential allies or sources of information (my normal behavior as an activist)? I chose the latter role—again, on the grounds that I should behave as I would in the absence of research, and that removing myself as a networker would simply bias the study in a different way.

But lines had to be drawn late in the interview process. It was one thing to tell Nuclear Free Zone advocates in Palo Alto that they might learn from mistakes of an earlier effort in Santa Monica, and to give them an address for the Santa Monica group. It would have been an entirely different matter, however, to yield to the request of an advocate of another initiative that I call him, after my interviews with potential allies in his area, to tell him of their decisions. Here he asked, quite blatantly, for a leak of advance information about a current campaign. The answer had to be no; I was willing to network, while studying movement activity, but unwilling to spy. Once again, networking was/is natural to most activists; spying is not. For the record, I "networked" on nine occasions. It is doubtful that it had much impact on the outcomes, except insofar as demoralized activists were glad to hear about, and make contact with, potential sources of help.

I have examined some of the costs of activist participation at some length; I now move to the happier topic of benefits. First, the question of access. Movement ties were helpful for the ease of fieldwork. Some movement people provided contacts with others I might have overlooked without their help. They provided moral support in the field, and in one case, gave me a room and meals in their home. Sometimes they took phone messages—a major plus given the time it took to set up my interviews.

Speedy access was also simplified by my ability to attend group meetings (and to find out in advance about those meetings), or to call for an appointment, on the grounds that I was a visiting Green, Quaker, or Sierra Club member, etc., with a legitimate reason for the call or visit. This became particularly important in the case of groups conducting illegal activities.

In Portland, Oregon, rumors of FBI surveillance of the peace movement preceded my arrival. Thus the contact for the local sanctuary movement (an unlawful effort to support Central American refugees) greeted my phone call with some suspicion. My statement that I was a Quaker, had attended the local Meeting for Worship earlier that week, and had obtained the contact name from the Meeting Bulletin, helped to allay some fears. It was only when I offered a letter of introduction from the Friends Meeting at Cambridge, however, that the contact person agreed to see me. Even with credentials in hand, it took considerable reassurance, including the oft-repeated "I am one of you," before sanctuary activists spoke frankly.

Sanctuary people elsewhere, and members of the Pledge of Resistance, were less wary, perhaps because I had earlier interviewed some of their allies. But again, their knowledge of my activism broke down barriers that might have remained for other, more "objective" observers. I spoke the language, exuded genuine sympathy, and could refer to my activities in the Boston-area Pledge (and in a past Cambridge sanctuary) where appropriate. It is noteworthy that one Earth First! contact whom I knew through my Greens' activism was friendly and cooperative; another, with whom I had no direct tie, was quite guarded throughout the interview, despite my status as a "mailing list member" of Earth First! and my obvious familiarity with the group's activities.[4]

Implications for the Study of Transformational Politics

One broad topic remains: the implications for those of us who study transformational politics, of relying on participant observation and other "soft" techniques, given the current stance of social scientists on objectivity and quantification. (I recognize the value of many of these soft techniques—narrative analysis, case studies, phenomenological research, and the like—and in fact, some of my consideration of the pros and cons of participant observation applies to them as well. I do not discuss them because of space limitations and because I have had little experience in using them.)

I have pointed out several benefits of activist observation: access to those who may not cooperate with others, and, via empathy, a grasp of the meaning of goals, strategies, and activities of activists. The disadvantages are the related questions of observer bias and the effect of the observer on the data. But there are more important issues of distance and objectivity, and of comparability of data obtained under differing degrees of involvement with the subject of research.

I have long since concluded that it is almost impossible, and probably not desirable, to be as distant or objective as many empirically oriented scholars would prefer. *All* sources of data have some inbuilt bias, whether we are discussing omissions of the census taker, deletions made in *The Congressional Record*, or low rates of response to mail questionnaires. On the conceptual level, we have yet to resolve the debate over imposing the researcher's framework versus somehow teasing out the meaning of political acts from the *actor's* perspective. Two solutions have been: first, to use a combination of methods in the hope that the flaws of each will be canceled by the other; and second, to choose observational techniques appropriate to specific research problems, and to the *audience or purpose to which research findings are directed*.

Multiple research strategies make sense because of problems of subjectivity and reliability. It is a rare project that does not (at the very least) check accounts of one respondent against another, or the researcher's field observations against media and other sources of data. In my own case, comparing several accounts of coalition work was important. For group involvement in referenda campaigns, official returns and reports on election expenditures were vital. Finally, I never relied on my own sense of the groups to which I belonged, but rather, interviewed activists from the group, using the same set of questions asked of leaders of other organizations.

But the dilemma remains: if the focus is on perspectives of relevant political actors, such perspectives are, by definition, subjective and even unstable, in that for some respondents, today's euphoria leads to tomorrow's despair. Thus self-assessment on topics like group success cannot be viewed as hard or "objective" data, although supplementary and independent information can reassure the researcher. (It should be noted, however, that this same problem exists for those who seek similar data via survey research.)

There really is little choice, however, about risking the bias, the subjectivity, and the lack of readily quantifiable data implied by both participant observation and unstructured interviewing techniques that seek the perspective of those studied—*if we want to study individuals and activities on the periphery of the political mainstream.* The point applies not only to movement groups but to those who have consciously withdrawn from politics-as-usual (into principled nonvoting, communes, etc.), and to revolutionaries and anarchists. It probably applies as well to those whose marginal status is involuntary (the poor, homeless, jobless, or incarcerated). There are two reasons for this: first, the question of access and candor in regard to outsiders, and second, the unique conceptual "eyeglasses" with which marginal actors are likely to view politics and society.

It is not surprising that new immigrants do not readily fit into traditional left-right categories, as measured by standard surveys; this lack of "fit" does not mean, however, that peripheral populations are unconcerned about political issues. They may simply order their priorities in a way that is almost incomprehensible because of the mainstream assumptions built into most survey instruments.

My final point concerns the audience to whom research findings are addressed and the use to which they are put. Most postbehavioral research seems directed to the quest for knowledge for its own sake, or to solving problems of public policy. The focus on objectivity, quantification and the like serves the felt need for work that is *cumulative* and that meets the test of falsifiability. But there are time-honored alternative goals for social research. I need only cite Kurt Lewin's (1948; 1953) "action research" on food habits, leadership, and other topics; Myrdal's (1944) work on race; Stouffers' on propaganda and morale in the Army (1949) to make the point that some social scientists have conducted research aimed at bringing about desired changes.

Tandon goes yet a step further, in a symposium on "Social Transformation and Participatory Research in arguing that "those who are directly affected by a problem have the right to acquire information about it for themselves" (1988, 20). (He accepts the idea of some division of labor—i.e., reliance on specialists in studying health or environmental problems.) We need not agree with his point to acknowledge one of his conclusions (1988, 26): "[F]undamental questions must be raised about what knowledge is produced, by whom, for whose interests and toward what ends. Such arguments begin to demand the creation of a new paradigm and organization of science." I have argued that it may be impossible to study certain kinds of political groups and·individuals using traditional research strategies, following standard caveats about objectivity. My reasoning has to do with access and empathy. It is unlikely, however, that mainstream scholars will accept nontraditional work as valid, except as a means of generating hypotheses to be rigorously tested in later studies. But, if the researcher is serious about wanting to provide concrete advice to the groups studied (or to take them as partners in designing the questions), it is unlikely that a monograph or scholarly journal is the appropriate place for disseminating findings.

This does not mean that bridging the gap between mainstream and transformational scholars is impossible. Unless we are prepared, as social scientists, to ignore a large part of the political world, on the grounds that it cannot always be studied objectively, some relaxation of "scientific" requirements may be needed, at least at this stage of research on new frontiers. The increasing number of avowedly policy oriented studies and the plethora of scholarly think-pieces on "how to fix what's wrong with America," lend credence to the idea that others share the view that we can no longer ignore difficult research problems.

Similarly, if and when oppressed or peripheral populations come to value our advice, activists may become tolerant about what now seems an overconcern with numbers, jargon, and conceptualization. I for one am weary of apologizing to activists about my academic mentality and supposed indifference to their needs. The two worlds can, and should enrich each other. And one would hope that we share a profound concern—with them and with our students—for the future of the planet which houses our politics and our lives, and with some of the oppressed and alienated individuals and groups who share it with us.

Notes

1. The main body of Berry's study was based on a survey of a large number of public interest lobbies; one portion of his work, however, was based on several months with two groups, a peace organization and an animal rights group.

2. For more details on how I inexorably acquired new organizational roles, and their consequences for my research, see Zisk (1992), Appendix. While many of the examples given in that work have been recounted here, this chapter is an updated account and assessment of participant observation, with somewhat more optimistic conclusions than those of 1992.

3. I recall no case where my vote or voice was crucial to the decisions by these consensual groups. There were two instances, however, where my arguments may have assisted in reaching consensus in a more timely fash-

ion than usual—namely, on the New England Greens' endorsement of the Massachusetts antinuclear initiative, and on the stance on abortion adopted by the Women's Caucus of the New England Greens.

4. Another cause for the difference, however, has become clear with subsequent events. Earth First! activities were in fact under FBI surveillance in one region (where the contact was wary) but not (to my knowledge) in the other. I am grateful to Christa Slaton for pointing out that interviewing illegal groups can sometimes be dangerous for a scholar. I have suffered no harm (yet) by consorting with those involved in illegalities, but some scholars have been jailed or found in contempt of court for refusing to provide information on their associates. Sam Popkin was a cause celebre, briefly, in the Boston area, for refusing to divulge his sources on *The Pentagon Papers*; he was sentenced to jail, for contempt, but released when the entire Harvard-MIT community came to his defense. I doubt seriously if those of us who chose to associate with Earth First! or sanctuary groups, or others now doing civil disobedience would find such scholarly support. Thus—beware. I assume an innocent stand; all scholars should. But the government may yet get us for our associations.

9

A Transformational Pedagogy:
The Politics of Gender

GALE HARRISON

Transformation signifies a radical, even revolutionary, change that cannot be undone except through another transformational experience or series of experiences. Transformation means that a person or society is fundamentally altered. The educational process can be one that leaves students and teachers unchanged—a few abstract facts are memorized, regurgitated for the test, and then promptly forgotten. But the process of education can also be an agent of change where new ideas are processed, old ideas are reevaluated, modified, and adapted to new ways of thinking; i.e., the student will never be quite the same again. This kind of change occurs at the affective as well as the cognitive level. Stafford Beer has defined "information as 'what changes us'" (Henry 1994, 97). Therefore, *real* education is always potentially transformational.

Teaching Gender Politics

As a professor of politics, International Studies, and Women's and Gender Studies, I initiated and currently teach a course in Women and Politics as one channel for fostering transformational change. Not only does the course provide the challenge of teaching about gender in political life in a comparative-international framework, but also there is a politics involved in the dynamics of the classroom, a politics of the academy as well.

While the composition of the Women and Politics class has ranged from two-thirds female, one third male to 60 percent male, 40 percent female, the most common sexual composition is about 50/50. Many of the men in the class are Justice Studies majors, seeking careers in law enforcement and corrections. Their backgrounds are often Southern, conservative, and rural—backgrounds that typically have not fostered positive attitudes towards feminism. On the other hand, I am a committed feminist and a liberal Democrat. Yet the course has been highly successful, filling to capacity quickly, often requested by men as well as by women.

In this course, as in my other teaching, I employ a feminist pedagogy based on feminist philosophy, epistemology, and methodology. Feminist pedagogy is based on several key factors: a philosophy that asserts that all human beings are equal and should be treated as such, an epistemology that proposes that there is no one correct truth or "way of knowing," and a methodology that values diverse methods (quantitative, statistical, qualitative, experiential, among others)—"the amplitude of empirical knowledge" that Louis Herman mentions in chapter 2. Such feminist philosophy is value-based as Christa Slaton notes in chapter 1, but so are all other pedagogical orientations.

Shan Overton and Christine Caron (1993) have spoken of the transformation that can occur by employing a feminist perspective. First, they assert that *power* and *authority* can be viewed as either control/power over or empowerment/power with, the latter implying a democratic model which they support. Secondly, in speaking of the *context* of learning, they assert that the context of knowledge, epistemology, and pedagogy can and should be shifted to communities of scholars (i.e., all of the participants in the class). Last, they find the locus of being *responsible* ("moral, legal, or mental accountability") as traditionally lying either with the teacher or the student. They assert that such individual responsibility should be shifted to a focus on responsiveness (which Webster's defines as "reacting"), a more interactive model, emphasizing the moral legitimacy of the students as well as the instructor.

The classroom I attempt to structure for teaching gender and politics fits the model supported by Overton and Caron, an environment where authority is based on expertise, experience, and commitment, not on techniques for control; power is defined as empowerment; the context of learning is group-oriented; and all participants share responsibility for the outcomes of the experience.

Critical Pedagogy

Paolo Freire's model of critical pedagogy expounded in the classic *Pedagogy of the Oppressed* (1970) lays the foundation for much feminist teaching. In this work Freire critiques what he labels the "banking" concept of education, which is the transference of collected knowledge from the authoritative teacher to the passive receptacle of the student. Such a model of education, he believes, acts to entrench the power of elites whose mission is to adapt the students to fit into the established power structure—a structure that benefits those in power. In contrast he postulates "liberating" or "problem-posing" education which works to free the scholarly community, both students and teachers, to pursue their own unique knowledge. Belenky et al. (1986) express much the same thought when they say that educators should ". . . encourage students to evolve their own patterns of work based on the problems they are pursuing." (229)

Such education proposes the egalitarian interactive approach which Overton and Caron value in feminist pedagogy. "[T]he problem-posing educator constantly re-forms his reflections in the reflection of the students. . . . Here, no one teaches another, nor is anyone self-taught. Men teach each other, mediated by the world, . . ." (Freire 1970, 67–68)

Freire argues that such an approach is transformational. Men "come to see the world not as a static reality, but as a reality in process, in transformation. . . . Problem-posing education affirms men as beings in the process of *becoming*— . . . [It] is revolutionary futurity." (Freire 1970, 71–72) ". . . Subjects . . . meet to *name* the world in order to transform it" (Freire 1970, 167). For a discussion of Freire's reevaluation of his use of "men" to the exclusion of women and his response to allegations of sexism, see bell hooks (1994.)

Such a pedagogy encompasses both reflection and action, which means praxis. Without reflection, mere activism remains; without action, only verbalism or empty abstraction remains. The educated must synthesize both thought and action to become a whole person (Freire 1970, 75–76). Richard Beth's "How Transformationalists Think About Transformation: Themes and Implications" (1995), gleans that "politics becomes transformational when it is rooted in participants' mindful engagement with their own political experience and practice" (Beth, 67). Clearly, critical pedagogy, political transformation, and feminist philosophy interface here. Nancie Caraway (1996, 21) says, "Rather than polarize antagonisms between feminists who 'think' and feminists who 'act,' we need to see reflection and resistance as equally valid requirements of political and civic experience."

Feminism and Transformation: A Democratic Paradigm

In Beth's study, eighteen out of twenty-four respondents (75 percent) linked feminism with transformation. ". . . It is the principles of feminism, not necessarily its specific issue positions, that tend to be regarded as specifically transformational" (Beth, 18). Beth, furthermore, asserts that "the core feminist principle, from a transformational perspective, is the emphasis on relationships of partnership and nurturance rather than of hierarchy, domination, or power" (Beth, 17). This is the democratic paradigm that Overton and Caron, as well as bell hooks, recommend. Hooks says, "Making the classroom a democratic setting where everyone feels a responsibility to contribute is a central goal of transformative pedagogy" (39).

The Women and Politics classes are structured to be as democratic as possible. While setting the agenda through the choice of textbooks, major discussion topics, testing tools, guest speakers and films, I encourage an interactive discussion that I moderate and facilitate. I also entertain students' self-initiated suggestions for speakers, topics, etc., as well as encourage students in the class to lead or facilitate certain segments of the course. For example, after synthesizing intensive library research and her own personal experience, a woman from India spoke on the status of women in her native country. What emerged was a stunning statement of oppression. Likewise, an African-American woman performed a powerful rendition of Sojourner Truth's speech, "Ain't I a Woman." Test dates can be rescheduled by majority vote of the class. Furthermore, I rely on student feedback from previous quarters in making pedagogical decisions; this is provided primarily by standardized department evaluation forms, enhanced by informal discussions with students. For example, as a result of complaints about too much reading, which I found to be a legitimate concern, I cut the reading load from five books to three.

Multiple Truths and Conflict-Resolution

Believing in a feminist perspective which honors the diverse and numerous "truths" we each construct to form meaning in our lives, I try never to imply that a student's statements, ideas, or feelings are totally wrong. As one respondent in the Beth study re-marked, one major assumption in group dynamics theory is that " 'in conflict, there is truth on all sides' " (Beth 1995, 55).

Rather I try to let the students *see* and *feel* each others' re-sponses to their statements. Once while the students discussed the social and legal tradition of a woman's assuming her husband's name at marriage, I asked how many of the women in the class would choose not to take their husband's name. At least four or five said very strongly that they would make that choice. After class one of the men told me that he was absolutely dumbfounded. "I never thought I would hear a woman say that," he said. If I had said, ". . . this percentage of American women believe this way," the men would have dutifully written that statistic in their notes and yawned. But these comments could not be discounted as the radical ideas of a feminist professor. These men were being confronted with women of their own generation asserting their independence. *That* had to be taken more seriously. In this pedagogy students learn from each other and hopefully learn to value their own contributions to academic discourse.

The level of emotion in these gender classes is often high—higher than in other courses. Because who we are sexually is such an intensely emotional subject, even previously rather quiet stu-dents join in the discussions that can be described in diplomatic terms as "frank and constructive." ". . . whenever we address in the classroom subjects that students are passionate about there is al-ways a possibility of confrontation, forceful expression of ideas, or even conflict." (hooks 1994, 39)

Both women and men sometimes complain of their discomfort in speaking because they fear a negative response from their class-mates (apparently more than a negative response from the teacher). One woman, who had told me that she was not going to speak again because she got "yelled at," verbally thrashed a man who said he did not think a company should have to pay a woman for maternity leave because *she* was the one that got pregnant. When I teased her about her outburst, she replied, "I just got so angry."

My policy is not to intervene when tempers flare. When I have inserted a remark, it is to affirm that in this class we employ "First Amendment freedom of expression." The professor's setting a tone of tolerance and good humor helps. As one man teased after an espe-cially intense discussion of affirmative action, "Well, let's all go to the parking lot and see whose tires have been slashed." The disci-pline then becomes the responsibility of the entire group and not solely that of the professor—the shared responsibility to which Overton and Caron refer. Clearly, the emotional intensity of the discussions indicates the affective, as well as the cognitive, nature of the process.

But the concept of radical relativism which postulates that all views are equally defensible presents a struggle for the feminist teacher. Nevertheless, I have so far never encountered a situation in which promoting "political correctness" outweighed the value of free discussion. The students have always proved mature enough to handle the sometimes difficult situations that arise. Other students tend to weed out offensive remarks by giving negative feedback to the offender, exemplifying a group responsibility for ethical behavior.

Teacher as Learner: A Community of Scholars

For many students, both male and female, the style and techniques, even the worldview, of the feminist professor are different from what they have been accustomed in traditional classrooms. The confrontation of feminist pedagogy with traditional students, used to traditional methods, creates an environment which can be conducive to transformation. In feminist pedagogy students are forced to confront "the Other." But professors are also forced to confront possibly disturbing perspectives.

One of the most conservative and outspoken men in one class was somewhat older than the others and working at the maximum security state prison. He had a no-nonsense, hard-shelled view of life. During a discussion of domestic violence, he stated dryly, "I think a lot of women just stay in these relationships because they have their own agenda. They can stay and then write a book and get a movie out of it," cynically referring to the film "What's Love Got to Do With It," the story of Tina Turner's relationship with an abusive husband. Later, a woman in the same class shared with me her own story—a life of sexual abuse and rape that made the life of Tina Turner look blessed. Nevertheless, on an exam question concerning violence against women, both this male and female student wrote high-quality answers, his reflecting the same kind of intelligence, sophistication of thought, and sensitivity that hers did. And over the course of the quarter I began to appreciate more and more the tough job he had dealing with the disadvantaged, mentally disturbed, "criminal" men he worked with daily. His knowledge to that point had been based on his daily work with the male prison population,

A Transformational Pedagogy   149

experiential knowledge. He proved on the written assignments that
he could integrate his background knowledge with scholarly writing
and synthesize the two into a fuller understanding of criminal behavior as it impacted women. As Barbara Knight says, a feminist
approach stresses the interrelatedness of our public and private
lives, of what we "learn" in a classroom and what we experience in
the everyday world. This man made a significant contribution to the
discussions, presenting a perspective that would have been lost in
the dialogue had we all been "sensitive liberal do-gooders," and I too
had broadened my perspective.

Studies document the passivity of female students in mixed-sex
classrooms. While feminine passivity usually has not been the case
in these classes, one section composed of 40 percent women, most of
whom were Southern-bred, did exhibit this pattern. One day one of
the men and I talked after class, and *he* raised the issue of the
women's silence, and I admitted that I was trying to encourage more
female participation, but not to much avail. The next day after several of the men had expressed opinions concerning the Family and
Medical Leave Act, he said very straightforwardly, "But none of us
who have been talking can get pregnant. I would like to hear what
some of the women have to say about this issue." Although most of
the women remained hesitant, slowly several did voice an opinion.
He and I threw each other a glance, as I acknowledged his support
in attempting to broaden the chorus of voices who would speak.
Again, the responsibility for the class outcome rested on interaction
between participants, not entirely on the professor.

The impact of gender is often manifest in the social dynamics of
the classes. A male student once astutely noted that when one of the
men made a point, there would be the instant team cheer: "Yeah,
that's right. You tell 'em." "But," he said, "the women don't support
each other when one of them makes a good point." He understood
that the support of the other men in the class might in fact make it
easier for them to come forward than for the women who might not
receive any overt support from their group.

He later told me that the teaching style that I and one other feminist in the department used provided the best classes he had taken
in college. "In the military," he said, "I do a good bit of teaching too.
And I know students don't learn much when the instructor simply
talks at them. But when they can get into the discussion and figure it
out for themselves, they will." Betty Smith Franklin (n.d.) explains
that ". . . Freirean process requires regular, supportive, peer based reflection focused on reading the world as experienced (Franklin, 5).

Recently I shared with a class a study of female and male high school students' foreign policy decision-making, which I had coauthored. As we discussed some unanticipated findings, an undergraduate woman gave a fresh alternative for explaining the results. Her insight will be included in a final draft, with appropriate credit to the student. Such academic collaboration between classroom and research stimulates increased knowledge in the academy. "Freire's work requires that students be included in the collegial relationships of the institution . . . as subjects participating in the continued rebirth of knowledge and value." (Franklin, 6)

Risks of Transformational Teaching

Transformational teaching does not come without its costs and pain as well as its potential enlightenment. A plaque on a colleague's door reads, "The truth shall make you free, but first it shall make you miserable." Whenever we seek to analyze, evaluate, and especially to redistribute society's power resources, some peoples' freedom can be others' misery.

During one class which was taught in the evening, we watched a movie about sexual harassment and afterwards discussed what harassment means and what public policies currently exist in that area. The next morning I received an obscene phone call. While it is possible the timing was coincidental, the fact that I had not received such a call in the previous three years led me to strongly believe, as did all of those with whom I conferred, that it came as a result of the previous night's discussions. I never received another call or any other threatening or harassing behavior, and this behavior has only occurred once in seven years. My *suspicion* is that the man who called was probably one who felt he could not speak out in the classroom and chose an inappropriate means of expressing his anger, frustration, and fear as a world he thought he understood and had some control over appeared to be collapsing around him.

Politics and Power in the Academy

Changing power relations are occurring not only in the society and polity as a whole but also within the academy. As Jeff Fishel so astutely points out in chapter 10, classrooms often reflect the political relationships in the larger society. Furthermore, Sandra Harding

asserts that feminists often perceive a "patriarchal association between knowledge and power" (Githens et al. 1994, 18–19).

A "gender politics" class seems an appropriate place for fostering change. Female professors often speak of the difficulty of setting
and maintaining authority in classes partially composed of males.
Traditional methods of ensuring authority such as the physical presence of the tall or large, usually older, male professor, the booming
voice of the lecturer, or the authoritative style of many male professors, often are not available to, or are not comfortable for, the female
instructor. The female professor is almost always physically smaller
than the male students and is sometimes younger than some of
them. While her voice may be strong, it may not carry in the lecture
hall to the same extent as a man's. Perhaps most importantly, many
feminists simply do not prefer the style often associated with the
traditional college professor. As a feminist, the professor may instead prefer a more democratic model of classroom interaction and
a different paradigm of authority, one based less on hierarchy and
formality and more on mutual respect.

In one section of this course 60 percent of the participants were
male. Two of the most assertive and talkative were older males in
their late twenties both of whom had served in the military and both
of whom were in law enforcement training. Each was intelligent and
self-confident, and each was considerably more conservative on social and political issues than the professor. In addition, they very
quickly became competitive to establish their claim for the role of
class leader.

While rapport with one grew rapidly, the other kept his distance,
never smiled during class and sat in the back of the room surrounded by a loyal cadre of lieutenants. While not openly confronta-
tional, he was disconcerting. I decided that if, by the end of the week,
the situation remained tense, I would ask him to talk with me pri-
vately. In the meantime, I continued my attempt to engage him after
class, utilizing the feminist approach of communication. Slowly, he
began to make comments back to me in the hall. While he continued
to play the loyal opposition in class, the tone changed and I no longer
felt uncomfortable. For the rest of the quarter we engaged in witty
repartee, not confrontation over expertise or authority. The camp in
the back left-hand corner became known affectionately as "The Rat
Pack."

Group process and conflict-resolution skills are invaluable in
dealing with the "living classroom." Role-modeling of good humor,
nondefensiveness, reciprocity, and tolerance is essential for success,

as is maximizing avenues of communication. Feminism's egalitarian approach is well-suited to this modeling. Beth argues that those who have discussed feminism's relationship to transformational politics have paid insufficient attention to feminist approaches to personal interaction (Beth 1995, 66).

There is the possibility that power in a classroom, as within the larger society, can be a non-zero-sum game—that the empowerment of students does not necessarily diminish the authority of the instructor and that the "power" of the professor is not exercised at the price of the submission or silencing of the students. It is this empowerment that feminist scholarship envisions.

Feminist Methodology

As stated before, feminist methodology values diversity. One aspect of methodology is to understand one's own perspective—situational positioning (Dukes 1996, 21)—and to claim one's own viewpoint and be able to communicate it openly and clearly. Vicky Randall (1994) notes that ". . . the feminist social researcher must take her own bias into account when gathering and interpreting information (Githens et al., 11)." Therefore, feminists claim the right to use the pronoun "I" in scholarly research and discourse. The use of personal pronouns has traditionally been prohibited in such research, and many, probably most, students have been taught never to use these pronouns in their academic papers. When I tell them they *can* use "I" in their work *if they want to*, I receive different responses. For some, usually women, the response is one of delight: "Oh, can we . . . really?" My inference is that these students find it comfortable to speak in a personal mode but have been kept from doing so in the past. But from the men I sometimes receive a very different response. One very good male student told me, "I just don't think I can do that. I have always been told not to." Another said, "Do we have to?" I found it necessary to reiterate my instructions several times in one class because operating from the mindset that the student *had to* do things the way the professor wanted them, they seemed to have a very difficult time understanding that I was not changing the form in which they *must* write, but instead offering options from which they were *free to choose*.

Students are also free to choose whatever methodology they find most appropriate for their research work, whether quantitative or qualitative. As Marla Brettschneider and Betty Zisk note, our knowledge can be enhanced by qualitative methods such as oral history, narrative, and case study. Participant observation, the methodology used in this study, is one example of such orientation. Often students combine methodologies. For example, one student did an empirical study of the status of women lawyers, enhancing his library findings with an in-depth case study of his sister's experience as a lawyer in California. Feminist pedagogy posits that there is not one right form in which to express one's ideas. The style chosen depends on personality and culture, among other factors. With this approach, hopefully students gain more control over their work than usual, leading to empowerment.

Feminism and Transformation

Stephen Woolpert in chapter 11 defines transformational politics as a politics of interconnectedness—which leads to sustainability, empowerment, synthesis, and transcendence. I believe that true transformation does sometimes occur in the Women and Politics classes. Furthermore, I believe that the transformational quality is, at least partly, the result of feminist philosophy and feminist teaching style. Feminist pedagogy, based on democratic principles and interaction, is structured to enhance interrelatedness and empowerment of students in the learning process and to lead to a community of scholars within the classroom.

A feminist epistemology is based first on the premise that there is no *one* correct way of explaining the world or of *knowing*. It is based on an awareness of cultural differences that filter the *facts* that we find, and it posits that knowledge can be gained from a variety of useful methodologies. Rather than engaging in the ongoing debate on the purpose of education (dissemination of information versus molding of students' character), I would prefer to move beyond the duality of that discourse to a convergence in which students would be exposed to a variety of knowledge (and encouraged to explore more), from which they could structure their own unique worldview that hopefully would meet theirs and society's needs to the optimum extent. Thus feminist epistemology encourages the integration of ideas and the holistic approach that Woolpert views as central to transformation. Such an approach is strikingly different from that of traditional political fractionalization. At the peak of an intense discussion, a male student once exclaimed enthusiastically, "Well, what you are talking about is complete revolution." By George, I think he has got it.

10

Transformational Teaching:
As if Students and Faculty Really Mattered[1]

JEFF FISHEL AND MORLEY SEGAL

No matter how important the research, and scholarly agenda of faculty, and no matter how important nonclassroom activities are to students, every week, month-after-month, year-after-year, faculty and students come together to cocreate potential learning communities in the classroom. A fatal flaw in this process is to assume that faculty are primarily responsible for what happens in class, "fatal" to students who thereby fail to develop self-responsibility for their own mutual education, and fatal to faculty whose egos and self-esteem regularly inflate and deflate depending on whether they and others see them as "spellbinding," "charismatic" or "powerful" in the classroom.

Research on the methods and philosophy of effective university teaching has grown substantially over the past 25 years (see Ramsden, 1992 for a review).[2] While faculty are not primarily responsible for what goes on in class, they are naturally the principal resource, particularly in terms of how a class will be organized and structured. The decision by an instructor to seek to build a learning community in the classroom, rather than simply replicating a conventional teaching formula, is the first step toward a transformational pedagogy, a point to which we return in the following.

We believe that faculty and students will be better served, that both will find more intellectual stimulation, meaning, creativity and satisfaction in the educational process, if political scientists are willing to learn from the extraordinary developments that are occurring outside academic life, particularly in the areas of management training, humanistic psychology, and adult education. A new field has developed in these areas—usually called Human Resources Development (HRD) or Organizational Development (OD)—which challenges conventional political science teaching in a number of important respects (Sikes, Drexler, and Grant, 1989).

The central thrust of HRD training is to combine traditional techniques with laboratory or experiential activities, to make learning a much more active, holistic, and personalized process. We concentrate here on the laboratory side of this equation because political scientists either know the standard regimen or can access established sources. We use the terms "experiential," "laboratory," and "participatory" synonymously throughout our article.

Laboratory Education and Learning Communities

Many political scientists can cite instances in which they have tried one or more participatory techniques and generated mixed or even very poor results. Students were unable to take a simulation seriously, or were unable to link their fieldwork experiences with the content or principles they were supposed to learn. This unfortunate outcome occurs because participatory and nontraditional techniques simply cannot be dropped into a traditional learning environment like most universities without careful planning. The groundwork must be laid by seeking to build a learning community in the classroom.

Learning communities are based on two key assumptions in laboratory education. The first is that events and interactions within the classroom are potentially as important as the conceptual and descriptive materials that are the substantive focus of the course. Experiential education is just as concerned with the process (including the instructor's "process") of learning as it is with substance. The dynamics within the classroom itself are an important part of the focus for learning because they are central to building community.

Second, community building means that the learning process must be personally integrative. Thoughts, feelings, and behavior are considered equally relevant for learning, and effective outcomes tend to involve an integration of all three. Learning is holistic, not simply a matter of cognitive understanding. The goal is to promote a sense of membership, belonging and *efficacy as a learner*. An added benefit of seeking to build a learning community is that traditional lecture discussion methods also are more likely to be effective in the context of a set of norms, processes, values, and behaviors that support the goal of classroom community. Laboratory education is *not* an alternative to traditional methods; its use can vary from the supplemental to the central in how instructors organize their classes, but it is essential to community building. Moreover, it is highly compatible with the main goals of transformational teaching, as discussed by Harrison in chapter 9, and among which we would list the following:

(1) Shifting *authority and power* from an instructor-dominated system to a more participatory one where empowerment of all participants ("power with rather than power over") is an important condition of democratic community.

(2) Shifting the *context* of learning (knowledge, epistemology, pedagogy) to the entire class to reinforce a sense of interconnectedness between everyone in the classroom.

(3) Expanding the *domain* of learning so that feelings and emotions (affect) are given equal priority with cognition and ideas can move education toward a more holistic approach in which students and faculty transcend old dichotomies. Any strategy of education that separates thinking-feeling, active-receptive, body-mind, empirical-normative, conscious-unconscious, inner-outer, to name but a few dichotomies, fragments and underestimates the capacity for learning and growth among *both* students and faculty.

(4) Expanding the *range of responsibility and choice* can lead to a more interactive process in class by emphasizing the ethical and psychological legitimacy of student's perspectives as well as the instructor's.

Concepts and Techniques

(1) Effective learning taps into existing psychological energy. We often start a class with a brief centering or awareness exercise asking each participant to state how they are feeling at that moment, or utilizing focused visualization which evokes such a feeling (see Pfeiffer, Goodstein, and Jones 1972–1995).[3] Such exercises are structured to bring forth potentially distracting elements such as reservations about the subject matter, or a task at home or the office left undone. By briefly discussing such feelings, the way is clear to proceed with the business at hand. During the class itself there are other opportunities to again insure that current energy is focused on learning.

(2) Learning is a process not a product. It involves the continuous creation of new personal knowledge from a synthesis of new and ex-

isting ideas. We reject the Lockean assumption of *tabula rasa*, which assumes a fixed state of knowledge, made up of basic mental atoms, which can then be recombined into new thoughts. The focus in management training and our teaching is more individual and personal. Management trainers usually use a practice of involving subordinates in decisions. To become aware and critically examine one's implicit theory is the beginning of learning. The next is to develop a new, equally personal but now more coherent and explicit theory and to compare that theory with the propositions and empirical data of others. Political scientists can use techniques of laboratory education to better exploit both sides of this process—identifying implicit theories and comparing it with other or new theories.

(3) Learning involves the resolution of conflicts between dialectically opposed modes of adapting to the world. Learning involves at least four different processes, and they are shown in Figure 10.1. We present them in the form of a circle to indicate that there is no order about which comes first, but if any of the four is missing the learning process is incomplete (Kolb 1984, 66).

The four processes reflect the fact that learning involves the reconciliation of observation and action, concrete experience and abstract concepts. A typical learning sequence might involve:

- An exercise or role play (concrete experience)

- A discussion of that experience (reflective observation).

- A discussion of concepts underlying the experience (abstract conceptualization).

- Action planning to put the above learning to use (active experimentation).

Ironically, this mixture of activity and reflection is reminiscent of educational strategies designed for precollege *and* adult populations. Only in graduate and undergraduate education is abstract conceptualization given a predominant role.

(4) Learning involves a transaction between person and environment. We stress this interaction by actively involving participants with each other and the rest of their environment in a wide variety of ways, including:

- Written inventories involving values, attitudes, traits, or behaviors that become meaningful as participants compare individual results and develop a group profile;

Figure 10.1
The Circle of Learning

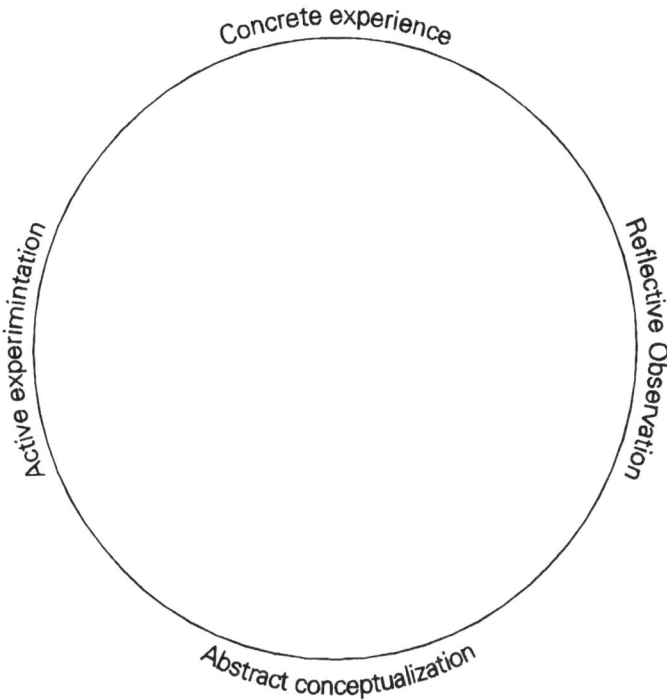

- Various patterns of homogeneous and heterogeneous groupings, e.g., biracial or multiracial; coeducational or gender-exclusive; partisan or bipartisan, etc.

- Exercises, role-playing and projects involving mutual exploration and sharing of information in dyads, triads, or small groups.

The net result of such efforts is that knowledge becomes less abstract, more personal and applied, and learning becomes less passive and more active.

Developing Classroom Resources

Traditional, as well as laboratory teaching, is improved when instructors carefully think about the appropriate use of resources.

We will focus upon five: (1) space; (2) time; (3) commitment; (4) differences among students; (5) using the class as a polity. A discussion of two techniques—Action Research and Process Consultation—also is included because they are widely used by HRD consultants to study organizational dynamics as they occur, dynamics that are central to managing the classroom as a polity.

(1) Space. Classrooms are assigned on the basis of the number of enrollees: thirty-five students will get a minimum of thirty-five chairs in rows all facing the front. Just as laws and regulations can provide a framework for political behavior, so the structural relationship of chairs in a classroom help control the frequency, pattern, and quality of interaction. If the instructor wants all communication to go through him or her, arrange the chairs in theater fashion (all facing the front). If the instructor wants people to react to each other's comments, arrange the chairs in a large circle so that individuals see each other. If the instructor wants students to engage in a potentially lively discussion with frequent interaction, put them in groups of five.

To space one can add purpose. If the instructor wants people to experience the emergence of leadership in a group, organize them in groups of eight to twelve. If the instructor wants to increase the likelihood of a lively discussion, then create groups who reflect a divergence of opinion (mixing people on the basis of policy, partisan, candidate preference, for example). Ask for a show of hands regarding opinions on a particular subject, and form groups composed of "for" "anti" and "indifferent." Another technique is to form homogenous groupings; the "fors" developing a position which can then be discussed with that of an opposing group. If the instructor wants all of the above, establish the norm that *space is a variable that can be controlled.* Chairs can be moved according to what is to be accomplished.

Space is a necessary but not a sufficient variable. The appropriate spatial structure does not guarantee the desired consequences but an inappropriate structure virtually precludes anything but an instructor-centered process.

(2) Time. Of all of the resources in the classroom, time is least under the control of the instructor. It takes a certain amount of time simply to identify the resources of the people in the class. The number of exercises or experiences which can be built into the fifty-minute lecture are limited. We prefer a two-hour session because it is essential for many structured exercises. There is no fixed or absolute time necessary for the experiential approach but what is necessary is a change in perspective. Instructors who want to share responsibility for

learning with their students must move from regarding class periods as fixed and unchanging, toward viewing time as a variable, the control of which is essential for differing results. We do not underestimate the administrative problems in altering class schedules but this does not preclude making a start, seeking two-hour seminar-style assignments. As an educational variable, time is too important to depend solely on a university bureaucracy and its norms.

(3) Commitment. Commitment is a major ingredient in the world of work. Without some internal desire to really commit oneself to the accomplishment of a task, most endeavors beyond simple manual labor have little chance of success. How then does this need for commitment affect the task for learning in a class?

Many factors are beyond the reach of an instructor; interest or lack of it in the subject, previous experiences in the classroom, extracurricular developments in the student's life are among the obvious. One factor, however, is in the hands of the instructor, and if properly handled this variable can offset or at least neutralize the negative impact of the rest. That factor is *the student's actual experience in your specific class.* The vehicle for dealing with feelings and attitudes resulting from that experience has often been termed the "psychological contract" (Schein 1980, 22). Whenever any of us enter a situation with mutual obligations and responsibilities, our willingness to commit is shaped by a series of assumptions and expectations. Often these are unspoken, and frequently all or part of these assumptions and expectations exist at an unconscious level in the classroom. One method we have found that is useful in surfacing expectations— students and faculty—is to make them more explicit.

The following "expectation exercise" illustrates one such method.

"Before we get started, I would like to spend a few minutes going over our expectations. Take out two sheets of paper. Don't put your names on these. On the first sheet I would like you to imagine that the class turned out to be the best course you have ever taken. Imagine what the class would be like in terms of:

- Subject covered

- Relationship with your fellow students

- Relationship with the instructor

"When you are through we will tape these to the wall. I am going to do the same thing" (give them approximately 5 minutes). "Now I'd like you to do the same thing on a second sheet but this time imagine that it is the *worst* class you have taken. What would it be like in terms of the same three dimensions."

The students and instructor write out their descriptions (expectations). The instructor then says "Now I'd like you to tape your positive expectations on the front of the room and your negative expectations on the back. I'll do the same with mine. Then everyone in the class should walk around, look at both sets without talking. Then we will sit down and discuss them."

(Once seated) "O.K. what seems to be the common qualities on both the positive and negative side? How do they compare with mine? Where do we have similar expectations? Where are they different?"

The discussion that follows can bring forth a process of psychological contracting. Both instructor and students have articulated their expectations, and both have an opportunity to explain why they think and feel the way they do. It is *not* necessary to assume that the expectations of students and the instructor will be the same. It is necessary for both to hear and understand the expectations of the other. Discovering and articulating expectations in this fashion allows instructors and students a process for developing commitment.

Differences Among Students

It often is argued that students can learn from one another yet this rarely occurs in the classroom. The basis for students acting as a resource for each other is *difference*; differences in origin, background, experience, reaction to the subject matter, and classroom experience. For these differences to serve an educational purpose, students must feel free to state them. There should be a framework or process for understanding the differences in terms of goals for the course. Some differences are based on group origin as commonly reported in demographic statistics: race, gender, age, economic class, status, work role, etc., and other differences involve values or attitudes, party identification, belief in capital punishment, etc. Finally, some differences that are particularly helpful relate to differences in learning styles. All of these differences can be used as a basis for learning.

Value and Attitude Differences

Such differences have a long history as a basis for political behavior. To legitimate their use in the classroom, individuals must self-identify in terms of whatever category one is using. If individuals can not identify themselves in a particular category, it is up to the instructor to supply some standard or criteria for differentiation tailored to the particular situation. For example, American University has a large population of very well-off students as well as those from families with more modest incomes. The division around family income is significant here, as it would be in many universities.

Closely related to income differences are differences in ideology, values, and attitudes. Here again students must be helped to differentiate themselves in a non-threatening manner. Written instruments and simple survey questions are particularly useful to accomplish this. There are also a number of value clarification exercises that allow individuals to identify subject-related values. These generally take the form of an imaginary story in which the student fills in the details and these details reveal the student's values (Simon, Howe, and Kirschenbaum 1972).

Differences in Learning Style

Among the most crucial differences in a learning situation, not surprisingly, are differences in learning style itself. Among academics, there is general acceptance of the notion that individual students differ in their manner or style of learning. Unfortunately, there are few tools available to political scientists to help alter one's teaching style in response to the composition of the class. HRD consultants have available a wide range of management and learning style instruments. "Style" in this context refers to a unique or different personal emphasis in accomplishing a task. The idea of "personal style" gained general acceptance in the 1950s and early 1960s as Blake and Mouton (1964), and others identified differing styles of managing. Closely related to how one manages is how one learns. A natural corollary to most management style instruments has been a set of parallel categorizations for learning. The Kolb learning style inventory (Kolb 1984), shown in Figure 10.1, developed as a way of identifying and understanding different styles of learning. While total learning involves all four of the orientations in Figure 10.1, individuals can and do differ in the mode they prefer to emphasize in the learning cycle. Kolb devised an instrument that measured individual preferences for initiating a learning experience with a particular style. The instrument has been widely used and validated. When a political scientist faces a class of thirty students, he or she can assume:

a. some people will learn best if they are *first* involved in a situation in an immediate and personal way (a simulation or role-play).

b. some people will learn best if they *first* can observe a number of situations and reflect upon them (case studies—data sets).

c. some people will learn best if they *first* can read or hear an explanation of a theory or set of principles (a lecture).

d. some people will learn best if they can *first* be involved in actively trying to influence or change something (an internship or field project).

Individuals with a preference for abstract conceptualization are likely to be attracted to university teaching (Kolb 1984, 123–131; Myers 1962, 64). It is no surprise, then, that the teaching of political science as well as most other college disciplines, is geared toward individuals who prefer abstract conceptualization. The result of this self-selection should be obvious: much less attention is devoted to the other three preferred styles of learning. Knowledge of multiple learning styles can be helpful to the instructor in three ways. First is *awareness for the instructor*. Most of us teach as we would like to be taught. Knowing this, instructors can take deliberate action to include other approaches in their presentation. Second is *awareness for students*. Knowing their own learning style, students can create opportunities to use it. Third is *a better understanding of the subject*. Learning is related to the political process because politics, among other things, demands learning. Understanding one's own learning style and using a framework that explains the learning styles of others, can help students and instructors gain a greater understanding of diverse phenomena.

The Class As a Polity

A final untapped resource are the thoughts, feelings, and behavior of students within the class itself. Classrooms can be viewed as partial microcosms of the larger political system. Naturally there are differences in size, scope, and legal impact between a classroom and the polity. There are also similarities. Classrooms have formal leaders who have limited and specified powers (the instructor), and a citizenry often apathetic but capable of becoming aroused (the students). Informal leaders emerge, decisions are made, subgroups and factions develop. People become alienated or enthusiastic. Classes are by no means mini nation-states but the resources are there to examine *some* of the dynamics of the larger system. Two methods which allow one to study these dynamics as they occur are: Action Research and Process Consultation (Schein 1969).

Action Research

The discovery of Action Research is usually attributed to the psychologist Kurt Lewin. Action Research involves gathering data from a group and then feeding that data back to the same group *in its entirety* so that the group can then discuss and react to it. It is not essential to have pretested unambiguous questions because the same individuals who filled out a questionnaire or were interviewed respond to the data. Rather than avoiding subjectivity, Action Research utilizes it; a group or organization studies itself in order to consider what, if any, changes need to be entertained.

Action Research can be used to study the political dynamics of a class as they occur. For a midcourse evaluation students can be asked two questions on a questionnaire, to be brainstormed in groups or to be posted on the wall. What aids my learning in this class? What hinders my learning in this class? If even some of the students trust the process—in fact, even if many do not trust it—the collective data can be quite provocative. This process will bring out the power dynamics of the class that usually exist slightly below the surface. The hardest part for the instructor who is new to such a process is to hear student reactions without feeling that he or she has to either change in response to student requests or defend that status quo (for detailed examples of building and using evaluations, Pfeiffer et al. 1986B).

Whatever the focus of the course, action research can be used systematically to bring out student thoughts, feelings, attitudes and values regarding the subject. Action Research is usually participative in management situations. Members of the work team participate in defining the questions, administering the questionnaire, and managing the feedback session. A similar process can take place in the classroom. Members of the class can manage the entire project from inception to feedback. The class can be treated as a microcosm to provide deeper views of the thoughts, feelings, and nuances behind visible behavior when one uses the methodology of Action Research.

Process Consultation

In management training, process consultation refers to observing, analyzing, and learning from the *process* by which a group operates as a system (Schein, 1969). To the extent a class also has some of the characteristics of a political system, process consultation can be a tool for learning about the dynamics of the political process. Process observation can come from the instructor or from students. Examples:

> 1. "Well we just had one of the more lively discussions of the semester. Let's look at what we did. There seemed to be some attempts at leadership. How did a person get to be a leader in this situation and what does that say about our class as a mini political system?"

> 2. "I noticed that our discussion of South Africa yesterday followed an interesting pattern of participation. Did anyone else notice that? Today we're going to discuss Roe v. Wade. I would like two volunteers to observe our process and give us a report at the end of class."

It is not ordinary for a class to focus on its own behavior as a means of learning but conducting a class in this way can be a powerful learning process. The key to creating a safe atmosphere is objective description without attributing motives to the individual being observed. Process consultation is the most difficult of the methods described in this article but it can also be the most rewarding. For a more detailed exposition, see Schein (1969).

Conclusion

The teaching of politics has much to gain from incorporating the experiential outlook of HRD. Using techniques of laboratory education increases the probability that learning *and* teaching will be more integrated, meaningful, and exciting, that the process and shared experiences in the classroom will unfold so that faculty and students really do matter.

What this philosophy and methodology ultimately aims for is human transformation, linking the personal experience of faculty and students to what Manfred Halpern in his chapter calls "the larger dramas of historical, political and sacred reality." Like political science, HRD is concerned with understanding the impact of individual thoughts, feelings, and behavior on the larger entity, and examining how the structure, its norms and power relationships, affect the individual. Traditional political science emphasizes knowing and understanding how "the system" works. Transformational pedagogy does not ignore cognitive understanding but places such understanding in the service of action. It draws on humanistic psychology to heighten inner and interpersonal awareness of feelings, identity, and personal efficacy.

It is one thing, for example, to read about the theory of political efficacy and speculate as to how this force influences voting behavior. It adds another dimension to realize how one's own sense of efficacy affects participation in the particular class in which you are sitting as a student. Conversely, to reformulate the question from the opposite causal direction is also important: how does class structure shape the student's sense of political efficacy? Transformational teaching grounds the personal and the collective in each person's experience, not to avoid generalizations about larger clusters (the usual approach of political science) but to give those generalizations direct, personal meaning.

David Abalos (1994, 31–32) puts the case well when he writes, ". . . that the politics of the classroom sets the agenda for the politics of the wider community . . . [this kind of education] is a fundamentally different choice from other modes of education. . . . The redeeming aspect of this choice [for faculty] is that teachers can come to know the choices they have been making . . . acknowledge their own fears and choose again to risk themselves as they pursue issues with students. This is what the politics of the classroom is all about: taking the next step, opting again and again to be honest and vulnerable, and refusing to stifle the emergence of students. This kind of education, created by students and teachers alike, prepares students to see politics not only as cooperation but also dissent, not only continuity, but also change."

Many educators have been eloquent in their conviction that teaching can move from the personal to the collective, uniting large structures and individual biographies in its vision and application. The creative use of experiential education suggests we can do far better than we have in translating this vision into classroom reality.

Notes

1. This is a revised and updated version of an article that originally appeared in "News for Teachers of Political Science," (*P.S.: Political Science and Politics*, spring 1987:11–14).

2. For political scientists, the quarterly publication on the profession, *P.S.: Political Science and Politics*, published by the American Political Science Association, regularly features a section on teaching.

3. *Organization Behavior Teaching Review*, is a useful source of new ideas for teaching organizational theory and practice experientially. Training in HRD and laboratory education is found inside and outside many universities but the central and creative role of the National Training Laboratories (now NTL Institute), founded shortly after World War II, has been substantial. Faculty development and training opportunities in NTL programs can be obtained by writing: NTL Institute/P.O. Box 9155/Arlington, VA 22209/703-527-1500. Other collections of exercises, particularly well suited for exploring psychological and group aspects of learning, are Stevens (1971), where Gestalt principles are emphasized; Ferrucci (1982), whose exercises are derived from the theory and practice of psychosynthesis, and Harman (1984); Goldberg (1983); Fanning (1988); and Pehrson (1995).

III

The Practice of Transformational Politics

11

The Practice of Transformational Politics:
An Overview

STEPHEN WOOLPERT

"Like the human heart, the world points beyond itself to something greater and more beautiful than its present condition. That something attracts us all, in different ways, and leads many of us to seek transformation . . . It becomes more and more evident that our own well-being is indissolubly linked to the health of society and our environment. It is possible, now, more than ever before, to see that our own growth is rooted in, and furthers, the whole world's advance."

—George Leonard and Michael Murphy

Introduction

Transitional periods, in which one age is merging into another, are by nature ineluctable and protean. Something is dying and something else is being born, but precisely what we cannot foresee. Political symptoms of the discontinuity between past and future are ubiquitous: the transition away from the Cold War, collisions between economic globalization and local cultures, the clash between industrialization and environmental well-being, the rise of feminism and multiculturalism, and technological revolutions in telecommunications and bioengineering.

What are the implications of such epochal shifts for the dynamics of political action and governance? How can people participate in bringing about a fundamentally better world? There is no single credo or orthodoxy to which transformationalists subscribe; however, three interrelated motifs run through the transformational literature on the shape of the postmodern political world: sustainability, empowerment, and transcendence.

The Politics of Sustainability

Faced for the first time in history with credible data warning of the possible demise of human civilization, polities are coming to recognize their interdependence with the biosphere. The greatest challenge facing the world is to create political and economic structures that function harmoniously in a viable ecosystem.

The unique character of transformational politics is well illustrated by its approach to this challenge. It recognizes that achieving sustainability is not essentially a problem of technological feasibility. Descriptions of sustainable economics, agriculture, architecture, technology, transportation, and resource management are plentiful (Adams 1992; Costanza 1991; Daley, Cobb, and Cobb 1994; Daly 1997; International Institute for Sustainable Development 1992; Lesh 1995; Trzyna 1995; van den Bergh and van der Straaten 1994).

Rather, the problems of overconsumption and environmental exploitation are seen as defects of a political system rooted in self-seeking materialism, patriarchal power, and alienation from nature. Thus, as Graham discusses in chapter 5, sustainability ultimately requires a transformation of our political values (Diamond and Orenstein 1990; Moorcroft 1992; Rifkin 1991; Sessions 1995). A new way of thinking about ourselves and our political institutions is necessary in order to respond to the environmental imperative. Unlike reform politics, therefore, transformational politics is not simply about adding environmental constituencies and interest groups to the conventional struggle for influence over public choices; rather, it is inextricably tied to a deeper shift towards postmaterialist values and priorities. Inglehart's multinational, longitudinal data show that global ecological awareness is "only one symptom of a much broader process of cultural change that is transforming not only attitudes but much of human behavior" (1995, 62; see also Elgin 1996; Milbrath 1986; Ray 1996).

The Politics of Empowerment

The shift to postmaterialist values calls into question the distribution of power: deep shifts in existing structures are needed to make and execute the kinds of choices that will lead towards sustainability. Therefore sustainability is inseparable from personal and collective empowerment. A revitalized democratic spirit, expressed in a myriad of forms, indicates the viability of a participatory political culture. Like environmental decay, powerlessness is a root cause of a broad array of political conflicts. And like sustainability, empowerment requires more than incremental change. It is not so much the ability to function in the existing political system as the ability to *renew* it, by developing the capacity for self-direction through interaction with others (Barber 1984; Freire 1970; Schwerin 1995).

The kinds of the opportunities society affords for expressing political preferences affect the very formation of those preferences (Bachrach and Botwinick 1992). Political institutions that isolate individuals reinforce patterns of domination and conflict, which in turn undermine the competencies required for self-government and ecological sensitivity. Conversely, increased participation in public decision making cultivates political efficacy and reduces the potential for destructive acts.

Individuals in an expansive democratic system do not so much discover the common good as create it, by interacting with each other and constructing shared purposes. Just as the empowering pedagogies described in Part II transform classrooms into participatory learning communities, self-governance in the public sphere helps transform conflicting interests into common ones while at the same time promoting individual autonomy and freedom. Personal and social transformation are thus reciprocally related.

The Politics of Transcendence

The web of transformational theories outlined in Part I reframes political problems and discloses new ways of addressing them in which old polarities find a new synthesis. The mechanistic view divides, dissects, and dichotomizes the world; we are prone to view ourselves as isolated egos surrounded by a world of objects. But where the competitive individualism of liberal politics promotes polarization and zero-sum thinking, the ecological view sees emergent, interwoven, open systems. Beneath the archetypal dramas of the political world lies a unified field. Traditional divisions between liberty and community, spiritual and secular, domestic and international yield to a more holistic politics (Becker 1991).

The search for a new political synthesis has been spurred by the breakdown of contemporary politics. The malfunctioning of policies and institutions is pervasive and widely felt; neither liberal nor conservative remedies promise relief. The transformational approach calls for pragmatic and synergistic responses that combine elements of conservatism and liberalism (Bellah 1991; Lerner 1996).

Transformational politics must also transcend the boundaries between local, national and global domains. Nation-states, in addition to exacting the costs described by Halpern in chapter 3, are confronting new environmental and economic conditions in which they increasingly find themselves incompetent to address threats to their peoples' well-being (Lerner 1992; Sakamoto 1994). Resources, interests, and conflicts are shaping politics with little regard for political boundaries; authority is diffusing away from states to other institutions, both subnational and transnational.

Finally, transformational politics expresses the universal need for loving human contact. Drawing on the current spiritual renaissance both inside and outside organized religions, it views our political predicament as a malaise of the soul, stemming from the relentless secularization and commodification of modern life. Spiritual politics entails a dialectic of inner work and outward action; contemplation and citizenship are both necessary for the good life. Like the ecological sensibility, it leads away from instrumental egoism toward a renewed appreciation of the sacred dimensions of life and the transcendent oneness of all being (diZerega 1991; Griffin 1990, Lerner 1996; McLaughlin and Davidson 1994; Wallice 1994).

Steps Towards Political Transformation

If the transformation envisioned here occurs, it will not be in a single great leap. But tangible evidence of this emerging perspective is noticeable throughout the political process: at the individual level, the group level, and the governmental level. Although transformation requires a response to the realities of globalization, the activities needed for such a response must begin close to home and move from the ground up.

The Personal Is Political

A major political insight of feminism is that the shift to a fundamentally better society is in many ways an "inside job." At the core of political conflict lie basic human needs. Individual and collective liberation, far from being in conflict, are complementary: individuals undergo self-transformation *in the process of* creating collectively a better society. As Gandhi observed, we must become the change we wish to see in the world. The interweaving of microlevel values and macrolevel politics is described by Knight in chapter 4 as "the integrity of self and polity." The following are but a few examples of the reciprocal relationship between psychological and political transformation.

The movements for appropriate technology (Berry 1992; Brand 1981; Schumacher 1973) and voluntary simplicity (Elgin 1993b; Sale 1985) are emblematic of the "bottom up" approach to the environmental crisis. Both seek to decentralize control of resource management (Harker and Natter 1995; Hubbard and Fong 1995; International Institute for Sustainable Development 1993). Both value "enoughness" rather than the relentless acquisition of material goods. Beyond emphasizing conservation, recycling, and renewable energy, they promote advances in human well-being which have minimal costs to the environment while preserving local cultures and personal self-determination.

Ecopsychologists work to dissolve the psychic numbing that prevents people from responding effectively to the natural world's suffering (Roszak, Gomes, and Kanner 1995). In addition, the spiritual sensibility of transformational politics inspires reverence for the wonder of nature and reaffirms the bond between humans and their planetary home (Berry 1981; Hughes and Swan 1986; Spretnak 1991). There is a renewed sacramentalism among many transformationalists that sees nature as a place of aesthetic enchantment, not a soulless mechanism.

The benefits of higher levels of psychological functioning are not limited to environmental politics. Building self-esteem reduces failure in school, teenage pregnancy, violent crime, chronic welfare dependency, and substance abuse (Mecca, Smelser, and Vasconcellos 1989); closely related is Sniderman's (1975) research on the correlation between self-esteem and democratic character. Meditation produces beneficial changes in prison behavior and recidivism among convicts (Dillbeck and Abrams 1987; Lozoff 1987). Crisis intervention training for police officers increases their self-awareness and interpersonal skills, improving their response to domestic disturbances and hostage situations (Woolpert 1980). The undogmatic spiritual program of Alcoholics Anonymous has proven to be the most effective method of treating alcoholism and a wide variety of obsessive/compulsive disorders. Alcoholics achieve sobriety by surrendering to a higher power of their own understanding. They maintain their recovery by making amends to those they have harmed, practicing prayer and meditation, and volunteering their services to other alcoholics (Alcoholics Anonymous World Services 1953).

The transformational effects of cultivating the inner life have also been demonstrated by political activists such as Gandhi, Tich Nhat Hanh, the Dalai Lama, Martin Luther King, Jr., and Cezar Chavez (Breggin 1992; Holmes 1990; Ingram 1990; Nhat Hanh 1991; Titmuss 1988). Far from being corrupted by power, such individuals exercise it in a way that helps liberate their followers and ennoble themselves. The peace and civil rights movements owe much to these exemplars of nonviolence, whose faith, compassion, and integrity have enabled them to seek enlightenment while engaged in the mundane world of politics. Rather than suppressing anger or venting it self-righteously, even in response to violent opposition, spiritually based activists transform their anger to create a strong inner space for peace work.

The Participatory Community

Personal growth is a necessary but insufficient condition for political transformation. Transformational politics also finds concrete expression in a variety of shifts in power designed to enlarge and enrich the democratic process (Boyce 1990; Boyte and Riessman 1986). Although not derived from a single master plan or ideology, they share the common purpose of creating public spaces where people can contribute their talents to the achievement of social goals, free from physical or psychological domination.

An important preliminary step towards empowerment is the mobilization of greater numbers of people for a wider array of public activities. Berry, Portney, and Thomson (1993) discuss successful systems of neighborhood government that incorporate citizens in public policy making. Experiments such as the Goals for Greater Milwaukee 2000 project have engaged citizens in community planning processes (Paulsen 1983; Bezold 1978). Lappé and DuBois (1994) offer stories of citizen problem-solving in schools, local government, and the workplace. Other mechanisms for broadening decision-making responsibility at the local level are bioregional planning practices, neighborhood-managed housing and justice centers, and community-based schools, police, architectural designs, food banks, land trusts, and credit programs (Fowler 1991; Osborne and Gaebler 1992; Scully 1994).

What distinguishes transformational from reformist organizations is their emphasis on the interconnected character of social problems rather than on piecemeal tinkering, and on the linkage between those problems and the broader transformation of personal values and political structures. The challenges facing transformational political organizations are examined from an archetypal perspective in chapter 15 on the Greens. The number of such nongovernmental groups, intergovernmental organizations, and international agencies continues to grow (Coleman 1994; Rensenbrink 1992; Parkin 1989; Richardson and Rootes 1995).

Transformational organizations have also blossomed in more traditional societies. The Grameen Bank in Bangladesh has pioneered a revolutionary program of microlending to help the poorest of poor women start their own businesses. Now dispersing $500 million annually to two million borrowers seeking to start their own businesses with no collateral, it has a near-perfect repayment rate (Counts 1996). The Sarvodaya Shramadana Movement in Sri Lanka developed a self-reliance model of community development. It balances the satisfaction of material and nonmaterial needs, primarily through Shramadana Camps in which the whole village gives their time and effort to accomplish something of collective value (Ekins 1992; Freidman 1992). Despite severe ethnic violence since 1983, millions of Sri Lankans have benefited from the "awakening" of their villages. The Comanche of Oklahoma have reincorporated traditional ways of direct participation in deciding about community affairs in order to emphasize harmony and affirm each person's identity as a tribal member. A consensus-building process known as Tribal Issues Management has replaced the tribal council system imposed by the United States government (Harris and Sachs 1994).

Spontaneous initiative and commitment are often more potent agents of transformation than formal institutions. Consequently the creation of alternative political spaces is a step towards empowerment. The formation of networks—loosely-aggregated webs of people with a common interest—has been facilitated by new information and communications technologies. In chapter 4, Knight outlines a theoretical understanding of networks, whose organizational characteristics are decentralized responsibility, permeable boundaries, tolerance of diversity, broad distribution of information and resources, and procedural informality (Limerick and Cunnington 1993; Lipnack and Stamps 1994).

In addition, thousands of participatory intentional communities around the world provide opportunities for empowerment not available in conventional social settings (McLaughlin and Davidson 1990; Shaffer and Anundsen 1993; Whitmyer 1993). The diversity in purpose and structure of such endeavors make them natural laboratories for experiments in cooperative governance.

In the field of conflict-resolution there is growing interest in noncoercive processes of dispute resolution that seek to bring about harmonious coexistence rather than conquest (Burton and Dukes 1990; Fisher and Ury 1981). Face-to-face mediation, which allows consideration of the full range of issues involved in a dispute, is an empowering alternative to formal dispute-management mechanisms which focus on narrow legal questions (Schwerin 1995). Mediation is not limited to local-level problem solving; Lederach (1995) examines its use resolving cross-cultural conflicts.

Dispersion of economic power is another bridge to transformation. Skilled work in post-industrial economies involves shifting objectives, flexible procedures and rapid information processing (Hage and Powers 1992; Rifkin 1995). Such unstable, complex workplace relationships require responsive leadership and collaboration among coworkers (Barrentine 1994; Marshall 1995). This in turn requires a workplace culture which designs meaningful jobs and values respectful relationships over competitive climbing up the corporate hierarchy.

Vast concentrations of productive resources treat both people and nature as expendable (Mander and Goldsmith 1996). Alternative forms of economic organization are more consistent with a cooperative approach and more easily bring ethical values into economic life. Small- and medium-sized cooperatives, community-based trusts, worker-owned businesses, and democratically managed organizations allow broader participation in economic decision-making processes. The Mondragón system of worker-owned and -controlled businesses and co-op retail stores in the Basque region of Spain is a robust example of successful economic democracy (Morrison 1991). Profit reserves in each firm furnish about half the investment capital; the rest comes from the Mondragón's own bank. By flattening the organizational hierarchy, democratic workplaces do not merely humanize relationships between managers and workers; they alter the underlying ownership patterns and reward structures. To insure the responsiveness of these enterprises to broader social and environmental concerns, public-interest representatives may participate in a comanagement system (Adams and Hausen 1992; Benello 1992; Muller 1991).

Good Governance

A transformed polity requires an integrated network of governing processes that are at once responsive to local communities and competent to deal with global issues. How might governments be transformed? Elections are a major focus for political transformation but, particularly in established liberal polities, the prevailing mood of anger and alienation cannot be dispelled simply by marginal changes such as "voting green," increasing voter turnout, or campaign finance reform.

However, numerous experimental procedures in teledemocracy expand decision making from a discrete event to a deliberative process. Unlike staged forums and referenda that have no binding effect on political outcomes, many of these projects have transferred real power to citizens. Using modern communications technologies to convey information, expand deliberation, and facilitate voting, they demonstrate that ordinary citizens generally reach reasonable, thoughtful, and widely acceptable solutions (Slaton, 1992). Several of these initiatives are discussed by Becker in chapter 12. Even on complex issues of science and technology normally controlled by elites, meaningful participation by the lay citizen is possible. Sclove (1995) describes various citizen-based technology policy procedures such as "consensus conferences" in Denmark, Dutch "science shops," and Sweden's Council for Planning and Coordination of Research.

In terms of outcomes, several examples can be cited of the innovative, pragmatic character of transformationally oriented policies.

a) The ecological approach to environmental policy making recognizes that sustainability is an emergent property of an entire system (Milbrath 1990). The shift in perspective from mechanisms and parts to wholeness and interdependence blurs the boundaries separating academic disciplines and policy-making networks. This requires new habits of mind in political decision making that appreciate nature's complex combinations of structure and openness, law and chance, order and chaos, determinism and probability.

Government subsidies, cost-benefit analyses, and measures of economic growth that encourage or disguise harmful activities are under attack (Cobb, Halstead, and Rowe 1995; Sheng 1995). Several countries have developed comprehensive, integrated sustainable development plans (Greenberg 1993; Johnson 1995). The most sweeping strategy was drawn up by the Dutch government in the late 1980s, consisting of hundreds of programs to achieve a matrix of goals, such as reducing waste volumes by 70 percent and reducing agricultural pesticide use by 50 percent.

b) In chapter 13 Cummings discusses the divisive and self-defeating assumptions underlying the current debate over affirmative action, challenging "political correctness" on both the left and the right. His explication of "fullness of opportunity" points to the need to change modern politics from an entropic to a synergistic basis. Similarly, Lerner (1996) argues that everyone suffers to some degree in a patriarchal, competitive system, so that a truly caring society must extend compassion not only to its obvious victims but also to those who are in some ways its beneficiaries. His "politics of meaning" combines liberal and conservative policy perspectives in a creative synthesis.

c) Communitarianism also exemplifies the search for an integration of liberal and conservative positions. Sparked by the publication of *Habits of the Heart* (Bella et al. 1985), which sold over 400,000 copies worldwide, it promotes both increased democratic participation and strengthened communities. Etzioni (1993, 1995) outlines the policy ramifications of the communitarian movement in the areas of education, public health and safety, multiculturalism, and property rights.

d) In the area of public safety, neither liberal nor conservative approaches to criminal punishment have resulted in penal practices that are defensible on grounds of cost-worthiness, humane treatment of criminals and victims, or public safety. But Victim-Offender Reconciliation Programs promote criminal restitution as an alternative sanction (Woolpert 1988). The primary purpose of restitution is restorative justice, that is, to obligate offenders to repair personally the damage caused by their crimes, although it is also an effective means of achieving both retribution and deterrence.

The remarkable success of the Delancey Street halfway house in San Francisco is also hard to explain in conventional conservative or liberal terms. As Hampden-Turner (1976) observes, it incorporates beliefs from the Right (the work ethic, the need for strong authority and self-discipline, opposition to big government, and contempt for welfare) and the Left (scorn for personal accumulation of wealth, a commitment to social justice and the plight of the underdog, and faith in the possibility of human growth).

e) The wellness movement credits the mind with a much larger role in health and healing than is recognized by conventional allopathic medicine (Goldman and Gurin 1993). Cost-conscious patients and health insurers are increasingly receptive to holistic health care approaches that treat mind, body, and spirit as inseparable—meditation, yoga, homeopathy, guided imagery, biofeedback, acupuncture, etc. (Benson and Stuart 1992). The wellness approach also challenges the assumption that the health of individuals can be treated apart from their environment. Mounting evidence shows the healing role played by factors such as community support, social activity, friends, and family (Bezold, Carlson, and Peck 1986; Duhl 1992).

After transformational policies have been designed, there is the problem of implementation. Institutional aggrandizement, inertia, and rigidity often prevent bureaucracies from responding intelligently and equitably to changing conditions. But alternative models are emerging for public sector agencies which go beyond mere changes in management style (Albo, Langille and Panitch 1993; Kiel 1994; Osborne and Plastrick 1997; Pinchot and Pinchot 1993; Troxel 1995). In these models hierarchical chains of command are replaced by fluid, decentralized systems of self-managing teams, collaborating with each other and with the public. Information, rewards, and opportunities to participate are widely shared, enabling learning and innovation. The role of central authorities is limited to establishing the rules and providing the supervision necessary to coordinate interconnected activities.

The decline in the ethos of public leadership has contributed to popular disaffection from political affairs. The problem, however, cannot be corrected by more regulations of official conduct, which only beget more sophisticated evasions. Executing transformational policies requires leadership qualities unlike those usually found in patriarchal institutions (Block 1993; Bryson and Crosby 1992; Chrislip and Larson 1994; Griffin and Falk 1993). It requires thinking in terms of future generations, whole systems, and dynamic nonlinear processes. Transformational leaders must create a compelling vision of a better society and empower their followers to pursue it. In his explication of the contrasts between "transactional" and "transformational" leadership, Burns says "Transforming leadership ultimately becomes *moral* in that it raises the level of human conduct and ethical aspirations of both leader and led" (1978, 20).

There are numerous exemplars of such leadership. Gilbert's analysis of Vaclav Havel in chapter 13 provides an understanding of the transformational principles that enable him to tap into his followers' sense of the higher good. Fishel (1992) provides an illuminating portrayal of John Vasconcellos, a humanistic leader in the California legislature. Wallace (1993) and Seabrook (1993) profile activists who exhibited distinguished leadership in preserving peace, environmental quality, and human dignity.

As the nation-state system evolves into a more complex polyarchy of diverse actors, democratic governance cannot be limited to the local or national levels. The goal of preserving a livable world—

the first practical interest shared by the entire human population—and the forces of economic and cultural globalization have provided the impetus for the creation of a global public sector that includes growing numbers of transformationally oriented organizations, most notably in the areas of peace, world hunger, human rights, and the environment. For example, over 13,000 nongovernmental organizations were represented at the 1992 Earth Summit in Rio de Janeiro (Henderson 1992; International Commission on Peace and Food (1994). De Oliveira and Tandon (1994) describe efforts to create a strategic alliance among these "third sector" actors, which are essential to building global democratic norms. Diamond and McDonald (1996) outline a systems approach to peacebuilding activities by economic, governmental, religious, educational and media groups, including the participation of ordinary individuals in citizen diplomacy. Use of the referendum/initiative process on global issues is examined by Rourke, Hiskes, and Zirakzadeh (1992).

A transnational democratic order requires steering mechanisms with a global reach. The prospects for world order are discussed in Falk (1992) and Laszlo (1994). Gurtov (1994) outlines a "global humanist" perspective on world politics that reconciles the forces for unity and diversity. Similarly, Bay (1981) envisions interdependent federations of small communities coupled with transnational authorities exercising worldwide or regional oversight, but with carefully limited powers.

Reconciling divergent interests in the global community also requires a transformed conception of human rights, one that is compatible with both western and nonwestern thought. Burns and Burns (1991) replace notions of rights based on due process and procedural fairness with "nurturing rights" based upon the universal human needs for survival, meaningful contact, and self-development. Nurturing rights are drawn from the ideals of a caring, trusting "extended household" (see also Said 1978). Hans Küng (1996) is taking a leadership role in promoting a "Global Ethic" in which rights are interwoven with responsibilities.

Conclusion

Thirty years ago, when the women's movement was just entering its second stage, it was the object of widespread ridicule and derision. Men have always had the power; changing such a fundamental political fact seemed unimaginable to many. There were—and still are—major disagreements over what feminism means, over goals, and over strategies. And yet, while patriarchy has hardly been eliminated, no one today can deny the broad and deep impact that the feminist movement has had. Fortuitously, a loosely-connected heterarchy of groups with diverse approaches and goals proved to be a remarkably successful political approach.

The transformational political movement finds itself in a position comparable to that of the early feminists. Our political journey has reached a crossroads. Although the direction envisioned by the contributors to this anthology is only one possible future, there is little doubt that what lies ahead will be qualitatively unlike what has gone before (Anderson 1996; Clark 1989; Elgin 1993a; Starhawk 1993). Therefore a spirit of innovation and tolerance of divergent strategies in the pursuit of a fundamentally better future is called for.

As with all transitional periods, the present age is one of heightened conflict, anxiety, and turbulence. Whether such turmoil yields beneficial or destructive outcomes depends on the kind of politics used to deal with it. In this introductory essay I have sought to identify briefly the major issues and themes in the transformational literature on the emerging postmodern world. Space does not permit a critical review of this burgeoning body of work, and much remains to be learned about the practice of transformational politics. "Laws and institutions," said Jefferson (1816/1989, 202), "must go hand in hand with the progress of the human mind. As that becomes more developed, more enlightened, as new discoveries are made, new truths disclosed . . . institutions must advance also, and keep pace with the times." The readings in Part III of this volume are offered in this spirit.

12

Transforming Representative Democracy: Four Real-Life Experiments in Teledemocracy

THEODORE L. BECKER

In the wake of the collapse of Soviet-style communism, modern representative democracies around the world are themselves experiencing great turbulence. In part these reflect the deficiencies of the nation-state system discussed in Halpern, chapter 4, and Woolpert, chapter 11. But I will argue that these difficulties are also due to structural flaws in those systems, and that all attempts at *reform* will fail to correct the problems. What is needed are corrections that will actually *transform* representative democracies into a synthesis between direct democracies and the present-day republican form of governance. In other words, modern representative democracies need a healthy dose of citizen empowerment through electronic communications and information technologies, new teledemocratic innovations that will transform them into substantially more democratic polities.

The Weaknesses of Modern Representative Democracy

Although some of the difficulties being experienced in modern representative democracies are inherent in their very essence, they were not felt in earlier times. As with the human body, when it is young it may not experience the deleterious consequences of some flaws in its genetic code. As it grows older, though, these deficiencies are exposed. Also, as the outside environment changes, it may place extra stress on the body, and the most vulnerable links are the first to deteriorate. This holds equally true with a body politic and is at the heart of the contemporary maladies being experienced in Western-style representative democracies everywhere.

After all, the first of them is now a few hundred years old. When the basic idea was born it was accurately perceived as a distinct improvement over monarchy and as a pragmatic alternative to direct democracy. The system worked reasonably well up to and into the early phases of the industrial revolution. However, as the readings in Part I demonstrate, the incredible advances in scientific knowledge and technology have all but demolished many of the key assumptions about humankind, including the ones that support republican institutions. Those who have traditionally controlled the principal levers of power within representative democracies have done their utmost to adjust to the times and to convince themselves and the citizenry that such a system is still the best one ever devised by the genius of humankind.

There is ample data, however, to show that governing elites are representative of selfish interests that have redistributed wealth upwards. Kevin Phillips traces how this has been done via tax policies from the early 1980s through the present (Phillips 1989) and Harrigan's recent study of American politics demonstrates a strong governing class bias against the bottom 60% of the American citizenry in all aspects of governance (Harrigan 1993). Hellinger and Judd (1991) refer to this false representative system as a "democratic facade."

As a matter of fact, every representative democracy in the world seems to be experiencing wider and wider gulfs of alienation between the government and the general public. Ordinary citizens fail to see their governments at the national, state/provincial, and even local levels as either understanding or reflecting their interests. There is a widely articulated sentiment that their governments are captive of extremely powerful, "special"—as opposed to the general—interests.

It seems fair to say that the breadth and depth of this "credibility gap" between citizens and governing elites may be reaching epic proportions. Osborne and Gaebler (1993, 1–2) describe this problem in the United States as follows: "Confidence in government has fallen to record lows . . . public fury alternates into public apathy." According to Sartori the widening "confidence gap" between citizens and representative governments is an "unprecedented trend . . . in a number of countries, disillusionment and distrust have currently swelled into a crescendo of frustration, anger and, in the end, an outright rejection of politics. In the end, then, we are confronted with a surge of anti-politics, with what we might call the politics of anti-politics" (Sartori 1994, 145).

How the Concept of "Televoting" Has Evolved

Ever since the invention of the radio it has been evident that the age of electronics would have strong effects on politics—some positive, some negative. One area of speculation concerned whether and in what ways electronic communication and information technologies might combine to become the electronic infrastructure for the improvement of both representative *and direct democracy.*

In 1940, R. Buckminister Fuller first envisioned the idea of what might be called "electronic town meetings" (ETMs) at the national level in the United States (Fuller 1963). He foresaw it as the next crucial evolution in Western governance; this vision was repeated in the 1960s and 1970s by such diverse political thinkers and activists as Erich Fromm (1955), Abbie Hoffman (1968), Alvin Toffler (1970) and Hazel Henderson (1970). But it was not until the early 1970s that serious experimentation began to see if electronic communications and information technologies could enhance citizen participation and/or provide an infrastructure for direct democracy at the nation-state level.

Some experimentation was of the laboratory type (Etzioni 1972). But most of it was done in collaboration with a wide variety of public and private political entities. The basic objective of this research was to see how various electronic components could be combined to involve citizens in a wide variety of political processes. Could electronic communications increase, inform, and improve citizen input into planning, dialogue, and decision making, and if so, how well? (Bezold 1978)

A large number of "teledemocratic" experiments were conducted from the mid-late 1970s through the mid-1980s. Here are the key findings of these major experiments:

- electronic media engage citizens in political processes who have not participated in conventional civic activities, e.g., attending public hearings, visiting their legislators, etc.

- citizens of all ages and backgrounds are willing to participate in teledemocratic experiences even where there is no guarantee that the results will influence the government.

- the overwhelming majority of citizens who participate in tele-democratic exercises are satisfied and/or excited by them and are willing to engage in similar processes in the future (Becker and Scarce 1986, 281).

There was, however, only inconclusive and spotty evidence as to the impact of these experiments on actual governmental behavior. Some consider this to be one of the major shortfalls of these experiments (Abramson, Arterton, and Orrin 1988; Arterton 1987). The truth of the matter is that the organizers were more concerned with seeing what design and mix of media would induce citizens to take part, i.e., to see how telecommunications could enhance a sense of citizen empowerment—even if it actually had little to no effect on government itself. This essay will present several of the most innovative real life experiments from the mid-1980s to the present time. This time, however, *success, i.e., citizen empowerment, will primarily be considered as a function of actual, positive, and direct impact on government.*

Real-Life Televoting Experiments

Essential to any "electronic town meeting" (ETM) are several key components. They are: (a) a group of citizens who are empowered via electronics to vote on (b) agendas, issues or candidates after they have had (c) time to deliberate over some facts and opinions concerning that issue or candidate and (d) to participate in or be privy to some discussion about the matter. At the very heart of the ETM is the simple act of "televoting," that is, voting-by-telecommunications. However, as the concept of "televoting" has developed over the years it has come to be almost synonymous with ETM.

For example, as far as I am aware, the initial usage of the word "televote" in an experimental setting was by Dr. Vincent Campbell in his famous San Jose Televote project in 1974, which was funded by the National Science Foundation. His "televote" was far more than simple voting via a telecommunications system. It involved a preregistration of voters, sending them information in a pamphlet, giving them a week to study the material, and then having them vote by phone into a computer tabulation system. In other words, it lacked only one of the key ingredients of an ETM—a method that encouraged or provided discussion (Campbell 1975).

Since the Campbell experiment, further refinements have been made on the concept of "televoting." The following four major experiments expand on this fundamental concept. All are designed to overcome some weakness in modern representative democracy, to empower ordinary citizens in its processes, and to make a real difference in governmental decision making.

Citizen Input Into Government Decision Making: Hawaii, 1985

The Hawaii Department of Health, faced with cutbacks in funding from the United States government, had to reduce medical services throughout the state. In one low-income area that had a high percentage of native Hawaiian and part-Hawaiian residents, they had tried to cut back drastically on their services in the local medical clinic. This was met by a strong, negative reaction from the citizens in that area which, in turn, led to some nasty political repercussions. Thus, the health officials were in a quandary over how to proceed in other areas with similar populations. They hypothesized that if they got the citizens themselves to participate in the decision-making process before the final disposition of the matter, the resulting policy might not meet with such hostility. But how were they to get high-quality citizen input on such a complex and controversial issue?

One of the main reasons that elected and administrative leaders pay so little attention to citizen attitudes about political and/or administrative issues is that conventional methods of public opinion polling are inadequate to get in-depth, considered views on complicated subjects. Instead, these opinions are seen as superficial, ill-informed and unreasoned (if not unreasonable). Besides, if a state agency was going to ask a local population how to cut its own medical services, they could readily predict the outcome: "Don't even think about it."

Fortunately for the Department of Health, a new type of political survey had been getting some local attention in the State of Hawaii. This was *the first* "informed, deliberative, scientific public opinion poll" of large samples: Hawaii Televote. Adapted from Campbell's methodology, Hawaii Televote recruited a random sample of 400 to 500 respondents by telephone, sent them packets of information by mail, gave the respondents as much time as they needed to think about the facts and opinions on the issue, *and also encouraged them to discuss the materials with friends, relatives,*

coworkers before formulating their opinions and relaying them back
to the survey team by telephone.

Eleven previous Hawaii Televote experiments had been completed from 1978 to 1985 (Becker and Slaton 1981). Some of the results of this new method of "deliberative polling" were that: (a)
highly representative samples participated; (b) many of the respondents had taken the time to read, think about and/or discuss at least
some of the materials and the issues; and (c) they had not only understood these complex issues, but many were able to transcend
their own personal situation and vote for alternatives that were
more in the public interest.

The design of Hawaii Televote is consistent with the subsequent
work of Daniel Yankelovich (1991). Yankelovich's goal has been to
convert conventional "mass public opinion" into "public judgment"
via a "working through" process. This is defined as providing the respondents with a limited amount of information and choices and encouraging them to take "the time and effort required for people to
absorb and accept all of the consequences of their own views" (118).

After that, James Fishkin developed another type of "deliberative opinion poll" (Fishkin 1991). According to Fishkin, "A deliberative opinion poll models what the public would think, if it had a
more adequate chance to think about the questions at issue" (1).
Fishkin's concept, like the other models, involves selecting random
samples of the population and presenting them with information,
opinions and alternatives, plus sufficient time to reflect and discuss
the issues. But unlike the other models, it also requires that the
random sample meet together in person for a period of a few days.

Sometime in the mid 1980s, the idea of deliberative polling had
come to the attention of some key administrators in the Hawaii Department of Health. Given their horrendous experience when they
had tried to cut back on health services in the mostly-Hawaiian
community of Nanakuli, they did not want a repeat of it in its sister
community of Waimanalo, where they also had to either decrease or
eliminate some health services or find an alternative mode of financing some part of them. Instead of the usual public hearings,
which did not work anyway, they needed a new way to filter some
ideas into the community, have the ideas discussed in depth, and get
the community itself to figure out how to face the inevitable federal
cuts. Thus was born the Waimanalo Hawaii Televote Project.

Waimanalo had roughly 2,500 households. We decided to ran-
domly sample 500 of them. Since this was a poor community with a
high degree of illiteracy and low reading levels, we did not expect to

get a high rate of agreement to participate. After all, the brochure we sent out was four full pages crammed with information, albeit cleverly illustrated and in full color. To our surprise, we obtained a higher percentage of telephone respondents who agreed to participate than in any of our prior Televotes. In previous Televote experiments we had averaged approximately a 55 percent rate of agreement; in this one, 75 percent of eligible respondents said they wanted us to send them a brochure. One major reason for such a big "turnout" was that this was the only time we had surveyed such a small community, and since we were calling hundreds of people in a community of 2,500 households, many of those we contacted had already heard about it because it was being discussed among some of their neighbors (Becker and Slaton, 1985).

Our final surprise came with the high rate of returns after the respondents had read and discussed the issue and had an opportunity to watch our specially designed cable TV "talk show" that was broadcast live into their community library. This reached the 75 percent level before we decided to terminate the call-backs (Becker and Slaton, 1985).

Why did a population with a relatively low level of education take part so enthusiastically in such a complicated "deliberative poll"? Unlike most telephone polls, which ask questions about political issues at the national, state or city level, this poll was sponsored by a government agency with direct control over something of great value to each participant: his or her family's most proximate center of health care—a **community** clinic. Moreover, that agency was asking them for their "considered opinion." Many were aware that this had **not** been done in a sister community. So they had reason to believe that their views would have some material consequence.

Because of this, and due to the nature of the poll, many in the Waimanalo community made it clear to the Department of Health that they understood the new fiscal realities by endorsing an alternative method of payment on certain services. In other words, 60 percent agreed that it was reasonable to charge a modest fee—on those who could afford it—for extra and continued services available to all members of the community. The Department of Health subsequently instituted without incident a system consistent with the view of the Waimanalo televoters.

This is a good example of how "televoting," as an information-opinion exchange system, can begin to close the chasm of trust and respect between citizens and governmental bureaucracies that plague representative democracies.

Enhanced Involvement in Public Hearings: Honolulu, 1988

The Honolulu City Council had been broadcasting public hearings on a regular basis to the citizens of the City and County of Honolulu over a cable television (CATV) channel for some time. However, very few citizens watched these hearings. And why should they? A major reason that anyone would take the time and trouble to attend a public hearing in person is that they have an opportunity to participate by speaking up. Viewing by TV removes that possibility. Or does it?

The producers of the live CATV hearings and I proposed two new dimensions to the televised broadcast. First, we would provide a direct telephone line into the hearing room that would be amplified so that the council and those attending could hear what the telephone caller had to say. We would then invite any citizen who wanted to testify at the hearing by telephone to do so by calling one of three telephone numbers flashed upon the screen. We believed that this would swell the "attendance" at the hearing and focus the attention of many in the viewing audience. We also hoped that the City Council would listen attentively to what the "electronic witnesses" had to offer.

It was our hypothesis that we could further boost the number of viewers by encouraging them to participate in a "straw poll" on the subject of the hearing. So we added several other telephone lines that the home viewers could call *after* they had watched a certain amount of testimony and debate. This would also provide an informal feedback mechanism to the council on how at least a self-selected sample of their constituency felt about the issue, which might influence their vote.

The City Council bought the idea. They, too, wanted to see if they could add to the attractiveness of the hearing process and to the limited capacity of the hearing room (approximately 100). Furthermore, they wanted to enhance the flow of information and opinion between government and the public. Besides, what harm could come from more citizens seeing the council in action on "live" television?

Information about the project was released to the press and there was a story or two in the media heralding the event. However, no money was allocated for advertising. Nevertheless, it became clear as soon as the hearing began that there was a huge pool of citizens who were eager to testify by phone. During the entire five-hour hearing, the telephone lines were continuously busy. Although the Council limited each home viewing citizen to a one-minute presentation, we were only able to get thirty-five TV witnesses to state their opinions—in addition to a like number testifying in person (who had no time limitations). It also became obvious that the home-based witnesses were spending their waiting time by listening carefully to the proceedings and by writing out their views, since they referred to specific points raised earlier in the hearings, rarely rambled or stumbled, and were extremely articulate. It was our estimate that several hundred citizens tried to get through but could not.

As to the "straw poll," even though we did not let the home viewers "vote" until they had heard a great deal of the testimony and discussion, approximately 7,000 votes were cast by phone. These three lines were also jammed continuously, so it was clear that many thousands more tried and failed to get through the telephone bottleneck. Thus, we know we increased the amount of informed, active participation in the hearings from at most 100 in the room, to several thousand citizens.

But there was another remarkable impact of this TV hearing: the response of the city council. First, just about every person in the hearing room represented interest groups favorable to the project (contractors, labor unions). Quite to the contrary, just about every citizen who managed to reach us through the telephone logjam was opposed to the project. The city council and the project organizers became quickly aware of this fact. It was also clear that the council was initially favorable to the project, but their remarks during the hearing began to be more neutral. Furthermore, the results of the straw poll, released the next day, made the sentiment of the citizenry even clearer: 3–1 opposed. Three weeks later the council turned the project down by a 6–2 vote.

A serious defect in the modern legislative process is that ordinary citizens do not have the time or resources to attend even important hearings. Moreover, they may have sound reasons to avoid attending or speaking up even if they have the capacity to do so. Cable television, telephones, and computers encourage anonymous home-based testimony and opinion-sharing. Simply put, they protect, inform, and provide access not heretofore possible.

Of course, special interest groups could try to prepackage or "stuff" the call-in testimony or straw-polling and get it to go their way. The best remedy for that is to set up a preselected random sample of citizens who agree to watch the program and then call in a special number and/or enter a Personal Identification Number

(PIN) before voting. This provides a scientific baseline so one can see what a truly representative sample of citizens thinks about the issue. This was precisely the method used by the Reform Party of Canada in a recent teledemocratic experiment in Calgary. (See "Mandating the Vote of Legislators by Televoting" later in this chapter.)

Voting-by-Telephone for Party Leader: Nova Scotia, 1992

The Liberal Party of Nova Scotia, Canada, had been out of power and the provincial elections were drawing closer. A number of candidates were ready to vie for the position of party leader. As usual, it would be a heated contest with many traditional factors present, including the demographic, geographical, and ideological rifts between party members in the metro area (Halifax) and those in the hinterlands.

On the other hand, there were some new elements that would come to play an important role in how the party would decide to choose its leader. For one thing, the incumbent Premier from the opposition party was seen by the public as being an honest politician who had waged a successful campaign against public corruption. Moreover, the Liberal Party did not have a favorable public image. One observer surmised that this was behind the Liberal Party's choice to use the "televote" (Stewart 1994).

But according to John Young, the President of the Liberal Party of Nova Scotia, the decision to try an electronic communications solution to the choice of leadership had an entirely different background. He and other top leaders wanted to "level the playing field" in selecting the party leader. Many people in the party had scant opportunity to become involved in the process because the traditional convention method excluded them. So the party leadership considered ways to change the system, including the use of a mail ballot or scattering ballot boxes systematically throughout the province.

A short time before this, Maritime Telephone and Telegraph (MT&T) had established a new section within the company to develop political applications for its high-tech computer equipment and technologies. Electronic Town Meetings were on their agenda and they learned of the discussion going on within the Liberal Party. So contact was made, and the leadership of the Party agreed to set up an entirely novel method of selecting a party leader in a representative democracy, one that utilized a state-of-the-art mix of telephones, television, and computers.

It worked like this: All dues-paying members of the party who wanted to vote for the leader of the party had to register by April 15th for the June 6th party election. They could pay either $25 if they wanted to vote from home or $45 if they wanted to come to the convention in Halifax and vote from a phone bank at that site. The convention was to be telecast live by the Canadian Broadcasting Company (CBC). Each party member who was registered to vote was expected to watch the nominations and the discussion and then vote by phone. A computer would then tally the results. The high road the Liberals were treading was that of pure teledemocracy—no backroom deals, just an open convention with direct democracy via telecommunications.

Nearly half of the party membership took advantage of this new system and registered to vote. So instead of a few party regulars some 7,500 Nova Scotians opted into the process. MT&T provided the equipment and the software package. The process looked failsafe. But the computer system took a nosedive—crashed and burned with no backup system in place. So, the party had to cancel the election.

I was an advisor to CBC that day, commenting on the debacle from the United States via a telephone hookup. Even a Yank could tell that the rank-and-file was having a temper tantrum. Some people had waited hours to vote. Others were repeatedly rejected by the computer. But no one blamed the Liberal Party for conducting the electronic election; all the rancor was reserved for MT&T. So the party and MT&T decided to give it another go in a couple of weeks—this time with a backup system and a $350,000 performance guarantee from MT&T to the Liberal Party. Fortunately, the second round of Televoting took place without a hitch. Well over 90 percent of the members who registered voted for the candidate of their choice and John Savage won a run-off with 52.7 percent of the vote.

It is not unimportant to note that Mr. Savage also won the election in 1993, upsetting the incumbent Premier. The televote was at least a factor in helping the Liberals overturn years of Conservative Party rule. But, according to Ian Stewart, there were more direct impacts of the televote on the political leadership selection process. One obvious effect was on who participated. Groups that were "empowered" by this teledemocratic method included: (a) those who lived a great distance from Halifax; (b) the elderly; and (c) people who were not "insiders" or party regulars. Furthermore, a statistical analysis of the support behind Mr. Savage indicates that these groups were a significant part of the coalition that elected him.

There were also two important longer-range effects of this major real-life experiment. First, Mr. Savage, despite evidence that he owed his power to a teledemocratically expanded electorate, apparently felt no need to consult that electorate once he was in office. In very short order, he came to be widely perceived by his own party members as being remote, arrogant, and arbitrary. On the other hand, the astonishing success of this televote process is highlighted by the ripple effect it has had in an amazingly short period of time. Since its inception in the spring of 1992, both the Liberal Party of British Columbia and the Conservative Party of Saskatchewan have elected their leadership in like fashion.

For the most part, though, representative democracies have not been truly open in their leadership recruitment. For example, the primary system in the United States, which was instituted to move the selection of party leaders out of "smoke filled" rooms and into the public realm, has failed to attract more than a minute percentage of citizens. And the "party caucus" method is even more exclusive. Using the "televote" is bound to attract a far wider constituency into this process and increase the image of political parties by bringing them as close to the general public as their telephone and TV set, and perhaps their personal computer as well.

Mandating the Vote of Legislators by Televoting: Canada, 1994

The Reform Party of Canada came to prominence in the 1992 national elections by winning approximately 15 percent of the seats in the national Parliament. The platform of the Reform Party included a promise to be more responsive to citizen input than any political party, in Canada or anywhere. To demonstrate this, the Reform Party held numerous "town meetings" to obtain citizen input into its potential legislative program if it gained power at the national level.

After its substantial electoral success, the leader of the party, Preston Manning, was determined to find new ways to keep its promises. A highly visible and successful project was to use a televote to involve several Reform Members of Parliament in an emotional, moral issue that was being hotly debated throughout the nation: whether a physician should be allowed to help a terminally ill patient end his or her life.

This particular design included the following elements: A television station agreed to carry a discussion on the issue, using documentary-type materials that both the studio and home audience would view. Then there was a professionally facilitated discussion between a panel of experts and the studio audience. A week or so before this TV program, random samples of citizens from the city and region were drawn and contacted by telephone. They were asked to watch the program and to vote on the issues flashed on the screen. In addition, they were mailed information prior to the program and were given a special telephone number to call in their votes. Thus, if a substantial portion of these televoters actually telephoned their votes during the program, the results would be from an informed scientific sample of voters who were privy to a televised face-to-face meeting in the studio. What made this adaptation so significant was the fact that the Reform Party of Canada, through its leader and through the agreement of five sitting MPs from the Calgary area, was willing to be *bound by the results of this televote as to how they would vote in Parliament even if their personal views were at odds with those of the televoters*. In addition, they made this commitment known in advance to the public at large and to the televoters themselves. This gave an added incentive to the televoters to participate. The main condition was that there had to be a "consensus"—although it was not stipulated in advance as to what precise percentage would be deemed to be such. Party leader Manning suggested that a mere majority would do for him, but another MP declared that it would have to be "an unquestionably clear majority." Furthermore, each Member of Parliament was permitted to compare the results of the random sample televote with the call-ins by the self-selected sample and with the results of a mail-in vote conducted among the party membership. Manning also noted that, if successful, he intended to use this method to turn "Calgary into the Athens of the 21st Century."

Unlike the Nova Scotia experiment, this one went off without any glitches the first time. The ETM and the televote were scheduled for a Sunday and it was broadcast live by a private CATV station in Calgary. ParticiCom had selected 700 to 800 televoters in each of the five districts represented by the five MPs and the vast majority of those cast teleballots. The tabulation of the televoters showed that 70 percent believed that doctor-assisted suicide should be legal in Canada; 21 percent were opposed; 9 percent were undecided. The self-selected call-in vote over the TV had about 60 percent of the viewers in favor of doctor-assisted suicide and the mail survey also had a considerable majority for the proposition. Thus, all five Reform MPs vowed that they would vote in favor of this issue when it came to a vote in Parliament *despite the fact that they are personally opposed to it.* As of this writing (January 1998), the ruling Liberal Party of Canada has not yet put this issue to a vote in Parliament.

Reforming versus Transforming Representative Democracies

The fact that modern representative democracies are ailing is not news to many citizens, political leaders, members of the media, and academics. Indeed, Benjamin Barber has referred to the weaknesses in this kind of polity as amounting to a "thin democracy" (Barber 1984). A number of remedies are usually prescribed, including: moving from single member districts to proportional representation, or moving from proportional representation to single member districts; term limits; public campaign financing; putting public hearings and legislative information banks "on line;" having legislators teleconference with constituents; and the like. Newt Gingrich, the current Speaker of the U.S. House of Representatives, has devised what he calls a "Virtual Congress," where representatives can talk to separate groups of their constituencies visually and simultaneously while at a great distance—via teleconferencing.

All of these are, at heart, *reforms* of the present system. They are dedicated to preserving the superstructure of the status quo. There is no change in structure here; the citizens have no new powers. However, if the system remains essentially unchanged, the systemic problems will not magically disappear. Thus, none of the aforementioned reforms are likely to close, to any substantial degree, the "Grand Canyon" of alienation that exists today between the major bulk of the citizenry of representative democracies and their governments. None is likely to lead to significant changes in strategic direction or policy. *This is because what is needed is a political transformation, not a political reformation.*

The difference between the two is that a political reform is quintessentially conservative, deferring to the past. It is *retroactive* by using superficial changes to maintain the traditional, fundamental structure of a governing system. In Kenneth Dolbeare's terms, reform is an "opiate" that eventually dulls the idea that there can be a change in the traditional values and structure of the system (Dolbeare 1974, 83–87).

A transformation, however, is future oriented and requires a fundamental change in the power structure to produce major changes in agendas and policies. However, a transformation differs from a revolution, since the latter changes the entire political system rapidly via a *total* restructuring of power. Those who propose transformation want to help ease the old system into a new phase by actually empowering citizens through various applications of televoting. Slaton calls this new permutation of representative democracy "the participatory representative state" (Slaton 1992, 114–120). This transformational approach also characterizes the empowering pedagogies discussed in Part II, as well as the political outlook of Czech President Vaclav Havel and the Greens, which are discussed by Gilbert in chapter 13 and Woolpert in chapter 15.

The key difference between teledemocratic reformers and transformers, then, is whether to empower citizens directly in major functions of the polity, such as strategic planning, agenda setting, hearings, policy making, implementing policies, and selecting leaders. Merely plugging unempowered citizens into the old processes by giving them freer access to more information will simply add to their confusion and helplessness. Plugging them into modern electronic communications and information retrieval systems will only lessen their estrangement if they have good reason to believe they have been granted greater political power beforehand.

It is my contention that these four separate experiments in televoting *serendipitously* comprise a package that would greatly improve what Knight in chapter 4 calls the "integrity" of representative democracy. It is also my view that if they were adopted together as regular features of any government, they would *transform* the structure, process, and policies of that polity, and its reputation in the eyes and hearts of its own citizens. In concert, they are a valuable downpayment on the long overdue promise of teledemocracy— the direct empowerment of the citizenry in major functions of representative democracies.

Each of these experiments show how modern telecommunications can do this in strategic areas of governance. Once this phase of political transformation is accomplished—by using this fourfold package or some other equally transformational processes—it will thereafter be of great value to give all citizens free access to all kinds of computer conferencing, interactive TV and electronic data retrieval, because only then will they know how much and what information they will need in order to carry out their new responsibilities in the participatory representative state. Only then will they be enabled, as Halpern puts it in chapter 3, "to participate in creating fundamentally new and better communities."

One final note: there are many other ways to improve and expand upon the uses of televoting and ETMs in modern governance, i.e., by using them to set up initiatives and referenda. These four are spotlighted here only because certain governments have been innovative and bold enough to try them. Perhaps within the next few years other applications will be used in real-life settings and provide even greater opportunities for transforming representative democracies through telecommunications.

13

Transformational Political Leadership: Insights from the Example of Vaclav Havel

ROBERT J. GILBERT

Introduction

Transformational political theory, described in Part I of this anthology, focuses on whole systems, including the personal and the sacred dimensions of politics. Consequently it is sometimes dismissed by political scientists as being too "idealistic," offering perspectives that are of little use in the rough-and-tumble real world. This attitude is, of course, a self-fulfilling prophecy: those who believe that politics must inevitably be based upon cynical self-interest will never attempt any progressive activity. In reality there are innumerable examples of successful transformational political activity, ranging from the abolition of human slavery to the freeing of entire nation-states from dictatorial control. Just as slavery was abolished by the determined effort of concerned individuals, so do contemporary transformational movements—such as the dissident movement in Eastern Europe which paved the way for the liberation of the former Warsaw Pact states from Soviet control (Rothschild 1993)—require pioneering individuals to take the lead.

Leadership is a risky thing, however. There is always the danger of a cult of personality, the elevation of a flawed human being to superhuman status. This way lies destruction, for transformational leaders must be without the desire for domination; political power brings out the worst in leaders who need to assert superiority over their fellow citizens. The best transformational political leaders, such as Mahatma Gandhi, Martin Luther King, Nelson Mandela, and (our present subject) Vaclav Havel, have all engaged in merciless self-examination and have committed themselves to transpersonal ethical goals in their respective societies. Such leaders do not lead through their personal power and charisma; rather *they lead through awakening in others the force of conscience and the understanding of a greater good* which, once grasped, can never be denied without the loss of one's integrity.

Just as adherents of power politics commonly dismiss transformational politics in general, so did they dismiss in the 1970s and early 1980s the idea that the Soviet Union's domination of Eastern Europe could be transformed without aggressive, militaristic power politics. The vast majority of Western political scientists, including those who considered themselves experts on the Soviet Union and Eastern Europe, were thus completely unprepared for—and uncomprehending of—the collapse of the Soviet Union and the self-liberation of the Warsaw Pact states in the late 1980s. One of the exceptions to this mass blindness on the part of political scientists was Zbigniew Brzezinski (1989). Significantly, Brzezinski is of Polish extraction; his analysis was derived from a deep knowledge of cultural and intellectual—in other words qualitative—aspects of the Eastern European situation, rather than purely quantitative measures of national strength.

It is now apparent that many leaders of the transformational movement in Eastern Europe understood certain essential human truths that are lost on most Western political analysts. Arguably the most successful, influential, and best-known of the Eastern European transformational political leaders is Vaclav Havel. Havel, whose work *The Power of the Powerless* inspired nonviolent resistance to Soviet domination, has led the Czech Republic into the most successful political transition of any Eastern European state; the conservative *Economist* magazine of London notes that the Czech Republic is the most politically and economically stable former communist country in the world, with an inflation rate in 1995 that was one-third that of Hungary and one-twentieth that of Russia (*The World in 1996*, 88).

Although the Czech transition to independence has not been without its problems (prominently among them the political split with Slovakia), Havel can be considered to be at least partly responsible for many of the best aspects of this transition. The virtually bloodless "Velvet Revolution" that liberated the country from Soviet rule, the positive perception of the Czech Republic's stability by the international community, and Prague's resurgence as a cultural magnet for the young and idealistic have all been influenced by Havel. Havel is not only an important case study of transformational leadership; his political thought is a veritable blueprint for the nonviolent democratization of repressive regimes. In this essay I inquire into the heart of Havel's leadership, particularly what is reproducible in his political approach that may help to foster political transformation elsewhere.

Transformation from Below: Havel the Dissident

Vaclav Havel became an advocate for the transformation of his country's political standards almost immediately upon attaining adulthood. In 1956 at the age of twenty he disrupted a Czech writers' conference, demanding recognition for writers whose works had been banned as "anti-Communist." After writing two full-length plays, Havel became in 1965 an editor of the noncommunist literary magazine *Tvar*. Inevitably the magazine was banned, but in his fight to keep the journal alive he realized an important political principle: "We introduced a new model of behavior: don't get involved in diffuse, general ideological polemics . . . fight only for . . . concrete causes, and be prepared to fight unswervingly to the end" (Havel 1988, 14). This then is the first principle of transformational activity in Havel's work:

1. Fight for concrete causes, not abstract polemics. By the mid-1960s Czechoslovakia led the way among Eastern European countries in progressive political activity, culminating in the 1968 "Prague Spring" during which Havel emerged as a national political figure. Czechoslovakia was being transformed from the bottom up by a wide range of progressive artistic/political projects; this era of renewed Czech political and cultural independence threatened to loosen the Soviet Union's grip on the entire Eastern bloc. Havel participated in forming the foundation for the Prague Spring movement by helping in 1967 to found the Circle of Independent Writers. Soon thereafter he published his influential article *On the Theme of an Opposition* (1991, 25–35) which demanded the establishment of a noncommunist political party based on the Czechoslovakian democratic tradition. The Prague Spring movement demonstrates a second principle:

2. Exert steady pressure (both artistic and directly political) to transform a corrupt political system. Havel was gaining the reputation

of being an articulate spokesperson for the highest aspirations of the Czech people. Liberal journalist Antonin J. Liehm wrote in 1968 that:

> [Some] people . . . deluded themselves into believing that Havel was an exception . . . That is a mistake . . . Havel expresses the feelings of his generation with absolute clarity across the lines of politics and other loyalties. And he speaks for the generation that follows him, too (Liehm 1968, 393–394).

This expression of the strivings of one's people is a demonstration of the transformational principle:

3. Represent the highest aspirations of one's community, rather than seeking power for oneself. Havel made clear during the Prague Spring of 1968 that he was not representing any preconceived political program in either his political or theatrical writings. Any *a priori* political viewpoint, he wrote, serves

> first of all as a filter through which reality is perceived, then as a principle on the basis of which reality is rearranged, and finally as part of the message which the artistic work is designed to transmit . . . [however] my presentation of reality naturally involves a certain amount of interpretation, but it is based solely on contemporary life without any preconceived ideological framework (Liehm 1968, 374).

Havel considers political problems as they present themselves in their natural interconnections rather than imposing ideological filters on his thinking. This avoidance of a predetermined ideology or program is one of the most important features of Havel's political vision. Paul Wilson, who has translated Havel's major works into English, notes the connection of this kind of unconditioned thinking to phenomenology:

> [P]henomenology is now a symptomatic, or typical, feature of the independent intellectual landscape in Central Europe today . . . Phenomenology offers a way of describing the world that frees thought (and, by implication, action) from the assumptions of the mechanistic determinism that still lie behind much of our scientific and political thinking (Havel 1988, 18).

This clear and unconditioned thinking is a major step towards developing a holistic insight into political/societal conditions—or any other topic (Bortoft 1986; Edelglass et al. 1992). Revealed here is the transformational principle:

4. View each situation afresh, without preconceived ideological frameworks that serve as reality filters. The Prague Spring period ended with the Soviet Union's dispatch of troops to occupy Czechoslovakia. Prominent dissidents such as Havel became targets of harassment. In 1969 Havel discovered a listening device in his Prague apartment; soon thereafter the Writer's Union was dissolved and Havel's plays banned from the stage. Nonetheless, Havel continued writing. His next public statement did not come until 1975, when he wrote an open letter to the General Secretary of the Czechoslovakian Communist Party indicting the communist system for replacing the true cultural life of his country with a "death principle" (Havel 1991, 50–83).

In 1977 Havel entered a period of deep contemplation regarding the picture of the human condition presented in Goethe's classic play *Faust*. The topic of humanity making a bargain with the devil in exchange for power and comfort moved Havel deeply; he soon resolved to write his own version of *Faust*. Eda Kriseova describes Havel's method of writing this play:

> [Havel] drew graphs of the individual actions, . . . represented the characters graphically, and drew in dots that determined the length of their future speeches . . . [He] first writes his plays in a sort of musical score and then, when he sees that they have structure and rhythm, rewrites these scores into words (1993, 216).

The remarkable imaginative mobility and range of Havel's thought processes—the ability to think in *pictures* and/or *sounds* rather than simply words—develops intuitive insight (Smit 1988; Steiner 1981, 1988). Havel's leadership stems in part from his having developed these expanded forms of awareness; his ability to think non-verbally combines synergistically with his phenomenological thinking to produce a deep level of understanding. From these considerations we may extract a fundamental principle of creative transformational work:

5. Develop a full range of thinking skills in order to attain expanded levels of insight. Havel titled his retelling of *Faust* in a modern Czech setting *Temptation*. The protagonist, Faustka, is a former Marxist who has become spiritually lost; secretly he engages in psychotronics, a synthesis of magic and technology. The play is remarkable for its unsettling effect upon audiences, and the subject itself seems to possess an elemental, archetypal power. Havel biographer Eda Kriseova notes that it is typical of Havel that he was the first to:

recognize what was in the air. He has the gift for looking at individual events from a bird's eye view, seeing them all at once, describing the links between them, and giving meaning to the whole (Kriseova 1993, 220–221).

Here then is the principle:

6. See individual events from a higher perspective which gives them context and meaning for everyday life. In 1977 Havel helped to found the internationally known forum for dissident activity in Czechoslovakia, Charter 77. This was followed by the formation of another progressive group, the Committee for the Defense of the Unjustly Prosecuted (VONS), in April of 1978. In addition to serving as a spokesman for these groups, Havel wrote in 1978 what was to become his most famous work and the seminal document of the Eastern European dissent movement, *The Power of the Powerless*.

This work presented the idea that any oppressive government can only function through the acquiescence of its citizens. Havel uses the example of a greengrocer who puts communist slogans in his store window; this helps him to get along in the system, but it is a lie. Simply through the means of citizens speaking and acting out of their true beliefs an oppressive political system must cease to function. "Living within the truth becomes the one natural point of departure for all activities that work against the automatism of the system" (Havel 1985, 45); if a critical mass of citizens honors this principle then any repressive regime can be overcome.

The Power of the Powerless was an intellectual key which helped open the door to the liberation of Eastern Europe. Polish Solidarity activist Zbygniew Bujak noted that:

> This essay reached us . . . at a point when we felt we were at the end of the road . . . Reading it gave us the theoretical underpinnings for our activity. It maintained our spirits; we did not give up . . . When I look at the victories of Solidarity, and of Charter 77, I see in them an astonishing fulfillment of the prophecies and knowledge contained in Havel's essay (Havel 1991, 125–126).

The phrase "Living in Truth" has come to represent the core of Havel's political philosophy, providing what may be the most crucial of all the transformational principles in this essay:

7. Live within the truth, maintaining self-integrity when confronting a repressive government. As might be expected, the Commu-

nists did not appreciate Havel's providing an intellectual foundation for undermining their authority. In 1979 Havel was imprisoned along with other prominent VONS members. In his letters from prison to his wife Olga, Havel was unflinching in his examination of his own faults, most notably providing an insightful account of his "fifteen bad moods." Here he describes to her his "worst mood":

> Essentially, it involves falling into a state of utter and complete self-doubt . . . Comparing myself to others, I am compelled to realize again and again how much better and more meaningfully they have acted in various situations, and how much they managed to achieve. I fault myself for lacking ideas and energy . . . I seem to lack strength, decisiveness and good humor and in general, I'm good for nothing and can expect nothing positive in life (Havel 1988,168).

This blisteringly honest self-examination is in stark contrast to the personal statements of many political leaders, who often strive to present a flawless persona to the world. Havel concludes this particular letter by noting:

> [T]hough I may occasionally succumb to this mood, it is never serious enough to have a destructive effect on my ability to make decisions, on my behavior or my actions . . . The point is I can't let my moods decide what I should do (Havel 1988:169).

These two observations by Havel reveal another principle:

8. Honestly recognize and admit all inner failings, while never falling prey to destructive moods. These letters from prison also contain remarkable meditations on the condition of humanity in the modern world, in which Havel acknowledges a belief in a higher order in the universe beyond his own personal "I." Indeed, his prison letters culminate in a profound spiritual understanding (Havel 1988, 375):

> Yes: man [sic] is in fact nailed down—like Christ on the cross—to a grid of paradoxes: stretched between the horizontal of the world and the vertical of Being; dragged down by the hopelessness of existing-in-the-world on the one hand, and the unattainability of the absolute on the other, he balances between the torment of not knowing his mission and the joy of carrying it out, between nothingness and meaningfulness.

Here we see an expression of the principle:

9. Remain aware of one's innate spiritual nature while struggling through the trials of everyday life.

Havel was released from prison in 1983 after a near-fatal illness precipitated an international demand for his release. The Czechoslovakian government had hoped that prison would break Havel's spirit and stop his dissident activity, but instead it only served to strengthen Havel's resolve and to increase recognition of his moral leadership. In 1985 Havel wrote *The Anatomy of a Reticence* describing why Eastern European peace and justice advocates sometimes had difficulty relating to their Western counterparts. Essentially, the Eastern Europeans sometimes felt that the Westerners were too self-congratulatory in their activism, and too rigid to have a sense of proportion:

> One of the traditions of the Central European climate . . . is . . . an intensified sense of irony and self-irony, together with humor and . . . an intensified fear of exaggerating our own dignity to an unintentionally comic stage . . . [W]hat is most earnest has a way of blending, in a particularly tense manner, with what is most comic (Havel 1986, 17–18).

Here we have a final—but critical—principle:

10. Have a sense of humor and proportion in transformational political activity. The political climate began to change throughout Eastern Europe in the mid-1980s as a result of Gorbachev's reforms. By 1989, the political situation in Czechoslovakia reached critical mass. Havel was again jailed for participating in an antigovernment demonstration, but international protest was so great that he was released after serving less than half of his eight-month sentence. Havel then helped to found an overtly political opposition movement called Civic Forum, leading a takeover of the government which was so peaceful and idealistic that it became known as the "Velvet Revolution." On December 29, 1989, Havel was unanimously elected President by the Federal Assembly; international reaction was overwhelmingly favorable (Brown 1991).

In summary, it is clear that the ten transformational principles embedded in Havel's thought and activity were influential in transforming the Czechoslovakian political system, as well as contributing to the transformation of the political systems of all the former Soviet-dominated states of Eastern Europe. These principles clarify a few of the lessons transformational political theorists and actors may learn from Havel. Havel's success in affecting his nation's political system as a dissident—"from below," so to speak—raises the question: How successful has he been acting "from above" as a national leader?

Transformation from Above: Havel the National Leader

Western political scientists and media commentators, although enthusiastic about Havel as an anti-Communist who rose to become the president of his country, have frequently been condescending in their evaluations of his political philosophy. It is common to find Havel caricatured as an uncomprehending novice in need of enlightenment regarding the cold realities of governance. This attitude is evident in comments such as those made by Thomas L. Friedman of the *New York Times* on the Feb. 23, 1990, *Washington Week in Review* program regarding Havel's ascension to the presidency: "You know, it's great to have a playwright up there, and it was all wonderful symbolism . . . but politics is not about poetry, it's about power, and it's about making hard choices, and not very pure choices sometimes" (Rosen 1990, 28).

Havel made clear from his first days in office that he intended to prove that an ethical and truthful form of political leadership was possible. Havel stressed that political means and political ends were one and the same, that "there is only one way to strive for decency, reason, responsibility, sincerity, civility, and tolerance, and that is decently, reasonably, responsibly, sincerely, civilly, and tolerantly" (Havel 1992d, 8). Havel was (and is) aware of how such ideas are dismissed in some quarters, but insisted nevertheless that "I am convinced that we will never build a democratic state based on rule of law if we do not at the same time build a state which is—regardless of how unscientific this may sound to the ears of the political scientist—humane, moral, intellectual, spiritual, and cultural" (Havel 1992b, 18).

Havel has done his best as President to maintain a clear phenomenological insight into contemporary political events, avoiding preconceived categories: "I have never espoused any ideology, dogma, or doctrine—left-wing, right-wing, or any other closed, ready-made system of presupposition about the world. On the contrary, I have tried to think independently, using my own powers of reason . . ." (1992b, 60). Havel's perception of economics, for example, makes clear that "the market economy is as natural and matter-of-fact to me as the air" (1992b, 65), but he then goes on to warn of the danger of a dogmatic approach:

> The cult of "systematically pure" market economics can be as dangerous as Marxist ideology, because it comes from *the same mental position*: that is, from the certainty that operating from theory is essentially smarter than operating from a knowledge of life . . . As if a general precept were more reliable than the guidance we get . . . from our understanding of individual human beings and the moral and social sensitivity that comes from such understanding (1992b, 66: emphasis added).

In 1992 Czechoslovakia split into two separate Republics despite Havel's strong objections; not wanting to play any part in this event, Havel resigned the presidency in protest. After the split Havel's moral authority remained undiminished; he was widely felt to be the most qualified person in the country to take the presidency of the now-separate Czech Republic. Havel was soon prevailed upon to accept the post, which he still held at the time of this writing (1998). As noted earlier, Havel has guided the Czech Republic through what is commonly acknowledged to be the most successful transformation of any formerly communist Eastern European nation, whether calculated in terms of political/economic stability or in terms of the cultural renaissance that nation has enjoyed. Inevitably, of course, Havel has been faced with a number of challenging situations over the last nine years in which to apply the principles of transformational leadership. While this topic is too large to be dealt with in depth in this essay, a sense of Havel's leadership can be conveyed by looking at two representative events in recent Czech foreign policy: the involvement of troops in the Persian Gulf War, and the official status of the Dalai Lama of Tibet.

The roots of Czechoslovakia's foreign policy are addressed in Havel's 1992 work *Summer Meditations*, in which he discusses the ethical conduct of policy as a head of state. Havel emphasizes that a nation's foreign policy must be based on common interests and not a self-absorbed "national interest":

> It should not, in other words, be a selfish, inconsiderate, mindlessly pragmatic foreign policy, to promote the interests of our own country unscrupulously, to the detriment of everyone else. It should rather be a policy that sees our own interests as an essential part of the common interest, one that encourages us at all times to become involved, even when there is no immediate benefit to be had from it (1992b, 98–99).

Havel was forced to apply this vision when faced with the decision of committing Czechoslovakian troops to the Persian Gulf War. Havel describes the action he took—and why:

> Human rights are universal and indivisible. Human freedom is also indivisible: if it is denied to anyone in the world, it is therefore denied, indirectly, to all people. This is why we cannot remain silent in the face of evil or violence; silence merely encourages them . . . We sent our units to the Persian Gulf to declare once more our support for that principle—not because we wanted to ingratiate ourselves with the Americans (1992a, 98).

Whereas Havel chose for moral reasons to join the international community's opposition to Iraq during the Persian Gulf War, he went his own separate way over the issue of the diplomatic status accorded Tibet's exiled spiritual leader, the Dalai Lama. The People's Republic of China has militarily occupied Tibet for decades, repeatedly threatening other nations not to recognize the political status of the Dalai Lama (Tibet's leader prior to the Chinese invasion). Havel broke ranks with other world leaders who (following the precepts of power politics) ostracized the Dalai Lama as a powerless exile with a powerful enemy. Here Havel describes the results of officially acknowledging the Dalai Lama as the leader of Tibet:

> China did not invade us in retaliation, nor did they cancel any contracts. But the Dalai Lama was subsequently received by many other heads of state. There was, of course, a certain risk in what I did, but I felt that, in the interest of a generally good thing, this risk could properly be undertaken . . . On the other hand, it is not usually a good idea to be too far ahead of the pack. True, it's an easy way to glory, but the risk can far outweigh the actual significance of the good intentions (1992b, 100).

Havel is "living in truth" by acknowledging the true moral status of the Dalai Lama despite diplomatic pressures to reject him; he also demonstrates humility and a sense of proportion in his comments regarding staying in touch with the larger community of political leaders so as to retain the possibility of influencing them positively.

In response to criticisms that his policies are too idealistic, Havel maintains that it is precisely "the kind of basic decency and humanity with which communism was overthrown here, and the moral direction of our foreign policy" which gives his nation the international prestige it enjoys (1992b, 101).

Conclusion

While Havel's empirical demonstration of the feasibility of transformational politics is of great importance, I do not intend to canonize Havel for his achievements nor to dismiss any personal or professional defects on his part. Transformational politics can benefit from positive role models, but of course the central concern of any truly transformational impulse must be that it comes from the people rather than from a leader who is somehow better than the average citizen. Indeed, one of Havel's greatest strengths is his humility and dedication to acting in the common interest.

Havel's actions, particularly as a national leader, can well be questioned from multiple perspectives. For example, Havel's involvement of Czech troops in the Persian Gulf War is highly problematic; Kuwait was liberated from the Iraqis only to be returned to the autocratic Kuwaiti government. Moreover, Iraq's infrastructure was so badly damaged that hundreds of thousands of Iraqi men, women, and children have died in the years following the War. In addition to criticism of what Havel *has* done, there are also complaints possible regarding what he has *not* done in office. For instance, there is a Czech law as of this writing that makes it a crime to criticize the government and/or the president. Although ostensibly opposed to this law, Havel has not made a determined effort to remove this repressive measure from the books.

In the final analysis, however, Havel remains an impressive ethical exception to the all-too-prevalent politics of power and cynicism. While we must retain our independence as political actors and freely critique all political individuals and institutions (for example, Cummings' critique of affirmative action in chapter 14), we must also respect and admire what is good, honorable and decent in life, particularly in the heavily compromised arena of political action. Havel's empirical legacy of positive political transformation—undertaken in the spirit of a universal "everyman," not of a Nietzschean "superman"—provides a blueprint for generations to come.

Finally, I cannot conclude without addressing the problem of how Havel's life work pertains to us as political actors. Westerners should feel cautious about relaxing into a warm glow about Havel's political activity, confident that our side of the old Iron Curtain has been a beacon of light to the world. Noam Chomsky has remarked that if Havel had been a dissident in one of the many Latin American police states that the United States trains, arms, and supports, he would never have lived long enough to become a popular political figure. In Latin America and elsewhere, dissidents similar to Havel are not simply harassed and imprisoned; they are commonly abducted in the middle of the night by death squads, their mutilated bodies left by the side of the road as a gruesome warning to others who might dare to engage in transformative political work.

If we as citizens of modern democratic states are to indeed "live within the truth," we bear the responsibility of recognizing—and voicing our opposition to—political injustice both within our own countries and in the world at large. Yet, despite the fact that the political environment of most citizens of North American and Western Europe is far safer than that which Havel had to contend with, who among us can claim to have achieved as much—or to have struggled in a just cause as faithfully—as Havel has? Such considerations lead us out of the safe confines of past history and our own abstract *intellectualization* about external personalities, into a *realization* of the pressing need for our own politically transformative activity in the here and now.

Which is where all politically transformative work begins.

14

Transforming Public Policy: Beyond Affirmative Action

MICHAEL S. CUMMINGS

The original, admirable intent of affirmative action was to transform injustice into justice. In many respects, unfortunately, this intent has itself been transformed into almost its opposite in the last thirty years. Meanwhile, a tendency toward political correctness on the Left has obscured the illogic, the injustice, and, ironically, the conservatism built into affirmative action as we know it today. The charge of racism against critics of affirmative action "has had a chilling effect on intellectual discussion of the place of race in American life" (Sniderman and Piazza 1993, 66). As Herman argues in chapter 2, "rather than avoid conflict we should struggle to question our most deeply held assumptions and actively seek out those who disagree."

From a transformational perspective, affirmative action exemplifies the limitations of piecemeal efforts to create a more collaborative and tolerant society. I will argue that affirmative action, far from being too liberal, is too conservative; that it helps to perpetuate the political economy of corporate capitalism; and that it should be replaced by a synergistic program of political transformation towards a healthier community—i.e., one that is both interdependent and diverse. I begin with a brief history of the original versus the current versions of affirmative action.

The Change in Meaning of Affirmative Action Since 1965

Presidents Truman, Kennedy, and Johnson all directed parts of their administrations to "act affirmatively" to root out racism. For instance, in 1953, Truman's Committee on Government Contract Compliance advised the Bureau of Employment Security "to act affirmatively to implement the policy of nondiscrimination" in numerous job-related functions (quoted in Marable 1995, 82). Kennedy's 1961 executive order 10925 stipulated: "The [government] contractor will take affirmative action to ensure that applicants are employed, and employees are treated during their employment, without regard to their race, creed, color, or national origin" (quoted in Mills 1994, 5). Note that race and other job-irrelevant factors are explicitly not to be considered. Similarly the Civil Rights Act of 1964, which banned Federal employment discrimination on the basis of race, color, religion, sex, or national origin, specifically declared that these protections did not grant "preferential treatment to any group because of race, color, religion, sex, or national origin" (quoted in Mills 1994, 6).

Marable (1995) characterizes this original conception of affirmative action as the government's "taking proactive steps to dismantle prejudice" (82). Marable's point is that in some form affirmative action has been around for a long time, and that its thrust was to prevent arbitrary factors like race and color from undermining equal opportunity. However, as the Voting Rights Act of 1965 was becoming law, President Johnson publicly departed from this original conception of affirmative action. In a speech at Howard University, he said: "[F]reedom is not enough. You do not take a person who, for years, has been hobbled by chains and liberate him, bring him to the starting line of a race and then say, 'You are free to compete with all others' and still justly believe you have been completely fair." Johnson argued that "not just legal equity" but "equality of result" was required for those who had been denied equal opportunity in the past (quoted in Mills 1994, 7). He implemented a new definition of affirmative action in which "benign" group preferences would now serve to compensate for, and overcome the lingering effects of, earlier hostile preferences.

From 1965 to 1980, the Johnson, Nixon, Ford, and Carter Administrations implemented or supported training, hiring, and admissions preferences for a variety of "protected" groups. Unquestionably, ending racism, sexism, and other forms of arbitrary discrimination should be high on the agenda of political transformation. And, by the late 1960s it had become clear to many Americans that ending de jure discrimination would not in itself end de facto inequality. In the 1970s and 1980s, champions of racial and gender equality argued that nonwhites and women needed and deserved preferential treatment in order to make up for their historically in-herited disadvantages. Legislatures wrote new laws, executives ad-ministered laws in new ways, and courts reinterpreted laws so as to permit or require special consideration—"reverse discrimination" in the eyes of critics—for the benefit of women and nonwhites.

Nathan Glazer's (1975) book titled *Affirmative Discrimination*, like Carl Cohens's (1995) *Naked Racial Preference*, underscored the reversal of the old concept of equal opportunity, according to which it had been wrong to judge individuals according to inherited group characteristics like race or sex. Many public and private institutions were now required to act affirmatively to increase their percentages of women and ethnic minorities, on the view that "[a]ffirmative ac-tion without numbers, whether in the form of quotas, goals, or timetables, is meaningless" (Hill 1992, 131).

Soon, other disadvantaged groups began to press the govern-ment for affirmative action on their behalf. These included senior citizens, the physically handicapped, veterans, members of various religions, and homosexuals. As we shall see, the winning of pro-tected status under affirmative-action guidelines has not followed any ethical or logical pattern, but rather has reflected different groups' relative political clout, the vagaries of different executives, legislatures, and courts, and the sympathies of the general public. Indeed, affirmative-action laws, policies, and rulings have differed widely and continue to be extensively litigated (Mezey 1992).

During this period, Supreme Court decisions varied dramati-cally in terms of permitting or disallowing "set-asides" and "propor-tional representation" for protected classes. In general, by 1980 the high court's decisions had turned more hostile to affirmative action, giving the Republican administrations of Reagan and Bush greater leeway to overtly oppose or tacitly undermine affirmative action.

As reported in the Los Angeles Times in July, 1995: "A Justice Department analysis of . . . affirmative action concludes the govern-ment will have a hard time defending its many programs that steer contracts to racial and ethnic minorities." One year later, the Court further muddied the waters by permitting states to ban the use of race or national origin as a factor in college admissions. "But be-cause the court didn't issue a ruling of its own, it left no nationwide guidance on the current validity of its 1978 Bakke ruling that col-leges could consider race as one of many factors in an effort to obtain a diverse student body" (Epstein 1996, 2).

Conservative opponents of affirmative action have enjoyed not only Court decisions limiting it but also a steadily increasing percentage of people opposed to group preferences. A sizable majority of Americans, though opposing discrimination against women and nonwhites, now oppose giving preferences to these groups (Sniderman and Piazza 1993; National Conference of Christians and Jews 1994; Los Angeles Times 1995). They especially oppose numerical set-asides, "proportional representation" according to race or gender, and quotas.

According to Sniderman and Piazza (1993), "[p]roposing to privilege some people rather than others, on the basis of a characteristic they were born with, violates a nearly universal norm of fairness" (134). It is true that President Johnson's metaphor of the mismatched runners underscored the important fact of institutional racism and sexism. Merely eliminating arbitrary discrimination would not cancel out the inherited disadvantages of groups formerly discriminated against. Unless disadvantaged groups like Blacks and women were given an extra boost, they could not be expected to compete on an equal basis with white males. But while this justification of affirmative action as preferential treatment may sound compassionate and reasonable, "[t]he idea that places should be, explicitly or implicitly, 'set aside' for minority (or women) applicants has never been accepted by a majority of Americans . . ." (Skocpol 1994, 296).

Contradictions of Affirmative Action

In response to charges of reverse discrimination, supporters of affirmative action have added to President Johnson's athletic metaphor of justification. University of Wisconsin labor-law professor James E. Jones, Jr. equates rejection of affirmative action with saying, "We stopped poisoning the lakes and we don't have to do anything to reverse what we've done" (Mercer 1994). Others argue, analogously, that the caboose of a train will never catch up with the engine unless it is placed on a separate track and given an extra push. In the past, say supporters of affirmative action, society has relegated women to the kitchen and Blacks to the back of the bus. Now it is time to give them seats in the corporate boardroom and at the front of the bus. Turnabout is fair play.

But is it? Who are the "we" who committed the original injustices, and to whom? An honest assessment of these questions reveals the unfortunate truths: (1) that historical injustices cannot be cleanly or fully righted in any case (Steele 1990); (2) that, as affirmative-action proponents charge, ignoring the present effects of history perpetuates old injustices; (3) that, as affirmative-action opponents reply, mitigating these effects creates new injustices; and that, consequently, (4) there is no "completely fair" cure for our history of racial and gender oppression. Believing otherwise is to believe in a Great Justice Maker in the Sky who can somehow right all the bad things that have happened in the area of unjust discrimination.

Refusing to give special consideration to women and nonwhites is unfair. But so is requiring innocent white males—especially those suffering from other disadvantages not of their own making—to sacrifice for the sins of their ancestors. And as we shall see, it is not only white males who are unfairly injured by affirmative action.

This dilemma amounts to a "choice of evils" created by an evil history. It is a serious problem made worse by those who refuse to recognize it. The Politically Correct Right denies the dilemma by positing, with Henry Ford, that "history is bunk," in the sense that the living should not be blamed for the sins of the dead. The Politically Correct Left denies the dilemma by claiming that all of today's white males have benefited from racism and sexism, even if they did not cause it, and thus owe a helping hand to all of today's women and nonwhites. Though both sides tout their views as ethically pure, simple logic casts doubt on such portrayals.

Groups Unprotected by Affirmative Action

Under affirmative action, what is the logic of protecting one disadvantaged group, for instance African-Americans, but not another, for instance people battered in childhood? Both conditions confer serious competitive disadvantages. Neither is a matter of choice. In both cases, more powerful groups—whites and adults, respectively—have abused less powerful groups, Blacks and children. In both cases, unusually blessed individuals within the oppressed group can sometimes surmount their disadvantages, while typical members of the deprived group continue to lag behind their nondeprived peers. Both Blacks and the previously battered suffer an average deficit in opportunity, self-esteem, and quality of life compared to other ethnic groups and compared to people who have been nurtured rather than brutalized in childhood.

In both cases, membership in the advantaged or disadvantaged group is unearned—a matter of pure chance. Contributing to both groups' suffering are biological facts—skin color and youth—poisoned by social conditions—white racism and adult cruelty. Government policies of omission and commission, supported by whites and adults, respectively, have further contributed to the plight of Blacks and abused children. The parallels between these two groups, as well as with other disadvantaged groups, are powerful.

There is no good reason why one such group should be protected and the other neglected by affirmative action. The list of anomalous comparisons could go on, matching the few protected classes with a much larger number of deserving but unprotected ones. Needy but generally unprotected groups include those who grew up in poverty, broken homes, orphanages, polluted environments, rural settings, or substandard educational districts, as well as those disabled by chronic bad health, addiction, anxiety, depression, physical abnormalities, and a wide variety of developmental impediments.

It is probable, of course, that a disproportionate percentage of women and nonwhites suffer from some of these additional categories of disadvantage. But why should women and nonwhites who are unusually advantaged in these other respects automatically get preferential treatment over Whites and men who are unusually disadvantaged? This anomaly of affirmative action means that many people who already enjoy a net competitive advantage are by government policy further advantaged, while many of the already disadvantaged are further disadvantaged!

Mounting evidence has convinced a number of observers on the Left that affirmative action has primarily benefited middle-class white females and middle-class Blacks, many of whom already enjoyed net competitive advantages before being further advantaged by affirmative action. Observers noting this anomaly include nonwhites and Whites, radicals and liberals alike (Carter 1991, hooks 1995, Kennedy 1996, Kessler-Harris 1994, Lerner 1996, Marable 1995, Skocpol 1994, Swain 1995). This perverse illogic of affirmative action plays into the hands of the political Right.

It is also essential to note that it is not only disadvantaged white men who are discriminated against by the arbitrarily limited number of protected classifications. A woman or person of color who suffers from a number of these additional, unrecognized disadvantages gets credit for only one or two of his or her many disadvantages. The fact that the arbitrary classifications of affirmative action discriminate against tens of millions of people who are neither white nor male helps explain why many women and people of color have become critical of affirmative action (Thomas 1994, Wilson 1987, Steele 1990, Carter 1991, Skocpol 1994, Chavez 1994, Njeri 1993,

Dinh 1994, Kessler-Harris 1994, Sowell 1994, Marable 1995, d'Souza 1994, Swain 1995).

The stereotyped notion that women and people of color must be either supporters of affirmative action or "sellouts" of their race or gender is promoted by leaders increasingly out of touch with those they purport to represent. Recent surveys show that in Australia, Germany, Italy, the United Kingdom, and the United States, "giving preferential treatment for jobs and promotions is massively unpopular," even among women (Sniderman and Piazza, 133–34). Carol Swain (1995) reports on a recent survey comparing the opinions of Black interest group leaders with those of the Black public: "Seventy-seven percent of black leaders supported preferential treatment of minorities, yet only 23 percent of the black public did" (12).

Each time an additional group, e.g., veterans or gays or dyslexics, wins protected status, the members of disadvantaged but still unprotected groups suffer yet another competitive setback (Kessler-Harris 1994). Each affirmative-action attempt to do the right thing for one new group does the wrong thing to these other disadvantaged groups.

Solution 1: A Logical and Just Affirmative Action Program

The purpose of affirmative action is to enable its beneficiaries to compete on an even playing field with those who are less deprived. Its method is to pass laws and administer policies that favor people who have inherited unfair disadvantages from arbitrary discrimination. Most Americans, like most people everywhere, present a rich mixture of competitive assets and liabilities. Fairness and logic require at the very least that affirmative action consider all of a person's major sources of advantage and disadvantage, not just some small number that have found political favor. Blacks, women, and seniors—especially the best-positioned of them—enjoy protected status because they have been able to organize and agitate more effectively than those suffering from dysfunctional families, anxiety, low self-esteem, addiction, phobias, childhood abuse, or youth itself. There is little justice to this anomaly.

A number of analysts have recently suggested changing or expanding the factors to be considered in affirmative action. Cornell West (1994b) advocates a "more wide-ranging affirmative action policy" (85). Clarence Page (1996), a supporter of affirmative action, concedes the "excesses of affirmative action . . . that . . . decline to take need as well as race into consideration" (234). John K. Wilson, a liberal, agrees with Dinesh d'Souza, a conservative, that class-based affirmative action would come closer to benefiting the truly needy (Wilson 1995, d'Souza 1994).

The most obvious problem with the redefined criteria for affirmative action that have been proposed so far is that they still do not—and, I will argue, cannot—go nearly far enough. In the late 1990s, being poor wins protection under affirmative action programs at certain institutions. This inclusion rectifies a major unfairness, but leaves many other sources of serious disadvantage untouched, including previous educational deficits, troubled and limiting environments, family dysfunction, and a wide range of developmental disabilities.

Roughly speaking, justice would require that each American be assigned a net Inequality of Opportunity, or Unearned Advantage, score reflecting all of his or her significant unearned competitive advantages or disadvantages—i.e., those resulting from something other than personal effort and sacrifice. The national Inequality of Opportunity score would be set at 0; i.e., zero net advantage or disadvantage compared to the average of all Americans. Maximum net-advantage and net-disadvantage scores might be set at +10 and –10. All citizens with a net-advantage score of (say) +1 or higher could then be required to enact an affirmative action program for all citizens scoring –1 or lower. The only neutral observers would be that small percentage of the populace at or very near the median. In effect, then, excluding these few exceptionally average citizens, the privileged half of the nation would carry out an affirmative action program for the underprivileged half.

Of course, the degree of protection, or compensatory aid, given or received by a particular person should be a function of his or her degree of net advantage or disadvantage. To attain the even playing field intended by affirmative action, a person just slightly below the Inequality of Opportunity median would need only a little affirmative-action relief, whereas someone scoring –9 would need massive help. Likewise, those just above the median would have only a slight obligation to help their fellows achieve equal opportunity, whereas those well above it would have a much heavier obligation. If this affirmative-action program were working well, few competitions would occur in which the competitors were markedly unequal in unearned advantages or disadvantages. Most significant differences in competitive assets would presumably be based on past personal dedication and effort. Justice, defined as substantially equal opportunity, would prevail.

The nation would also be exhausted and bankrupt! The technology, bureaucracy, and sheer energy required to carry out such a program would become the central focus of public life. Indeed, much of what we now consider private life would have to become public, in order for society to ascertain just how advantaged or disadvantaged each of us really is, and then to correct each of us upward or downward.

In a sense, Americans would be united by a shared national prohibition: "No unearned advantage or disadvantage in the marketplace of life." There would be a perhaps unintended consequence of this less arbitrary, more nearly complete system of affirmative action. The resulting distribution of winners and losers would be far less assailable by the new class of deserving losers. Having had equal opportunity, these losers could beg only mercy, not justice. Competitive justice would truly reign supreme. A natural aristocracy, in the original sense of the rule of the best, would be free to emerge, effortfully (Henry 1994).

Solution 2: Entitlement to Conditions of Maslowian Dignity

Some recent thinkers, notably William Julius Wilson (1994) and Theda Skocpol (1994), have grasped the tragic dilemma of our evil history as well as the contradictory quality of affirmative action's attempt to correct the evil consequences. They have proposed programs intended not so much to equalize opportunities—an elusive goal at best—but to secure absolute equality in one vital sense. They believe that a rich society has an obligation to provide every citizen with the minimum requisites for a dignified life.

The programs Wilson has advocated for over a decade would go a long way toward satisfying citizens' basic needs according to Maslow's (1943) hierarchy of human needs: survival, security, affection, and respect. "Full employment policies, job skills training, comprehensive health-care legislation, educational reforms in the public schools, child care legislation, and crime and drug abuse prevention programs—these are the race-neutral policies likely to begin making a difference for the poor, black and white" (Wilson 168). Despite Wilson's role as an advisor to President Clinton, Clinton has resisted pressure to reform affirmative action along with welfare.

Skocpol (1994) agrees with Wilson that the group preferences of affirmative action have played into the hands of conservative Republicans. For both moral and political reasons, she, like Wilson, favors replacing affirmative action with a set of universal social policies: "To help less privileged minorities through government programs, the first step is to establish a baseline of broad benefits and services that span classes and races (and that can be supplemented by targeted services for the elderly, children, and other vulnerable people)" (297).

In effect, this approach to helping the disadvantaged promotes the kind of political development James Davies (1986) recommended based on the universality and validity of Maslow's hierarchy of human needs. A more highly developed political system, according to Davies, is not one that maximizes economic or technological development, but one that creates the conditions under which all citizens have an opportunity to develop their higher-level needs for self-actualization.

At this point, a defender of affirmative action may well ask whether Wilson's and Skocpol's alternative of universal social policies would not permit racial and gender differences to persist, so that, even with citizens' basic needs fulfilled, white males would still have historically inherited, unfair advantages in the quest for self-actualization. This question brings us to a final, transformational alternative to affirmative action.

Solution 3: Fullness of Opportunity

I supported affirmative action for twenty years both as a political activist and a university administrator, but with increasing ambivalence. I would probably support Solution 1, a broadened affirmative action, but with continuing ambivalence. For, on the one hand, the addition of each new protected class would remove a source of injustice for that class but would automatically intensify the injustice faced by all remaining classes who are disadvantaged but still unprotected. Yet, on the other hand, comprehensively expanding the realm of protected classes would soon make affirmative action prohibitively costly for the nation as a whole. I support Solution 2 with no ambivalence whatsoever. Indeed, providing for all citizens' basic needs is a necessary precondition for Solution 3, which would help transform both the entropic culture and the oppressive institutions of United States society. Before examining Solution 3, let us pinpoint the single most invidious aspect of affirmative action as it has developed in the last thirty years: its promotion of division among actual and potential beneficiaries and thus its mostly unwitting alliance with the political economy of corporate capitalism. Said differently, while affirmative action tries to change the composition of society's winners and losers so as to make life less unjust, it does not challenge the system of winners and losers itself. In fact, affirmative action legitimizes and strengthens this system by claiming to cleanse it of injustice. John Rensenbrink (1992) argues that "the affirmative action mechanism has been used to alienate those from one another who could, and need to, help each other: African-Americans and Euro-Americans who have the insight and strength to be friends. By keeping them absorbed in the minutiae of affirmative action legislation and litigation, the powers-that-be have sought, often successfully, to undercut the intent and impact of affirmative action. They have stymied the overall efforts of creative spirits to join forces to fight for real alternatives" (81).

Indeed, by conferring group benefits on some and denying them to others, affirmative action has often pitted different ethnic groups against each other. Bell hooks (1995) notes that affirmative action has encouraged a kind of competitive victimization, in which different groups try to outdo one another "in the competition for favors and reparations from the white male power structure" (55). Ironically, she notes, this currying of favor with Whites seems to have encouraged anti-Black racism by women and non-Black people of color.

In a more general and unfortunate irony, recent surveys indicate that "members of minority groups are more likely than whites to hold negative stereotypes about other minority groups, including religious minorities" (*Washington Post*, March 3, 1994). Hooks (1995) believes that Native, Asian, and Hispanic Americans "consistently seek to distance themselves from blackness" because they are "jockeying for white approval and reward" (199). She warns: "Until racist anti-black sentiments are let go by other people of color, no transformation of white supremacy will take place" (201).

Many white females, even those who do not particularly identify with their own race, may understandably resent racial favoritism that works against them. Similarly, many Black and Hispanic males resent favoritism toward women with whom they are contending for positions or promotions. In the words of Viet Dinh (1994, 280), ". . . affirmative action can fan the flames of racial animosity. Each racial and ethnic group looks on the others as competitors rather than allies in the fight for a share of the American pie."

An increasing chorus of nonwhite activists and intellectuals have joined in arguing against what they see as affirmative action's racially demeaning implication that nonwhites are incapable of competing with Whites on their own merits (Carter 1991; Murray 1994; Steele 1990). Carter points out that in practice affirmative action has benefited the least disadvantaged members of protected classes more than it has the most disadvantaged members:

> What has happened in black America in the era of affirmative action is this: middle-class black people are better off and lower-class black people are worse off. . . . And at the elite educational institutions . . . the [affirmative action] programs are increasingly dominated by the children of the middle class. One need not argue that affirmative action is the cause of increasing income inequality in black America to understand that it is not a solution (71–2).

These African-American reactions to affirmative action, along with the increasing white and male backlash against it (Faludi 1991), suggest that affirmative action has been operating on the surface, not at the roots, of the problem. As Herman observes in chapter 4, the transformational paradigm asks and answers questions at a more fundamental level than the old paradigm. What is most fundamentally in need of change is the system of conquest itself, the system of gratifying ourselves by defeating others, the system of exploiting our own advantages to the detriment of our fellow human beings. Affirmative action has had the justifiable goal of redressing an unjust demography of winners and losers. But the goal of equal opportunity to "kick butt"—in Olympic skater Tonya Harding's memorable phrase—would be an unworthy one even if it were practical, which it is not.

Beyond Affirmative Action: Synergy and Community

A number of thinkers are beginning to point us in a new direction. Defending affirmative action at Berkeley, Chancellor Chang-Lin Tien (1994) argues that "[t]he synergy of women and ethnic minorities in traditional disciplines has breathed new vitality into the social sciences and humanities as well [as women's studies']" (241). I will argue that synergy is ultimately the key to transcending the entropic dilemmas of affirmative action.

Drew Days (1994), warns that we must overcome "an acceptance of civil rights as a zero-sum game." He notes that under affirmative action "the larger structural issues have been avoided" (277). Likewise, Lani Guinier (1994) stresses that a progressive politics needs to become "positive-sum, in which everyone wins something"

(186). She adds that "politics need not be forever seen as I win, you lose. . . ." (190). Her proposed system of "cumulative voting," which I proposed in less detail in 1980 (Cummings 1980, 55–6), successfully addresses the problem of differential intensities of preference that had befuddled Robert Dahl (1961). Intense minorities can thereby fight their oppression by bundling their votes on issues of special concern. What Guinier does not do, however, is to challenge the existing, socially produced distribution of preferences, many of which are racist, sexist, and generally entropic.

Bell hooks (1995) believes that racial and gender victimization and recrimination need to give way to creating an inclusive "culture where beloved community flourishes" (271). She asserts that "[i]n a beloved community solidarity and trust are grounded in profound commitment to a shared vision" (272). The synergistic transformation I propose would improve the chances of realizing hook's vision.

Are positive-sum games possible? Many people believe so, but few have developed credible strategies for moving an entire society in this synergistic direction. One of the clearest-headed critics of affirmative action's tendency to promote division among the disadvantaged is Michael Lerner (1996). He charges the Left with stressing institutional solutions while overlooking the "crucial focus on values" (90). And he gives examples of values that would be positive-sum, or synergistic: "the major focus of politics must be on creating a society committed to loving and caring" (90).

Lerner believes that the alternative to valuing "wealth and power above all" is to value "ethical and spiritual reality" (89). Most likely, if people could be made into saints, some religion or ideology would have done so by now. But as anthropologist Charles Erasmus (1977) has convincingly shown, large-scale attempts to "provision the common good" by moral exhortations alone—"Do unto others as you would have others do unto you" or "From each according to ability, to each according to need"—founder on the legitimate self-interests and market forces they attempt to ignore.

Authentic transformation depends upon realistic assumptions about human nature and human potential. I leave it to the reader to determine whether my own alternative to affirmative action, corporate capitalism, and Lasch's (1979) "culture of narcissism" is any more realistic than Lerner's.

We are not equal, and we will never be equal, in competitive assets. Competitive success as a goal is not about equality or inequality, fairness or unfairness; it is about winning and losing as the central focus of our lives. If equal opportunity is unattainable, and equal opportunity to "kick butt" unworthy, what can we do to redress past injustices without creating new ones? We can trade in the flawed goal of equal opportunity for the nobler one of fullness of opportunity.

The keynote of a society based on such a goal would be institutional socialization of values whose pursuit, while not necessarily altruistic, would be synergistic rather than entropic, positive-sum rather than zero-sum. Borrowing from physics' second law of thermodynamics, I define an entropic value as an inherently competitive one whose pursuit causes social conflict, friction, and collective loss of usable energy. Borrowing from biology, I define a synergistic value as one whose attainment by one person *increases* the likelihood of its attainment by others. Woolpert in chapter 11 refers to this as "the politics of transcendence." A key assumption is that with basic "dignity" needs guaranteed and with most citizens' value pursuits at least compatible and often reinforcing, far fewer people would be looking over their shoulders to see how well they were doing compared with others. Instead, they could be more concerned with how fully they were realizing their own unique potentials.

Without making heroically altruistic assumptions, let us examine briefly the difference between entropic and synergistic values. Entropic values like power, wealth, and status are characterized by the fact that one person's success in gaining them necessarily entails others' failure; there are no powerful people without powerless ones, no wealthy without poor, no high-status without low-status. (I am referring here to such values as ends; as means to an end, one's power, wealth or status may be used for synergistic, even altruistic purposes.)

Halpern in chapter 3 questions how fulfilling such values are even when achieved. A society primarily fostering such entropic values will be a society divided into winners and losers, a society divided against itself. Those who are losers in their own eyes and the eyes of others will experience and act out a wide variety of social pathologies, including crime, violence, child abuse, alcoholism, drug addiction, broken homes, psychological distress, and suicide. Communities will lack solidarity, and patriotism will be superficial and hypocritical.

Synergistic values like knowledge and wisdom, creativity and craftsmanship, simple pleasures like gardening and fishing, and friendship, love, or family are characterized by the fact that, on balance, one person's attainment of them makes it more likely that others will attain them too. As Knight says in chapter 4, "the whole gives meaning to the parts." The knowledge or wisdom you gain makes it possible for you to share it with me. My own enhanced creativity or craftsmanship may rub off on you. With the exception of the deeper, inherently altruistic forms of love and friendship, these values operate synergistically whether they are pursued primarily in self-interest or primarily in concern for others. Eisler's (1987) "partnership model," adapted from ancient Minoan Crete, is based on a matriarchal culture of synergistic values.

I do not deny the possibility of deformations of synergistic values by which my knowledge is used to preserve your ignorance (e.g., advertising), my creations are themselves destructive (e.g., weaponry), and so forth. But it is precisely conditions of social injustice that encourage such deformations—conditions endemic in corporate capitalism, or more generally what Halpern in chapter 3 calls "Act One."

Two points about this choice of values deserve special attention. First, people whose basic needs are fulfilled and who are pursuing synergistic values will be minimally concerned with whether their opportunities or achievements are exactly equal to the those of their neighbors. Interpersonal and intergroup comparisons will persist, but with less fervor, frenzy, arrogance, and envy. Friendlier forms of competition will typically breed enjoyment and excellence more than conquest and resentment.

Second, the mostly ominous centralization of business, government, and the media makes more possible a broad and rapid transformation of values. The joint implication of these two points is that transformationalists would do better to refocus their energies and resources—including those currently expended on affirmative action—on a values offensive directed especially at schools and mass media, but also at other major agents of socialization. Of course, the earliest and most immediate socializer remains the family, whose values are continually shaped by these larger, more centralized institutions. Nothing has disintegrated the family more dramatically than the ever-increasing pursuit of power, wealth, and status that is the essence of corporate capitalism and its offspring, the culture of narcissism and mass consumption.

We cannot ignore the bureaucratized institutions of business, government, media, education, and the "helping professions"; indeed, we must penetrate them physically and normatively. But neither can we rely on them exclusively. We must rebuild our families and our neighborhoods from the ground up and create new, decentralized "communities of competence" (Lasch 1979, 396).

Continued reliance on affirmative action implies a continuing dependence on the bureaucratic authorities who will bless its bene-

ficiaries with jobs, admissions, and other rewards—while alienating
these beneficiaries from most of their natural allies. By contrast: "In
order to break the existing pattern of dependence and put an end to
the erosion of competence, citizens will have to take the solution of
their problems into their own hands" (Lasch, 396). Or, in the words
of Randall Kennedy, "The essential element of this transformation is
the creation of a sentiment of community strong enough to enable
each group to entrust its fate to the good faith and decency of the
other . . ." (1994, 66).

Lasch's recommended "traditions of localism, self-help, and community action" (397) are now complemented by hundreds of thriving
intentional communities, worker- and consumer-owned cooperatives;
numerous experiments in co-housing, community gardening, and organic farming; and thousands of neighborhood-improvement associations, many of which are referred to in Woolpert's chapter 11.
Where such communities have empowered their residents to meet
their own needs and set their own agendas, they offer microcosmic
models whose features can inform and inspire larger and very different communities. Especially promising is the recent tendency of
racial and sexual "separatist" groups to reach out and form alliances
with other groups committed to cultural diversity and democratic
empowerment (Fellowship for Intentional Community 1995). Overlapping with these alliances have been many Green parties and
Green associations in Europe and North America, discussed by both
Graham and Woolpert in this volume. Moreover, as Becker shows in
chapter 12, electronic democracy also helps to reinvigorate citizen
participation in community governance.

Strong neighborhoods and face-to-face communities do permit
one feature of affirmative action to be realized, perhaps better than
do the affirmative-action programs themselves. Friendly neighbors
and coworkers know one another's needs and abilities, advantages
and disadvantages, far better than do distant bureaucrats. Just as
the "objective" researcher simply has different biases from those of
a participant-observer, as Zisk points out in chapter 9, the "impersonal" affirmative action administrator has different biases from
those of one's friends and neighbors. The informal, voluntary tradition in rural communities, small towns, and ethnic neighborhoods of
helping one another out may often fulfill the legitimate intent of affirmative action—leveling the playing field for those in need—better
than do official programs of group preferential treatment. Far from
creating divisions, such local self-help is part of the glue that bonds
these communities together, in part by creating "a public sphere in

which conversation and empowering struggle are possible," in Brettschneider's wording (chapter 7).

The synergistic vision does not rely on heroic quantities of pure altruism, but it does call for a more robust and widespread incidence of reciprocal altruism, which both historical and contemporary evidence suggests is the best basis for "provisioning the common good" (Erasmus 1979). While interpersonal comparisons and competitions would endure, socialization would not teach us that their outcome—superiority or inferiority, victory or defeat—is the key to happiness. The criterion for Solution 3's vision of the Good Life, rather, would be how well we do with what we have, assuming that all of us have available to us Solution 2's guaranteed means for a decent, dignified life. This change at the level of basic values promoted by social institutions would mean a transformation of our society from one of acquisitive individualists to one of self-actualizing compatriots.

15

Transformational Political Groups: The Political Psychology of the Green Political Movement[1]

STEPHEN WOOLPERT

Nothing is more difficult to handle, more doubtful of success, nor more dangerous to manage, than to put oneself at the head of introducing new orders.

—Niccolo Machiavelli, *The Prince*

Introduction

The global Green movement is the most significant organizational manifestation of transformational politics. It therefore provides a valuable opportunity to inquire into what Halpern in chapter 3 calls the "archetypal drama" of political action in the service of fundamental and comprehensive change. The focus of this chapter is on the interplay between the Greens' internal dynamics and their performance in the political arena.

Green parties and nonelectoral movements began to appear in the 1970s and 1980s, most successfully in Europe, but also in the United States and New Zealand (Kemp 1992; Rensenbrink 1992; Rudig 1995; Parkin 1989; Richardson and Rootes 1995; Zisk 1992). European Green parties achieved impressive successes in the late 1980s, but many have faced difficulties sustaining their support as environmental issues became less salient in the early 1990s. In the United States elections of 1994, Green parties competed in eighteen states, receiving more than one million votes and electing eight candidates to local offices; they nominated their first Presidential candidate, Ralph Nader, in 1996.

Despite the legal and institutional barriers blocking newcomers' entry into established party systems, Green parties are active in 75 countries, including many poor and developing nations of Africa and Latin America (Affigne 1995). These parties are affiliated with a myriad of transformationally oriented direct action and educational groups who eschew electoral politics but share the same political stance, embodied by the slogan "neither Left nor Right, but Out in Front."

The Green movement is not easy to define because it is young and still organizationally mutable. In chapter 5 Graham has explicated the holistic, ecocentric paradigm that distinguishes the Green's ideology from the Democratic Left. The four basic "pillars" of Green politics are: 1) ecology, denoting both environmentalism and a holistic approach to political processes; 2) social responsibility, which means the support of economic, legal, and political equality as well as the duty to contribute to the common good; 3) grassroots democracy, i.e., expanded opportunities for direct participation in public decisions; and 4) nonviolence, which entails opposition to both violent behavior and structural oppression.

The North American Greens in 1984 expanded this list to ten "Key Values" with the addition of community economics, respect for diversity, postpatriarchal values, decentralization, global responsibility, and sustainability. In addition, an overarching theme often identified in the literature on the Green movement (e.g., Spretnak 1986) is a spiritual emphasis on reducing ego-centeredness and increasing regard for the oneness of all being.

Brettschneider demonstrates in chapter 7 that transformational groups cannot properly be evaluated simply according to narrow political criteria, such as their longevity or size. Accordingly, the framework I use here, which is based on Carl Jung's concept of "the shadow," not only illuminates the internal dynamics of transformational groups but also indicates ways of improving their effectiveness in *transformational terms*. Jungian thought lends itself to an understanding of transformational politics because it recognizes the spiritual dimensions of human existence, the need to transcend opposing tendencies in order to achieve wholeness, and the importance of nonrational ways of knowing, such as intuition and imagination. In Part I of this volume, Herman, Halpern, and Knight each incorporate Jungian elements into their essays. Although Jung himself emphasized individual transformation as the *sine qua non* of political transformation, his thought also sheds light on the organizational dynamics of transformational groups.

My argument is that, first, members of all political groups tend to develop a collective ego-ideal or "persona," comprised of traits that are consistent with the core values of each group's political ideology. Second, members of political groups are prone to repress into the "shadow" those psychological qualities in themselves that are at variance with their collective persona. Third, denial and projection cause groups to perceive their political opponents as embodying those very qualities that they themselves have lost or disowned. Fourth, shadow material, if not integrated into consciousness, tends to be expressed in dangerous and self-defeating ways.

I begin with a brief overview of Jungian thought. I then infer the Greens' collective persona from their core political values. Using Jungian archetypes, I identify two major components of the Greens' collective shadow and discuss the negative political consequences of repression and projection within the Green subculture. Finally I suggest ways for transformational groups to integrate shadow material.

The Shadow in Jungian Psychology

Appreciation of Jung's concept of the shadow is impossible without an understanding of his idea of the collective unconscious, which he defines in Campbell (1971, 44–55), as:

> the deposit of all human experience, right back to its remotest beginnings. . . . The collective unconscious contains the whole spiritual heritage of mankind's [sic] evolution, born anew in the brain structure of every individual. . . . [It] is the source of the instinctual forces of the psyche and the forms or categories that regulate them, namely the archetypes.

Archetypes are inborn, universal, *a priori* modes of perception. They are not thoughts but the infrastructure of patterns within which thought occurs. They precede and structure ideas in the same way that instincts structure behavior. Archetypes enter into consciousness by means of symbols and mythological forms.

The "shadow" and the "persona" are archetypes so central to the human psyche that Jung treats them as separate subsystems. The shadow refers to the wild, primitive side of the psyche. The term connotes its roots in the dark recesses of our past. The quality of the shadow is daimonic and untamed. It also connotes invisibility; we repress this unpleasant psychic material because it stands in contrast to social norms and customs. From these approved elements each individual forms a social mask, or persona, which is presented outwardly, facing the light of public expectations, while the undesirable elements remain hidden. So the relationship between the persona and the shadow is compensatory: Whatever is overexpressed, underexpressed, or lacking in the former is complemented appropriately in the latter (Jung 1964).

Repression of shadow elements does not destroy them. Indeed, whenever the shadow is deprived of a conscious outlet, it is "transformed into something essentially baleful, destructive, and anarchical" (Odajnyk 1976, 59). The more intensely it is repressed, the greater its dynamic energy becomes.

As with all archetypes, the exact content of the shadow differs from one person to another. What is universal is the presence of the shadow itself, its dynamic tension with the persona, and its potential danger. Of crucial political importance, however, is that when an entire group represses the same attributes, its members have a collective layer to their shadow, and they will tend to deal with it in similar ways.

The common, albeit unhealthy, method of coping with repressed material is projection: the futile effort to banish it from oneself by externalizing it. Falsely attributing one's disowned urges, feelings, or ideas to others preserves one's persona, while at the same time directing the emotional energy associated with the shadow material away from the self. However, denial and projection also cause the shadow to grow larger and darker. In individuals it can lead to neurosis and psychosis. In political communities it can express itself in collective violence, corruption, fanaticism, authoritarian submission, and moral decay.

The Persona of the Green Political Culture

The first step in applying this framework to transformational politics is to draw from the core values of the Green movement a picture of their collective ego ideal. One central feature of Green politics is the absence of the will to power in its traditional sense.

Control of others is incompatible with Green values. They reject hierarchical, monolithic institutions and criticize the destructive effects of manipulative power relations. The Greens aim at transforming what Cummings in chapter 14 calls "entropic" politics into the win-win politics of a synergistic community in which influence is widely and equitably shared. Aggressive, "dominator" behavior runs counter to the Green's "partnership" ethos (Eisler 1987).

A second characteristic of the Greens' ego-ideal is the strong need for rectitude. This follows from their emphasis on political emancipation and spiritual growth. Fidelity to Green political values requires openness and honesty, following the political "high road." Their search for collective self-actualization is incompatible with dirty tricks, double-dealing, and hardball politics-as-usual.

A third element of the Greens' ego-ideal is the high priority given to affiliation. This reflects their egalitarian ethos and respect for diversity. Greens seek to transcend the divisive politics of intolerance and us-against-them, favoring a synthesis of policies from various points along the traditional ideological spectrum. Green politics is inclusive of ethnic, cultural, religious, racial, and gender differences. Directive leadership is discouraged in favor of collaborative, consensus-based decision making.

Finally, the Greens' commitment to personal empowerment and community cohesion outweighs their desire for expediency in achieving political objectives. Proper political means are not to be subordinated to successful goal-attainment. Their view is that ends cannot justify means, because only a participatory, egalitarian political process can determine what political goals should in fact be achieved.

The motivational profile of the Green ego ideal, then, in comparison with that of other political groups, is above average in the need for rectitude and affiliation, but below average in the need for power and achievement. The persona that one would expect from this combination of motives and values is sincere, kind, gentle, cooperative, open-minded, and unselfish. The extent to which members of the Green movement conform to this collective persona is an empirical question. It is likely, however, that active members would feel greater pressure to conform than inactive members, and that the deep ecologists (known as "fundis") would exhibit such traits more strongly than the less spiritually oriented Left Greens (known as "realos"). Let us now consider what clues this persona provides about the content of the Greens' collective shadow.

The Shadow of the Green Movement

In exploring the shadow we enter an obscure world of myths and symbols. Virgil guided Dante on his journey into the underworld of the Inferno; who is better qualified to guide us in appreciating the Greens' shadow than the master of the dark side of politics, Niccolo Machiavelli? Machiavelli's prince, in stark contrast to the Green ego-ideal, ranks high on both power and achievement motivation and correspondingly low on the need for rectitude and affiliation. And of equal importance, his metaphorical prose is well-suited to the analysis of archetypal political material.

Of central relevance here is his advice (Machiavelli 1952, 92) "to know well how to act as a beast," i.e., to appreciate the baser side of politics. Specifically, he argues that it is necessary to "imitate the fox and the lion." The fox, Machiavelli explains, is good at avoiding traps; the lion knows how to protect himself against wolves. Each of these archetypal symbols epitomizes political attributes which have been split off from the Green persona.

The fox represents the trickster archetype (Jung 1959). The trickster is a Dionysian figure, elusive and protean. According to Hynes (1993, 34–42), the mythic trickster is: 1) ambiguous, anomalous, and polyvalent; 2) a consummate liar, deceiver, and cheater; 3) a shape-shifter, the "master of metamorphosis"; 4) an inverter of situations, values, and social orders; 5) a messenger from the gods and a mediator between the sacred and the profane; and 6) a blasphemer who mocks taboos and forms creative innovations, thereby focusing attention, often humorously, on the nature of conventional ideals.

The lion symbolizes the archetype of the hero. The lion is Apollonian: strong, proud, and stout-hearted. Mythologically the lion is associated with the image of the inspirational, invincible leader who commands the center of both human and divine attention. (Campbell 1973). Heroes overcome obstacles through courage, charisma, skill, and perseverance. Tollefson (1993) finds four traits shared by heroes around the world: Heroes do something worth talking about, they serve powers or principles larger than themselves, they live lives worthy of imitation, and they are catalysts for change.

Neither of these archetypes is compatible with the Greens' persona. Their opposition to dominance and hierarchy relegates the heroic forcefulness of the lion into the darkness. The fox's shrewdness and deception are incongruent with their spiritual values and their rejection of expediency.

The political consequences are severe. First, when archetypes enter the shadow they become distorted, destructive forces. The hero becomes a symbol of savage ferocity and violent oppression; followers fear their leader's power. The trickster becomes emblematic of fraud and treachery. Mistrust and intrigue permeate the political community. Second, shadow archetypes are projected onto outgroups: *they* are coercive and domineering, *they* are duplicitous and sneaky, we are not. Third, shadow archetypes are underexpressed in the collective persona. Thus, when the political energy of the lion is repressed, this deficiency is outwardly expressed by the archetype of the innocent lamb: docile, timid, and weak. Similarly, if a group persona has relegated the fox to the shadow, it will lack adroitness, shrewdness, and acumen. In its place is the archetype of the inept, ingenuous fool.

For groups such the Greens denial of these archetypes is especially costly, because both the hero and the trickster are cultural transformers. Heroes serve as pathfinders who show the way to new knowledge and new destinations. Their courageous self-sacrifice and moral strength galvanize and inspire group commitment in the face of daunting challenges. Tricksters empower by exciting the imagination and pointing out new possibilities. By outwitting more powerful adversaries, tricksters represent hope for the oppressed. The trickster's role as an antidote for the pomposity and moralism which often characterize visionary movements is exemplified by Vaclav Havel's recognition of the importance of humor as a safeguard against self-inflation, as noted by Gilbert in chapter 13.

Certain empirically testable propositions about the Greens' political dynamics follow from this analysis:

1) Because of their repression of the hero, the Greens should be prone to mistrust powerful leadership. Difficult political conflicts are apt to be avoided rather than confronted.

2) Denial of the trickster is likely to cause the Greens to encounter unusual difficulty with issues of trust and tactics. This should show up in the form of intrigue and mutual suspicion, as well as confusion over organizational and strategic choices.

3) If Greens do in fact project these archetypes onto outgroups and/or opponents within their own movement, they should express particular anger toward those perceived as exhibiting top-down leadership or overbearing control, and towards those perceived to be engaging in deceptive, fraudulent political conduct.

I have not been an active participant in the Green movement; however, the literature on the Greens by those closest to it, particularly Capra and Spretnak (1984), Rensenbrink (1992), Satin (1990) and Slaton (1992), support each of these hypotheses. The struggle over leadership and power issues in the Green movement is frequently mentioned. Greens mistrust expertise, hierarchy, and worldly success (Satin 1990, 2). Aggressive leadership styles are criticized as oppressively masculine. Greens are prone to resent heroic conduct. Capra and Spretnak (1984, 135) observe:

> People who are too charismatic, too effective, too noticeable, too creative in their theories, or too sought after by the media are often attacked and to an extent devoured by the Greens.

Rensenbrink (1992, 198) also refers to Greens as "fiercely ready to pounce on the actions and words of those who take initiative." Slaton (1992, 110) cites the following analysis by a Green activist: "There are leaders around but they leave regularly because of [the Greens'] penchant for stoning them." Their antipathy towards heroic leadership is further reflected in their practice of frequent rotation of official positions. Concentration of power is avoided, but at the price of lost seniority, experience, and hence influence.

The avoidance of conflict is also a common problem among Greens. Slaton alludes to their "laid-back' 1960s attitudes. Rensenbrink (1992, 113–115) describes the side effects of the Greens' "longing for a new perfect harmony":

> Differences are muted when they shouldn't be, conflict is assumed to have been transcended when it hasn't been, and the member finds it necessary to conform, lapse into passivity, or get out.

Elected Green officials in Germany have complained that the desire for congeniality discourages grassroots members from listening to their problems and conflicts. One German Green noted that "there are a lot of soft people in the Greens without much juice in them" (Capra and Spretnak 1984, 150).

Regarding tactical issues, Greens have been vexed by the tension between their transformational principles and the search for effective methods of political engagement. For example, initiatives that faithfully demonstrate their opposition to violence and injustice, such as direct action tactics, may produce no tangible political results. On the other hand, unbridled expediency, even in the pursuit of worthwhile goals, runs counter to the Greens' view that means are inseparable from ends.

This tension has divided Greens in both Europe and the United States over whether to participate as a political party in the established power system. Coalitions with political groups whose tactics may be at variance with intrinsic Green values have raised similar problems. The left "realos" devote much more time and energy to discussing strategy and tactics than do the more visionary/holistic "fundis" (Capra and Spretnak 1984). Rensenbrink describes the Greens' reluctance to "face that part of the political which gives spiritually minded people the most trouble: strategy" (1992, 238–244; see also Affigne 1995).

There is also evidence of internal mistrust and intrigue (Capra and Spretnak 1984; Rensenbrink 1992; Slaton 1992). Cleavages exist between local and national elements, activists and intellectuals, "fundis" and "realos," men and women members. Slaton describes the bickering among the United States Greens as incessant, malicious, and brutal.

The Greens' attitude towards outgroups is a revealing anomaly. Their commitment to recognizing interdependence and celebrating diversity should discourage hostility towards perceived enemies. Nonetheless, there are political groups whom Greens staunchly oppose: polluters, arms manufacturers and dealers, bigots, oppressive oligarchies, multinational corporations, and monolithic bureaucracies. Not surprisingly, Greens fault such groups for the power-seeking and duplicity they deny in themselves. Moreover, the factions within the movement have self-destructively demonized one another. Manifestations of the lion or the fox by their opponents arouse anger, even hatred, among Greens (Rensenbrink 1992).

Shadow-Work: Recovering the Lion and the Fox

In light of the many failures of previous nonviolent, grassroots democratic movements, the difficulties posed by the Greens' collective shadow should not be overlooked. The Jekyll-and-Hyde disjunction between their values and their group dynamics, plus their failure to learn from past mistakes, indicate that the transformation of their own group dynamics is inextricably connected to the transformation of politics writ large. Just as Vaclav Havel brought his personal "dark moods" to light (see chapter 14), what follows are ways of integrating shadow material at the group level.

The contemporary dream appreciation movement exemplifies a classic Jungian approach to domesticating the shadow. In dream groups members read their dreams aloud and discuss their significance (Hillman 1990; von Franz 1991; Sanford 1978). For example, Jeremy Taylor (1983; 1992) has led hundreds of community-based dream groups, working with Blacks and Whites, Palestinians and Israelis, and warring prison gangs, among others. By bringing shadow material to consciousness in subtle, nonideological ways, the shared exploration of dreams overcomes the dynamics of group denial and projection, thereby reducing animosity. Taylor claims that dreamwork is most fruitful in groups with a commitment to social action.

A second approach is the use of rituals, ceremonies, and body movement exercises. Like dream work, and the "Shamanic disciplines" referred to by Herman in chapter 3, such collective activities are an avenue to archetypal energy, bypassing the rational mind. They are a familiar component of many groups in the feminist movement and the mythopoetic branch of the men's movement (Cahill and Halpern, 1990; Harding, 1992; Stein, 1990). Whether the focus is on drumming and chanting, poetry and visual arts, bioenergetics or breathwork, these processes are powerful tools for assimilating repressed primitive material and freeing up blocked group energy.

Eisler and Loye (1990) employ another kind of group exercise as a means of creating "partnership rather than "dominator" practices. In this activity participants use storytelling and role-playing to portray the hero/heroine archetype, first in the context of a patriarchal dominator society and then in the context of a postpatriarchal partnership society. The second part of the exercise imbues the courage and boldness of the lion archetype with contents appropriate to the transformed culture envisioned by the Greens, such as the adventurous heroine or the nurturing hero. Chinen (1996) also provides stories depicting the heroic feminine.

Political applications of the trickster's shrewdness are described by Fisher and Ury (1981, 111–12). They distinguish "positional bargaining," which typifies conventional power politics, from "negotiation on the merits," a method congruent with collaborative decision making. The negotiating tactics associated with this approach allow the fox's elusiveness and cleverness to be expressed. For example, they suggest a trickster technique called "negotiation Jujitsu" which artfully sidesteps the other's attack and deflects it against the problem. That is, don't attack the other's position, look behind it; don't defend your ideas, invite criticism and advice; recast an attack on you as an attack on the problem; ask questions and pause.

Other empowering approaches to transforming conflicts are reviewed in Schwerin (1995). All the preceding activities help to develop what Herman in chapter 2 and Graham in chapter 5 call "wisdom"—the intuitive insight that Gilbert argues in chapter 13 is a key to Vaclav Havel's success as a transformational leader. Unquestionably, much remains to be learned about shadow work. These approaches are meant only to be suggestive of ways in which transformational groups can foster familiarity with their shadow. It bears repeating that the danger lies not in the shadow material itself but in a one-sided consciousness that refuses to own its dark side.

Conclusion

The future of the Green movement hinges on a number of interlocking factors, of which psychological dynamics are only one subset. However, it is possible to envision three scenarios, each the product of a different response to the tension between the Green's ego-ideal and their collective unconscious.

1) The first and historically most common is convergence. Here, in order to achieve their political goals, Greens adopt the tactics of the dominant political culture. They become more and more like the groups they oppose. In time, the Greens are merely one more voice in the not-so-heavenly chorus of interest group pluralism, retaining some of their distinctive range and timbre but losing their "outsider" stance. Cooptation and goal displacement occur as the Greens gain mainstream respectability. Their persona requires less repression of Machiavellian impulses, and their shadow blends gradually into that of the larger political culture.

2) The converse scenario is that of polarization, in which Greens maintain fealty to their ego ideal and avoid political contamination. But the price is political irrelevance. While Greens are narcissistically preoccupied with their chronic leadership and strategy issues, global environmental destruction and oligarchic politics continue unabated. Unable to be effective in practical politics, they leave others to make the critical decisions, attributing all bad deeds to their opponents and only good ones to themselves. This is the outcome one would anticipate simply by extrapolating from the dynamics of the Green movement.

3) A third possibility exists which transcends the dangers of the first two. It presupposes successful assimilation of the lion and fox archetypes into the Green persona. These shadow elements are thereby robbed of their destructive force, allowing their positive qualities to be incorporated into the Green's political repertoire. In

this scenario, "Green warriors" (Rensenbrink 1992, 226–31) empower their companions, boldly diffusing responsibility throughout the organization. A diverse array of heroines and heroes derive their authority from flexible, collaborative relationships, and political acumen. Conflict is expected, but because it is not loaded with repressed shadow energy, it is neither vindictive nor chronic.

"Wise as serpents, gentle as doves," Greens deftly maneuver through the pitfalls of power politics, upending conventional practices, outwitting stronger opponents, and all the while transforming the rules of the game. Their trickster energy is appropriately targeted to deflate grandiosity—their own as much as their adversaries'. Occasional breaches of shared values bring the underside of their dominant norms to the surface. Far from losing ethical sensitivity, Greens see constructive irreverence as a remedy for the maladies of self-righteousness and perfectionism.

Affigne's (1995) account of recent meetings between United States Greens and other third parties in order to bridge differences, foster dialogue, and encourage interparty cooperation provides evidence of possible movement in this direction. Further short-run steps include establishing links with groups proficient in the various techniques previously discussed. To my knowledge, however, no Green organizations are presently following this path.

If commitment to authentic democratic participation continues to spread, and if ecological problems persist, political support for Green parties is potentially substantial. But "wolves" and "traps" are as much a part of the political terrain today as they were in Machiavelli's Florence; his admonition to learn about the political underworld must still be heeded. Consequently, Jung's understanding of the collective unconscious sheds much-needed light on crucial problems facing transformational political groups. In order for their political vision to be realized, they must come face to face with the undomesticated forces hidden deep in their collective shadow; they must learn to transform politics from the inside out. Innovative efforts to transform group consciousness therefore play a critical role in the transformation of politics.

Note

1. I am grateful to Betty Zisk and John Rensenbrink for their comments on an earlier draft of this paper.

Bibliography

Abalos, David T. 1992. Rediscovering the Sacred Among Latinos: A Critique from the Perspective of a Theory of Transformation. *The Latino Studies Journal* 3: 1–25.

———. 1993. *The Latino Family and the Politics of Transformation*. New York: Praeger.

———. 1994. Teaching and Practicing Multicultural and Gender Fair Education from the Perspective of Transformational Politics. Presented at the Annual Meeting of the American Political Science Association. New York.

———. 1996. *Strategies of Transformation: Toward a Multicultural Society*. Westport, CT: Praeger.

Aberbach, Joel D., and Bert A. Rockman. 1978. Bureaucrats and Clientele Groups: A View from Capitol Hill. *American Journal of Political Science*. 22:818–32.

Abram, David. 1990. "The Perceptual Implications of Gaia." In *Darma Gaia*, ed. Alan Hunt Badiner. Berkeley, CA: Parallax Press.

Abrami, Philip C., et al. 1993. *Using Cooperative Learning*. Dubuque, IA: Brown & Benchmark.

Abramson, Jeffrey, Christopher Arterton, and Gary Orren. 1988. *The Electronic Commonwealth*. New York: Basic Books.

Adams, Frank, and Gary Hausen. 1992. *Putting Democracy to Work*. San Francisco: Berrett-Koehler.

Adams, W. M. 1992. *Green Development: Environment and Sustainability in the Third World*. London: Routledge.

Adler, Patricia A., and Peter Adler. 1987. *Membership Roles in Field Research*. Newbury Park, CA: Sage.

Affigne, Anthony DeSales. 1995. "Transforming the American Political Landscape." Paper Presented at the Annual Meeting of the American Political Science Association. Chicago, IL.

Albo, Gregory, David Langille, and Leo Panitch, eds. 1993. *A Different Kind of State? Popular Power and Democratic Administration*. Toronto: Oxford University Press.

Alcoholics Anonymous World Services. 1953. *Twelve Steps and Twelve Traditions*. New York: The A. A. Grapevine.

Almond, Gabriel. 1988. Separate tables: Schools and Sects in Political Science. *PS: Political Science and Politics*: Fall.

———. 1990. The Nature of Contemporary Political Science: A Roundtable Discussion. *PS: Political Science and Politics*: Fall.

Anderson, Walter Truett. 1996. *Evolution Isn't What It Used to Be: The Augmented Animal and the Whole Wired World*. New York: W. H. Freeman.

Argyris, Chris, and D. Shon. 1991. Participatory Action Research and Action Science Compared: A Commentary. In *Participatory Action Research*, ed. W. F. White. Newbury Park, CA: Sage.

Armstrong, Susan, and Botzler, Richard, eds. 1993. *Environmental Ethics: Divergence and Convergence*. New York: McGraw Hill.

Aronowitz, Stanley, and William DiFazio. 1994. *The Jobless Future: Sci-Tech and the Dogma of Work*. Minneapolis: University of Minnesota Press.

Arterton, E. Christopher. 1987. *Teledemocracy*. Newbury Park, CA: Sage.

Astin, Alexander. 1987. Competition or Cooperation. *Change*. (September/October):12–19.

Bachrach, Peter, and Aryeh Botwinick. 1992. *Power and Empowerment*. Philadelphia: Temple University Press.

Bacon, Francis. 1960. *The New Organon*. New York: Macmillan.

Bahro, R. 1984. *From Red to Green*. London: Verso/New Left Books.

Balka, Christie, and Andy Rose. 1989. *Twice Blessed: On Being Lesbian, Gay, and Jewish*. Boston: Beacon Press.

Bandura, Albert. 1986. *Social Foundations of Thought and Action*. Englewood Cliffs, NJ: Prentice-Hall.

Barber, Benjamin. 1984. *Strong Democracy: Participatory Politics for a New Age*. Berkeley, CA: University of California Press.

———. 1992a. *An Aristocracy of Everyone*. New York: Ballentine Books.

———. 1992b. Going to the Community. *The Civic Arts Review* 5(4):10–12.

————, and Richard Battistoni. 1993. A Season of Service: Introducing Service Learning into the Liberal Arts Curriculum. *PS: Political Science & Politics* (June):235–40, 262.

Barrentine, Pat, ed. 1994. *When the Canary Stops Singing: Women's Perspectives on Transforming Business.* San Francisco: Berret-Koehler.

Bay, Christian. 1981. *Strategies of Political Emancipation.* Notre Dame: University of Notre Dame Press.

Beare, Hedley, and Richard Slaughter. 1993. *Education for the Twenty-First Century.* London: Routledge.

Beck, Evelyn Torton, ed. 1982. *Nice Jewish Girls: A Lesbian Anthology.* Freedom, CA: Crossing Press.

Becker, Theodore. 1991. *Quantum Politics: Applying Quantum Theory to Political Phenomena.* Westport, CT: Praeger.

————. 1997. Televote: Interactive, Participatory Polling. In *Teaching Democracy by Being Democratic*, eds. Theodore Becker and Richard Couto. Westport, CT: Praeger.

————, and Richard Couto, ed. 1997. *Teaching Democracy by Being Democratic.* Westport, CT: Praeger.

————, and Richard Scarce. 1986. Teledemocracy Emergent. In *Progress in Communication Sciences* Vol. VIII. eds. Brenda Dervin and Melvin J. Voigt, Norwood, NJ: Ablex Publishing.

————, and Christa Slaton. 1981. Hawaii Televote: Measuring Public Opinion on Complex Policy Issues. *Political Science* (NZ) 33:52–83.

————. 1985. *Hawaii Health Decisions 1985: A Report to the State of Hawaii Department of Health.* Honolulu, HI.

Beer, Stafford. 1995. Managing Modern Complexity. In *Public Administration and Public Affairs*, ed. Nicholas Henry. Englewood Cliffs, NJ: Prentice-Hall.

Belenky, Mary F., Blythe M. Clinchy, Nancy R. Goldberger, and Jill M. Tarule. 1986. *Women's Ways of Knowing: The Development of Self, Voice, and Mind.* New York: Basic Books.

Bellah, Robert, et al. 1985. *Habits of the Heart.* New York: Harper and Row.

————, et al. 1991. *The Good Society.* New York: Alfred Knopf.

Benello, C. George. 1992. *From the Ground Up: Essays on Grassroots and Workplace Democracy.* Boston: South End.

Benson, Herbert, and Eileen Stuart. 1992. *The Wellness Book.* New York: Fireside.

Berman, Morris. 1984. *The Reenchantment of the World*. New York: Bantam.

Berry, James. 1993. Religion's Unacknowledged Obligation to the Universe. *C.F.R.S.L. Newsletter* No. 15512.

Berry, Jeffrey M. 1977. *Lobbying for the People*. Princeton, NJ: Princeton University Press.

———. 1981. Beyond Citizen Participation: Effective Advocacy before Administrative Agencies. *Journal of Applied Behavioral Sciences* 17:463–77.

———, Kent Portney, and Ken Thomson. 1993. *The Rebirth of Urban Democracy*. Washington: Brookings.

Berry, Thomas. 1989. *The Dream of the Earth*. San Francisco: Sierra Club.

Berry, Wendell. 1981. *The Gift of Good Land*. Berkeley, CA: North Point.

———. 1992. *Sex, Economy, Freedom, and Community*. New York: Pantheon.

Beth, Richard S. 1995. How Transformationalists Think About Transformation: Themes and Implications. Presented at the Annual Meeting of the American Political Science Association. Chicago, IL.

Bezold, Clement. 1978. *Anticipatory Democracy: People in the Politics of the Future*. New York: Random House.

———, Rick Carlson, and Jonathan Peck. 1986. *The Future of Work and Health*. Dover, MA: Auburn House.

Blake, Robert, and Mouton, Jan. 1964. *The Managerial Grid*. Houston: Gulf Publishing Company.

Bleier, Ruth, ed. 1988. *Feminist Approaches to Science*. New York: Pergamon.

Block, Peter. 1993. *Stewardship: Choosing Service Over Self-Interest*. San Francisco: Berrett-Koehler.

Bond, Doug. 1993. Transforming Struggle in Comparative Perspective. Presented at the Annual Meeting of the American Political Science Association. Washington, DC.

Bookchin, Murray. 1986. *The Modern Crisis*. Philadelphia: New Society Publishers.

———. 1990. *The Philosophy of Social Ecology*. Montreal: Black Rose Books.

Bortoft, Henri. 1986. *Goethe's Scientific Consciousness*. Kent, England: The Institute for Cultural Research.

Boyce, Harry. 1990. *Commonwealth: A Return to Citizen Politics*. New York: Free Press.

Boyer, Ernest. 1987. *College: The Undergraduate Experience in America*. New York: Harper and Row.

Boyte, Harry C. 1980. *The Backyard Revolution: Understanding the New Citizen Movement*. Philadelphia: Temple University Press.

————, and Frank Riessman. 1986. *The New Populism: The Politics of Empowerment*. Philadelphia: Temple University Press.

Brand, Stewart, ed. 1981. *The Whole Earth Catalogue*. New York: Random House.

Breggin, Peter. 1992. *Beyond Conflict*. New York: St. Martin's Press.

Brettschneider, Marla. 1993. Using Feminist Methodology in the Study of Political Groups. Paper presented at the Midwest Women's Studies Association Regional Conference. Vermillion, SD.

————. 1996. *Cornerstones of Peace: Jewish Identity Politics and Democratic Theory*. New Brunswick, NJ: Rutgers University Press.

Briggs, John. 1992. *Fractals*. New York: Simon and Schuster.

————, and F. David Peat. 1989. *Turbulent Mirror*. New York: Harper and Row.

Brown, J. F. 1991. *Surge to Freedom*. Durham, NC: Duke University Press.

Brown, Lester. 1990. Picturing a Sustainable Society. *The Elmwood Newsletter* 6(1):1,4,10.

Brown, W. P. 1985. Variations in the Behavior and Style of State Lobbyists and Interest Groups. *Journal of Politics* 47:450–68.

Bruffee, Kenneth. 1993. *Collaborative Learning: Higher Education, Interdependence, and the Authority of Knowledge*. Baltimore: Johns Hopkins University Press.

Bryan, Frank, and John McClaughry. 1991. From Vermont, a radical blueprint to reinvigorate democracy. *Utne Reader*: (Jan/Feb).

Bryson, John, and Barbara Crosby. 1992. *Leadership for the Common Good*. San Francisco: Jossey-Bass.

Brzezinski, Zbigniew. 1989. *The Grand Failure*. New York: Collier Books.

Bullurd, Robert D., and Beverly H. Wright. 1992. The Quest for Environmental Equity: Mobilizing the African-American Community for Social Change. In *American Environmentalism: 1970–1990*, eds. Riley E. Dunlap and Angela Mertig. Washington, DC: Taylor and Francis.

Bunyard, Peter and Edward Goldsmith. 1988. *Gaia: the Thesis, the Mechanisms, and the Implications*. Camelford, Cornwall, U.K.: Wadebridge Ecological Centre.

Burns, James MacGregor. 1978. *Leadership*. New York: Harper and Row.

———, and Stuart Burns. 1991. *A People's Charter: The Pursuit of Rights in America*. New York: Alfred Knopf.

Burton, John, and Frank Dukes, eds. 1990. *Conflict: Practices in Management, Settlement, and Resolution*. New York: St. Martin's Press.

Burtt, Edwin A. (1954). *The Metaphysical Foundations of Physical Modern Science*. New York: Doubleday Anchor.

Butterfield, Herbert (1957). *The Origins of Modern Science 1300–1800*. New York: The Free Press.

Cable, Sherry, and Charles Cable. 1995. *Environmental Problems: Grassroots Solutions*. New York: St. Martin's Press.

Cahill, Sedonia, and Joshua Halpern. 1990. *The Ceremonial Circle*. San Francisco: HarperCollins.

Caldecott, Leonie, and Stephanie Leland, eds. 1983. *Reclaim the Earth*. London: Women's Press.

Campbell, Joseph. 1973. *The Hero with a Thousand Faces*. Princeton, NJ: Princeton University Press.

———, ed. 1971. *The Portable Jung*. New York: Penguin.

Campbell, Vincent. 1975. *Televote: A New Civic Communications System*. Palo Alto, CA: Stanford Research Institute.

Cancian, Francesca M., and James W. Gibson. 1990. *Making War Making Peace*. Belmont, CA: Wadsworth.

Capra, Fritjof. 1982. *The Turning Point: Science, Society, and the Rising Culture*. New York: Simon and Schuster.

———. 1991. *The Tao of Physics*. Boston: Shambhala Publications.

———. 1992–1993. Five Criteria of Systems Thinking. *The Elmwood Quarterly* 8(4):9–10.

———, and Charlene Spretnak. 1984. *Green Politics*. New York: Dutton.

Caraway, Nancie. 1996. The Riddle of Consciousness: Racism and Identity in Feminist Theory. In *Women in Politics: Outsiders or Insiders*, ed. Lois Lovelace Duke. Englewood Cliffs, NJ: Prentice-Hall.

Carter, Stephen. 1991. *Reflections of an Affirmative Action Baby*. New York: Basic Books.

Caspary, William R. 1995. John Dewey as a Comprehensive Transformational Theorist. Presented at the Annual Meeting of the American Political Science Association. Chicago, IL.

———. 1997. Students in Charge. In *Teaching Democracy by Being Democratic*, ed. Theodore Becker and Richard Couto. Westport, CT: Praeger.

Chase, Steve. 1995. Can Capitalism Be Reformed: Notes on Creating a Green Economy. *The Trumpeter*. 12(1):3–10.

Chavez, Linda. 1994. Just Say Latino. In *Debating Affirmative Action*, ed. Nicolaus Mills. New York: Bantam.

Chinen, Allen. 1991. Men's Mid-life Initiation into the Deep Masculine. In *To Be a Man: In Search of the Deep Masculine*, ed. Keith Thompson. Los Angeles: Jeremy Tarcher.

———. 1996. *Waking the World: Classic Tales of Women and the Heroic Feminine*. Los Angeles: Tarcher.

Chrislip, David, and Carl Larson. 1994. *Collaborative Leadership*. San Francisco: Jossey-Bass.

Cigler, Allan J., and Burdett A. Loomis. 1983 and 1986 editions. *Interest Group Politics*. Washington, DC: Congressional Quarterly.

Clark, Mary. 1989. *Ariadne's Thread: In Search of a Greener Future*. New York: St. Martin's Press.

Clark, P. B., and J. Q. Wilson. 1961. Incentive Systems: A Theory of Organizations. *Administrative Science Quarterly* 6 (June):129–66.

Cobb, Clifford, Ted Halstead, and Jonathan Rowe. 1995. *The Genuine Progress Indicator: Summary of Data and Methodology*. San Francisco: Redefining Progress.

Cohen, Carl. 1995. *Naked Racial Preference: The Case Against Affirmative Action*. Lanham, MD: Madison Books.

Coleman, Daniel. 1994. *Ecopolitics: Building a Green Society*. New Brunswick, NJ: Rutgers University Press.

Conley, Verena A. 1997. *Ecopolitics: The Environment in Post Structuralist Thought*. London: Routledge.

Cooper, J. L., P. Robinson, and M. McKinney. 1994. Cooperative Learning in the Classroom. In *Changing College Classrooms: New Teaching and Learning Strategies for An Increasingly Complex World*, ed. D. F. Halpern. San Francisco: Jossey-Bass.

Costanza, Robert, ed. 1991. *Ecological Economics: The Science and Management of Sustainability*. New York: Columbia University Press.

Counts, Alex. 1996. *Give Us Credit*. New York: Random House.

Couto, Richard A. 1993a. Learning in Service as a Context for Learning. In *Rethinking Tradition: Integrating Service with Academic Study on College Campuses*, ed. Tamar Y. Kupiec. Providence, RI: Campus Compact.

————. 1993b. The Transformation of "Transforming Leadership": Reclaiming a Lost Theoretical Term. Presented at the Annual Meeting of the American Political Science Association. Washington, DC.

————. 1997. Service Learning: Integrating Community Issues and the Curriculum. In *Teaching Democracy by Being Democratic*, eds. Theodore Becker and Richard Couto. Westport, CT: Praeger.

Crenson, Matthew A. 1978. Social Networks and Political Processes in Urban Neighborhoods. *American Journal of Political Science* 22:578–94.

Criden, Yosef, and Saadia Gelb. 1976. *The Kibbutz Experience: Dialogue in Kfar Blum*. New York: Schocken.

Crozier, Michael, Samuel Huntington, and Joji Watanuki. 1975. *The Crisis of Democracy*. New York: New York University Press.

Cummings, Michael S. 1980. Democratic Procedure and Community in Utopia. *Alternative Futures: The Journal of Utopian Studies*, 3(4):35–57.

Cummings, Michael S. 1995. Political Correctness and Political Transformation. Presented at the Annual Meeting of the American Political Science Association. Chicago, IL.

Cuseo, J. Winter 1992. Collaborative and Cooperative Learning in Higher Education: A Proposed Taxonomy. *Cooperative Learning and College Teaching* 2(2):2–5.

Dahl, Robert. 1961. *Who Governs?*. New Haven, CT: Yale University Press.

Daly, Herman, John Cobb, and Clifford Cobb. 1994. *For the Common Good: Redirecting the Economy toward Community, the Environment, and a Sustainable Future*. Boston: Beacon.

————. 1996. *Beyond Growth: The Economics of Sustainable Development*. Boston: Beacon.

Daly, Mary. 1997. *Gyn/ecology: The Metaethics of Radical Feminism*. Boston: Beacon.

Dator, James A. 1984. Quantum Theory and Political Design. Paper presented at the G. Dutweiller Institute.

Davidson, N. 1994. Cooperative and Collaborative Learning: An Integrative Perspective. In *Creativity and Collaborative Learning: A Practical*

Guide to Empowering Students and Teachers, ed. J. S. Thousand, R. A. Villa and A. I. Nevin. Baltimore: Brookes.

Davies, James C. 1986. Roots of Political Behavior. In *Political Psychology: Contemporary Problems and Issues*, ed. Margaret Hermann. San Francisco: Jossey-Bass.

Days III, Drew. 1994. Civil Rights at the Crossroads. In *Debating Affirmative Action*, ed. Nicolaus Mills. New York: Bantam.

de Chardin, Teilhard. 1975. *The Phenomenon of Man*. New York: Harper.

Denzau, A., and M. Munger. 1986. Legislators and Interest Groups: How Unorganized Interests Get Represented. *American Political Science Review* 80:89–106.

De Oliveira, Miguel Darcy, and Rajesh Tandon, eds. 1994. *Citizens Strengthening Global Civil Society*. Washington, DC: CIVICUS.

Der Derian, James, ed. 1995. *International Theory: Critical Investigations*. New York: New York University Press.

Devall, Bill, and George Sessions. 1985. *Deep Ecology*, Salt Lake City: Peregrise Smith Books.

Dewey, John. 1966. *Democracy and Education*. New York: Free Press.

Diamond, Irene, and Gloria Ornstein, eds. 1990. *Reweaving the World: The Emergence of Ecofeminism*. San Francisco: Sierra Club.

Diamond, Larry. 1994. The Global Imperative: Building a Democratic World Order. *Current History* 93:1–7.

Diamond, Louise, and John McDonald. 1996. *Multi-Track Diplomacy: A Systems Approach to Peace*. West Hartford, CT: Kumarian.

Diamond, Stanley. 1974. *In Search of the Primitive*. New Brunswick, NJ: Transaction Books.

Dietz, Mary G. 1991. Hannah Arendt and Feminist Politics. In *Feminist Interpretations and Political Theory*, eds. Mary Lyndon Shanley and Carole Pateman. University Park: Pennsylvania State University Press.

Dillbeck, Michael, and Allan Abrams. 1987. The Application of the Transcendental Meditation Program to Corrections. *International Journal of Comparative and Applied Criminal Justice* 11:111–32.

Dinh, Viet D. 1994. Multiracial Affirmative Action. In *Debating Affirmative Action*, ed. Nicolaus Mills. New York: Bantam.

Dionne, E. J. 1991. *Why Americans Hate Politics*. New York: Simon and Schuster.

———. 1996. *They Only Look Dead*. New York: Simon and Schuster.

diZerega, Gus. 1991. "Integrating Quantum Theory with Post-Modern Political Thought and Action: The Priority of Relationships over Objects." In *Quantum Politics*, ed. Theodore Becker. Westport, CT: Praeger.

d'Souza, Dinesh. 1994. "Sins of Admission." In *Debating Affirmative Action*, ed. Nicolaus Mills. New York: Bantam.

———. 1995. *The End of Racism*. New York: The Free Press.

Dodds, E. R. (1966). *The Greeks and the Irrational*. Berkeley, CA: University of California Press.

Dolbeare, Kenneth M. 1974. *Political Change in the United States: A Framework for Analysis*. New York: McGraw-Hill.

———, and Hubbell, Jane R. 1996. *USA 2012: After the Middle Class Revolution*. Chatham, NJ: Chatham House.

Drengson, Alan R. 1991. Introduction: Environmental Crisis, Education, and Deep Ecology. *The Trumpeter* 8(3):97–98.

Duerr, Hans Peter. 1985. *Dreamtime: Concerning the Boundary between Wilderness and Civilization*. New York: Basil Blackwell.

Duhl, Leonard. 1992. *Health Planning and Social Change*. New York: Human Sciences.

Dukes, E. Franklin. 1996. *Resolving Public Conflict: Transforming Community and Governance*. New York: St. Martin's Press.

Durning, Allan. 1993. The Worth of the Earth. *World Watch Journal* 6(4):39–40.

Easton, David B. 1969. The New Revolution in Political Science, *American Political Science Review* 63 (December): 1051–1061.

Eckersley, Robyn. 1992. *Environmentalism and Political Theory*. Albany: State University of New York Press.

Edelglass, Stephen, Georg Maier, Hans Gebert, and John Davy. 1992. *Matter and Mind: Imaginative Participation in Science*. Hudson, NY: Lindesfarne Press.

Ehrlich, Paul R., and A. H. Ehrlich. 1990. *The Population Explosion*. New York: Simon and Schuster.

Eisler, Riane. 1987. *The Chalice and the Blade*. San Francisco: HarperCollins.

———, and David Loye. 1990. *The Partnership Way: New Tools for Living and Learning Together*. San Francisco: HarperCollins.

Eison, James A., Fred Janzow, and Charles Bonwell. 1990. Active Learning Development Workshops: Or Practicing What We Teach. *The Journal of Staff, Program, and Organization Development* 5, no. 2 (Summer).

Ekins, Paul. 1992. *A New World Order: Grassroots Movements for Global Change*. London: Routledge.

Eleff, Bob. 1985. Economics and Environmental Values. *Human Economy Newsletter*. 6(3):9

Elgin, Duane. 1993a. *Awakening Earth: Exploring the Evolution of Human Culture and Consciousness*. New York: Morrow.

———. 1993b. *Voluntary Simplicity*. New York: Morrow.

———. 1996. *Global Paradigm Change: Is a Shift Underway?* San Anselmo, CA: Indicators Project.

Eliade, Mircea. 1964. *Shamanism: Archaic Techniques of Ecstasy*. Princeton, NJ: Princeton University Press.

Elon, Amos. 1981. *The Israelis: Founders and Sons*. New York: Penguin.

Epstein, Aaron. 1996. "Affirmative Action Ban Upheld." *The Denver Post*, (July) 2, 2.

Erasmus, Charles. 1977. *In Search of the Common Good: Utopian Experiments, Past and Present*. New York: Free Press.

Etzioni, Amitai. 1972. Minerva: An Electronic Town Hall. *Policy Sciences*, 3:457–74.

———. 1993. *The Spirit of Community*. New York: Crown.

———, ed. 1995. *Rights and the Common Good*. New York: St. Martin's Press.

Ezorsky, Gertrude. 1991. *Racism and Justice: The Case for Affirmative Action*. Ithaca, New York: Cornell University Press.

Falk, Richard. 1992. *Explorations at the Edge of Time: The Prospects for World Order*. New York: Crown.

Faludi, Susan. 1991. *Backlash: The Undeclared War Against American Women*. New York: Crown Publishers.

Fanning, Patrick. 1988. *Visualization for Change*. Oakland: New Harbinger Publications.

Fellowship for Intentional Community. 1995. *Directory of Intentional Communities*. Rutledge, MO: Fellowship for Intentional Community.

Fenno, Richard F. 1978. *Home Style: House Hembers in Their Districts*. Boston: Little, Brown.

Ferguson, Marilyn. 1980. *The Aquarian Conspiracy: Personal and Social Transformation in the 1980s*. Los Angeles: J. P. Tarcher.

Ferruci, Piero. 1982. *What We May Be*. Los Angeles: J. P. Tarcher, Inc.

Fishel, Jeff. 1992. Leadership for Change: John Vasconcellos (D-CA) and the Promise of Humanistic Psychology in Public Life. *Political Psychology* 13:663–92.

Fisher, Roger, and William Ury. 1981. *Getting to Yes*. Boston: Houghton Mifflin.

Fishkin, James. 1991. *Democracy and Deliberation*. New Haven, CT: Yale University Press.

Forbess-Greene, Sue, ed. 1986. *Encyclopedia of Icebreakers*. San Diego: University Associates.

Fowler, Robert. 1991. *The Dance with Community*. Lawrence, KA: The University Press of Kansas.

Fowler, Linda, and Ronald Shaiko. 1987. The Grassroots Connection: Environmental Activists and Senate Roll Calls. *American Journal of Political Science* 31:484–510.

Franklin, Betty Smith. n.d. Paolo Freire and the Undergraduate Education of the Elite. Emory University. Typescript.

Freeman, Jo, ed. 1995. *Social Movements of the Sixties and Seventies*. New York: Longman.

———. 1995. *Women: A Feminist Perspective*. Mountain View, CA: Mayfield.

Friedan, Betty. 1963. *The Feminine Mystique*. New York: Norton.

Freidman, John. 1992. *Empowerment: The Politics of Alternative Development*. Cambridge, MA: Blackwell.

Freire, Paulo. 1970. *The Pedagogy of the Oppressed*. New York: Herder and Herder.

———. 1973. *Education for Critical Consciousness*. New York: Continuum.

———. 1985. *The Politics of Education: Culture, Power and Liberation*. Handley, MA: Bergin and Garvey.

Fromm, Erich. 1955. *The Sane Society*. Greenwich, CT: Fawcett Publications.

Fuller, R. Buckminster. 1963. *No More Second Hand God and Other Writings*. Carbondale, IL: Southern Illinois University Press.

Furst, Peter. 1976. *Hallucinogens and Culture*. San Francisco: Chandler and Sharp.

Galtung, Johan. 1996. *Peace by Peaceful Means: Peace and Conflict, Development and Civilization*. London: Sage.

Gaventa, John. 1993. The Powerful, the Powerless and the Experts: Knowledge Struggles in an Information Age. In *Voices of Change: Participatory Re-*

search in the U.S. and Canada, eds. Peter Park, Mary Brydon-Miller, Budd L. Hall, and Ted Jackson. Westport, CT: Bergin and Garvey.

Geiser, Kay. 1983. Toxic Times and Class Politics. *Radical America.* 17(1–2):39–50.

Gelb, Joyce, and Marian Leif Palley. 1977. Women and Interest Group Politics: A Case Study of the Equal Credit Opportunity Act. *American Politics Quarterly* (July):331–52.

Giroux, Henry A. 1981. *Ideology, Culture, and the Process of Schooling.* Philadelphia: Temple University Press.

———. 1983. *Theory and Resistance in Education.* Hadley, MA: Bergin and Garvey.

———. 1988. *Teachers as Intellectuals.* Hadley, MA: Bergin and Garvey.

———. 1994. School for Scandal: Whittling Away at Public Education. In *Disturbing Pleasures: Learning Popular Culture*, ed. Henry Giroux. New York: Routledge.

Githens, Marianne, Peppa Norris, and Joni Lovendushi, eds. 1994. *Different Roles, Different Voices: Women and Politics in the United States and Europe.* New York: HarperCollins College.

Glazer, Nathan 1975. *Affirmative Discrimination.* New York: Basic Books.

Gleick, James. 1987. *Chaos.* New York: Viking.

Goldberg, Philip. 1983. *The Intuitive Edge.* Los Angeles: J. P. Tarcher.

Goldman, Daniel, and Joel Gurin, eds. 1993. *Mind Body Medicine.* Yonkers, NY: Consumer Reports.

Gore, Al. 1992. *Earth in the Balance: Ecology and the Human Spirit.* Boston: Houghton Mifflin.

Gormley, W., J. Headle, and C. Williams. 1983. Potential Responsiveness in the Bureaucracy: Views of Public Utility Regulation. *American Political Science Review* 77:704–17.

Goulet, Denis. 1977. *The Uncertain Promise: Value Conflicts in Technology Transfer.* New York: IDOC/North America.

Graham, Daniel N. 1986. The Green Challenge to Left Politics: Ecological and Egalitarian Perspectives. In *Ecopolitics Conference Proceedings*, August 30–31, ed. Mark F. Carden. Brisbane, Australia: School of Australian Environmental Studies, Griffith University.

———. 1989. Class, Gender, and Nature Conflicts: Democratic Left and Eco-Feminist Responses. In *Research In Inequality and Social Conflict*, Vol. 1, ed. Wallimann and Dobkowski. Greenwich, CT: JAI Press.

———. 1995a. Greens and The Politics of Ecology and Equality. PhD. Dissertation, University of North Carolina.

———. 1995b. Environmental Education: Rethinking Nature, Humans, and Human Nature. *On The Horizon* 3(5):10–11.

Greenberg, Philip A. 1993. *Toward a U.S. Green Plan: Thinking About a U.S. Strategy for Sustainable Development.* San Francisco: Resource Renewal Institute.

Griffin, David Ray. 1990. *Sacred Interconnections: Postmodern Spirituality, Political Economy, and Art.* Albany: State University of New York Press.

———, and Richard Falk, eds. 1993. *Postmodern Politics for a Planet in Crisis.* Albany: State University of New York Press.

Guarasci, Richard, and Craig Rimmerman. 1997. Applying Democratic Theory in Community Organizations. In *Teaching Democracy by Being Democratic,* eds. Theodore Becker and Richard Couto. Westport, CT: Praeger.

Guinier, Lani. 1994. *The Tyranny of the Majority.* New York: Free Press.

Gurtov, Mel. 1994. *Global Politics in the Human Interest.* Boulder, CO: Lynne Reinner.

Haas, Michael. 1970. *Approaches to the Study of Political Science.* Scranton, PA: Chandler Publishing Co.

Haenke, David. 1989. Ecological Economics. *The Egg* 9(1):5–7.

Hage, Jerald, and Charles Powers. 1992. *Post-Industrial Lives: Roles and Relationships in the 21st Century.* Newbury Park, CA: Sage.

Hall, B. L. 1981. Participatory Research, Popular Knowledge, and Power: A Personal Reflection. *Convergence,* 14(3):6–17.

Hall, John A. 1993. Liberalism. In Joel Krieger, ed. *The Oxford Companion to Politics of the World.* Princeton, NJ: Princeton University Press.

Halpern, Manfred. 1991. Why Are Most of Us Partial Selves? Why Do Partial Selves Enter the Road Into Deformation? Presented at the Annual Meeting of the American Political Science Association. Washington, DC.

———. Forthcoming. *Transformation: Its Theory and Practice in Personal, Political, Historical and Sacred Being.* Princeton, NJ: Princeton University Press.

Hampden-Turner, Charles. 1976. *Sane Asylum: Inside the Delancey Street Foundation.* New York: Morrow.

Harding, Charles, ed. 1992. *Wingspan: Inside the Men's Movement.* New York: St. Martin's Press.

Harding, Sandra. 1986. *The Science Question in Feminism*. Ithaca, NY: Cornell University Press.

———. 1994. The Instability of the Analytical Categories of Feminist Theory. In *Different Roles, Different Voices: Women and Politics in the United States and Europe*, eds. Marianne Githens, Pippa Norris, and Joni Lovenduski. New York: HarperCollins.

Harkavy, I., and J. L. Puchett. 1991. Toward Effective University-Public School Partnerships: An Analysis of a Contemporary Model. *Teachers College Record*, 92:556–581.

Harker, Donald, and Elizabeth Natter. 1995. *Where We Live: A Citizen's Guide to Conducting a Community Environmental Inventory*. Washington, DC: Island Press.

Harman, Willis. 1984. *Higher Creativity*. Los Angeles: J. P. Tarcher.

Harrigan, John J. 1993. *Empty Dreams, Empty Pockets: Class and Bias in American Politics*. New York: Macmillan.

Harris, LaDonna, and Stephen Sachs. 1994. Harmony through Wisdom of the People: Recreating Traditional Ways of Building Consensus among the Comanche. Paper presented at the annual meeting of the American Political Science Association. New York.

Hart, John. 1984. *The Spirit of the Earth*. Ramsey, NJ: Paulist Press.

Havel, Vaclav. 1985. *The Power of the Powerless*. Armonk, NY: M. E. Sharpe.

———. 1986. *Anatomy of a Reticence*. Stockholm: The Charter 77 Foundation.

———. 1988. *Letters to Olga*. New York: Alfred A. Knopf.

———. 1991. *Open Letters*. New York: Alfred A. Knopf.

———. 1992a. The Effort to Exercise Power in Accord with a Vision of Civility. *The New York Times*, (July) 26.

———. 1992b. *Summer Meditations*. New York: Alfred A. Knopf.

Hayles, Katherine. 1990. *Chaos Bound*. Ithaca, NY: Cornell University Press.

———. ed. 1991. *Chaos and Order*. Chicago: University Press.

Hayward, Jeremy. 1990. Ecology and the Experience of Sacredness. In *Darma Gaia*, ed. Alan Hunt Badiner. Berkeley, CA: Parallax Press.

Heclo, Hugh. 1978. Issue Networks and the Executive Establishment. In *The New American Political System* ed. Anthony King. Washington, DC: American Enterprise Institute.

Hellinger, Daniel, and Dennis R. Judd. 1991. *The Democratic Facade*. Pacific Grove, CA: Brooks Cole Publishing.

Henderson, Hazel. 1970. Computers: Hardware of Democracy, *Forum 70: The Management Monthly on Information Systems*, 2(2):22–24, 46–51.

———. 1981. *The Politics of the Solar Age: Alternatives to Economics*. Garden City, NY: Anchor Press.

———. 1987. Futurely Assured Development. *Ploughshare Press* 12(4):39–48.

———. 1991. *Paradigms in Progress: Life Beyond Economics*. Indianapolis, IN: Knowledge Systems, Inc.

———. 1992. At Rio NGO's Were Again Out Front. *Christian Science Monitor*: (June) 25:19.

———. 1996. *Building a Win-Win World*. San Francisco: Berrett-Koehler.

Henry III, William A. 1994. *In Defense of Elitism*. New York: Anchor Books.

Herman, Louis. 1996. Personal Empowerment. In *Teaching Democracy by Being Democratic*, eds. Theodore Becker and Richard Couto. Westport, CT: Praeger.

Herndon, J. F. 1982. Access, Record and Competition as Influences on Interest Group Contributions to Congressional Campaigns. *Journal of American Politics* 44:996–1019.

Heschel, Joshua. 1984. *Man is Not Alone: A Philosophy of Religion*. New York: Farrar Straus and Giroux.

Heschel, Susannah, ed. 1983. *On Being a Jewish Feminist*. New York: Schocken Books.

Hesse, Herman. 1974. *Demian*. New York: Bantam.

———. 1981a. *Steppenwolf*. New York: Bantam.

———. 1981b. *Narcissus and Goldmund*. New York: Bantam.

Hill, Herbert. 1992. Race, Affirmative Action and the Constitution. In *American Politics: Classic and Contemporary Readings*, eds. Allan Cigler and Burdett Loomis. Boston: Houghton-Mifflin.

Hillman, Deborah Jay. 1990. The Emergence of the Grassroots Dream Movement. In *Dreamtime and Dreamwork*, ed. Stanley Krippner. New York: Jeremy Tarcher.

Hinkley, Barbara. 1978. *Stability and Change in Congress*. New York: Harper and Row.

Hoffman, Abbie. 1968. *Revolution for the Hell of It*. New York: Dial Press.

Holm, Hans Henrik, and Georg Sorenson. 1995. *Whose World Order? Uneven Globalization and the End of the Cold War*. Boulder, CO: Westview.

Holmes, Robert, ed. 1990. *Non-Violence in Theory and Practice*. Belmont, CA: Wadsworth.

hooks, bell. 1984. *Feminist Theory: From Margin to Center*. Boston: South End Press.

———. 1994. *Teaching to Transgress: Education as the Practice of Freedom*. New York: Routledge.

———. 1995. *Killing Rage: Ending Racism*. New York: Henry Holt.

Horkheimer, Max. 1972. *Critical Theory, The Social Function of Philosophy*. New York: Seabury Press.

Hubbard, Alice, and Clay Fong. 1995. *Community Energy Workbook: A Guide to Building a Sustainable Economy*. Snowmass, CO: Rocky Mountain Institute.

Hughes, Charles J. 1985. Gaia: A Natural Scientist's Ethic for the Future. *The Ecologist* 15(3):92–103.

Hughes, J. Donald, and Jim Swan. 1986. How Much of the Earth Is Sacred Space? *Environmental Review* 10:247–259.

Hynes, William. 1993. Mapping the Characteristics of Mythic Tricksters: A Heuristic Guide. In *Mythical Trickster Figures*, eds. William Hynes and William Doty. Tuscaloosa, AL: University of Alabama Press, 1993.

Inglehart, Ronald. 1977. *The Silent Revolution, Changing Values and Political Styles Among Western Publics*. Princeton, NJ: Princeton University Press.

———, and Paul Abramson. 1994. Economic Security and Value Changes. *American Political Science Review* 88:336–354.

———. 1995. Public Support for Environmental Protection: Objective Problems and Subjective Values in 43 Societies. *PS: Political Science & Politics* 28 (March):57–72.

Ingram, Catherine. 1990. *In the Footsteps of Gandhi: Conversations with Spiritual Social Activists*. Berkeley, CA: Parallax.

International Commission on Peace and Food. 1994. *Uncommon Opportunities: An Agenda for Peace and Equitable Development*. London: Zed.

International Institute for Sustainable Development. 1993. *Sourcebook on Sustainable Development*. Winnepeg, Manitoba: IISD.

Isaak, Alan C. 1985. *Scope and Methods of Political Science*, 4th ed. Homewood, Ill: Dorsey.

Israel, B., S. J. Schwrman, and M. K. Hugentobler. 1992. Conducting Action Research: Relationships between Organization Members and Researchers. *Journal of Applied Behavioral Science.* 28:74–99.

Jefferson, Thomas. 1816/1989. Letter to Samuel Kercheval. In *American Political Thought*, ed. Kenneth Dolbeare. Chatham, NJ: Chatham House.

Johnson, David W., and Roger T. Johnson. 1989. *Cooperation and Competition: Theory and Research.* Edina, MN: Interaction Book Co.

———, Roger T. Johnson, and Karl A. Smith. 1991. *Active Learning: Cooperation in the College Classroom.* Edina, MN: Interaction Book Co.

Johnson, Huey. 1995. *Green Plans: Greenprint for Sustainability.* Lincoln, NE: University of Nebraska Press.

Jung, Carl G. 1959. *Four Archetypes.* Princeton, NJ: Princeton University Press.

———. 1964. The Fight with the Shadow. In *The Collected Works of C.G. Jung*, vol. 10, ed. H. Read, M. Fordham, and G. Adler. London: Routledge.

Kassiola, Joel J. 1991. *The Death of Industrial Civilization, The Limits to Economic Growth, and the Repoliticization of Advanced Industrial Society.* Albany: State University of New York Press.

Kazis, Richard, and Richard Grossman. 1982. *Fear at Work.* New York: Pilgrim Press.

Keepin, William. 1994. David Bohm: A Life of Dialogue Between Science and Spirit. *Noetic Sciences Review* 30:16–19.

Keller, Evelyn Fox. 1985. *Reflections on Gender and Science.* New Haven, CT: Yale University Press.

Kellert, Stephen. 1993. *In the Wake of Chaos.* Chicago: University Press.

Kelley, Sean. 1991. Science, Wisdom and the Ecocentric Paradigm: The Signal Contributions of Hegel and Morin. *The Trumpeter* 8(1):26–28.

Kelly, Petra. 1989. Foreword. In *Healing the Wounds: The Promise of Ecofeminism*, ed. J. Plant, ix–xi. Philadelphia: New Society Publishers.

Kemmis, Daniel. 1990. *Community and the Politics of Place.* Norman, OK: Oklahoma University Press.

Kemp, Penny, ed. 1992. *Europe's Green Alternative.* Montreal: Black Rose.

Kennedy, Randall 1994. Persuasion and Distrust: The Affirmative Action Debate. In *Debating Affirmative Action*, ed. Nicolaus Mills. New York: Bantam.

Kessler-Harris, Alice 1994. Feminism and Affirmative Action. In *Debating Affirmative Action*, ed. Nicolaus Mills. New York: Bantam.

Kieffer, Charles. 1984. Citizen Empowerment: A Development Perspective. *Prevention in Human Services* 3:9–36.

Kiel, L. Douglas. 1994. *Managing Chaos and Complexity in Government: A New Paradigm for Managing Change, Innovation, and Organizational Renewal*. San Francisco: Jossey-Bass.

Kim, Tae-Chang, and James A. Dator, eds. 1994. *Creating a New History for Future Generations*. Japan: Institute for the Integrated Study of Future Generations.

Kitto, H. D. F. 1966. *The Greeks*. Baltimore: Penguin.

Klare, Michael T. 1994. *Peace & World Security Studies: A Curriculum Guide*. Boulder, CO: Lynne Reiner.

Klepfisz, Irena, and Melanie Kay-Kantrowitz, eds. 1986. *The Tribe of Dina*. Sinister Wisdom 29/30. Reprint 1989. Boston: Beacon.

Knight, Barbara. 1995. Liberalism and the Politics of Integrity. Presented to the Annual Meeting of the American Political Science Association. Chicago, IL.

Knorr, Klaus, and James N. Rosenau, eds. 1969. *Contending Approaches to International Politics*. Princeton, NJ: Princeton University Press.

Kolb, David A. 1976. *The Learning Style Inventory: Technical Manual*. Boston: McBer and Company.

———. 1984. *Experiential Learning: Experience as the Source of Learning and Development*. Englewood Cliffs, NJ: Prentice-Hall.

Kolton, Elizabeth, ed. 1978. *The Jewish Woman*. New York: Schoken Books.

Korten, David C. 1994. Sustainable Development: Conventional versus Emergent Alternative Wisdom. *Human Economy* (Summer):1,8:14.

Kothar, R. 1981. Environment and Alternative Development. *Working Paper #15*, New York: Institute for World Order.

Kreisberg, Seth. 1992. *Transforming Power: Domination, Empowerment, and Education*. Albany, NY: State University of New York Press.

Kriseova, Eda. 1993. *Vaclav Havel: The Authorized Biography*. New York: St. Martin's Press.

Kuhn, Thomas A. 1970. *The Structure of Scientific Revolutions*. Chicago: University of Chicago Press.

Küng, Hans, ed. 1996. *Yes to a Global Ethic*. New York: Continuum.

Labor Committee for Safe Energy and Full Employment. 1980. Report on First National Labor Conference for Safe Energy and Full Employment. Washington, DC: author.

Lahar, Stephanie. 1993. Ecofeminist Theory and Grassroots Politics. In *Environmental Ethics: Divergence and Convergence*, eds. Susan Armstrong and Richard Botzler. New York: McGraw Hill.

Lame Deer, John, and Erdoes, Richard. 1972. *Lame Deer Seeker of Vision: Life of a Sioux Medicine Man*. New York: Simon and Schuster.

Landau, Martin. 1961. On the Use of Metaphor in Political Science. *Social Research* 28:331–353.

Lappé, Frances Moore, and Paul Martin DuBois. 1994. *The Quickening of America*. San Francisco: Jossey-Bass.

Lasch, Christopher. 1979. *The Culture of Narcissism: American Life in an Age of Diminishing Expectations*. New York: Norton.

Laszlo, Ervin. 1994. *Vision 2020: Reordering Chaos for Global Survival*. Langhorne, PA: Gordon and Breach Science.

Lather, Patricia Ann. 1991. *Getting Smart: Feminist Research and Pedagogy*. New York: Routledge.

Lederach, John. 1995. *Preparing for Peace: Conflict Transformation across Cultures*. Syracuse, NY: Syracuse University Press.

Lee, Martha. 1995. *Earth First: Environmental Apocalypse*. Syracuse, NY: Syracuse University Press.

Leopold, Aldo. 1949. *Sand County Almanac*. New York: Oxford University Press.

Lerner, Michael. 1996. *The Politics of Meaning*. Reading, MA: Addison-Wesley.

Lerner, Steve. 1992. *Beyond the Earth Summit: Conversations with Advocates of Sustainable Development*. Bolinas, CA: Common Knowledge.

Lesh, Donald. 1995. *Sustainable Development Tool Kit*. Washington, DC: Global Tomorrow Coalition.

Lewin, Kurt. 1948. *Resolving Social Conflicts: Selected Papers on Group Dynamics*. New York: Harper and Row.

———— 1953. Studies in Group Decision. In *Group Dynamics: Research and Theory*, eds. Dorwin Cartwright and Alvin Zander. New York: Harper and Row.

Liebow, Elliot. 1967. *Tally's Corner: A Study of Negro Streetcorner Men*. Boston: Little, Brown.

Liehm, Antonin J. 1968. *The Politics of Culture*. New York: Random House.

Limerick, David, and Bert Cunnington. 1993. *Managing the New Organization: A Blueprint for Networks and Strategic Alliances*. San Francisco: Jossey-Bass.

Lincoln, Yvonna, and Egon Guba. 1985. *Naturalistic Inquiry*. Beverly Hills, CA: Sage.

Lipnak, Jessica, and Jeffrey Stamps. 1994. *The Age of the Network: Organizing Principles for the 21st Century*. Essex Junction VT: OMNEO.

Locke, John. 1690/1964. *An Essay Concerning Human Understanding*. New York: Meridian.

Lopez, George A., Jackie G. Smith, and Ron Pagnucco. 1995. The Global Tide. *Bulletin of the Atomic Scientist* 51 (July/August):33–39.

Lozoff, Bo. 1987. *We're All Doing Time: A Guide for Getting Free*. Durham, NC: Prison-Ashram Project.

Luke, Timothy. 1983. Notes for a Deconstructionist Ecology. *New Political Science* 11:21–32.

Luthans, Fred. 1977. *Organizational Behavior*. New York: McGraw Hill.

Macy, Joanna. 1991. *World as Lover, World as Self*. Berkeley, CA: Parallax.

Machiavelli, Niccolo. 1952. *The Prince*. New York: New American Library.

MacKinnon, Catharine A. 1987. *Feminism Unmodified*. Cambridge, MA: Harvard University Press.

———. 1989. *Toward a Feminist Theory of the State*. Cambridge, MA: Harvard University Press.

Malecki, Edward S., and H. R. Mahood. 1972. *Group Politics: A New Emphasis*. New York: Scribner.

Mander, Jerry, and Edward Goldsmith, eds. 1996. *The Case Against the Global Economy*. San Francisco: Sierra Club.

Mansbridge, Jane. 1980. *Beyond Adversary Democracy*. Chicago: University of Chicago Press.

———. 1990. Democracy and Common Interests. *Social Alternatives* 8:20–24.

Marable, Manning 1995. *Beyond Black and White*. New York: Verso.

Marshall, Edward. 1995. *Transforming the Way We Work: The Power of the Collaborative Workplace*. Chapel Hill, NC: AMACOM.

Masini, Eleonara. 1993. *Why Future Studies?* Grey Seal Books.

Maslow, Abraham. 1943. A Theory of Motivation. *Psychological Review*, 50:370–396.

Matthews, Donald R. 1960. *U.S. Senators and their World*. New York: Vintage.

Mayhew, David R. 1974. *Congress: The Electoral Connection*. New Haven, CT: Yale University Press.

McClure, Laura. 1985. Unions and Environmentalists Working Together. *World Press Review*, (July): 10–12.

McCullough, Thomas E. 1991. *The Moral Imagination and Public Life*. Chatham, NJ: Chatham House.

McGlennon, John, and Ronald Rapoport. 1983. The Party Isn't Over: Incentives for Activism in the 1980 Presidential Nominating Campaign. *Journal of Politics* 45:1006–15.

McKenna, Terence. 1992. *Food of the Gods: The Search for the Original Tree of Knowledge*. New York: Bantam.

McLaughlin, Corinne, and Gordon Davidson. 1990. *Builders of the Dawn: Community Lifestyles in a Changing World*. Summertown, TN: The Book.

———, and Gordon Davidson. 1994. *Spiritual Politics*. New York: Ballentine.

McLellan, David, ed. 1977. *Karl Marx: Selected Writings*. Oxford: Oxford University Press.

Mecca, Andrew, Neil Smelser, and John Vasconcellos. 1989. *The Social Importance of Self-Esteem*. Berkeley, CA: University of California Press.

Mercer, Joye. 1994. "Assault on Affirmative Action." *Chronicle of Higher Education*, (March) 16.

Merchant, Carolyn. 1980. *The Death of Nature: Women, Ecology and the Scientific Revolution*. New York: Harper and Row.

Mezey, Susan Gluck, 1992. *In Pursuit of Equality: Women, Public Policy, and the Federal Courts*. New York: St. Martin's Press.

Mies, Maria, and Vandana Shiva, eds. 1993. *Ecofeminism*. London: Zed Books.

Milbrath, Lester W. 1984. *Environmentalists, Vanguards for a New Society*. Albany: State University of New York Press.

———. 1986. Environmental Beliefs and Values. In *Political Psychology*, ed. Margaret Hermann. San Francisco: Jossey-Bass.

———. 1989. *Envisioning a Sustainable Society: Learning Our Way Out*. Albany: State University of New York Press.

Miller, D. Patrick. 1991. What the Shadow Knows: An Interview with John Sanford. In *Meeting the Shadow*, eds. Connie Zweig and Jeremiah Abrams. Los Angeles: Jeremy Tarcher.

Miller, John. 1993. The Wrong Shade of Green: Orthodox Economics Puts Profits before Sustainability. *Dollars and Sense* (185):6–9.

Mills, C. Wright. 1959. *The Sociological Imagination*. New York: Oxford University Press.

Mills, Nicolaus, ed. 1994. *Debating Affirmative Action: Race, Gender, Ethnicity, and the Politics of Inclusion*. New York: Bantam.

Moffett, James. 1994. *The Universal Schoolhouse*. San Francisco: Jossey-Bass.

Moorcroft, Sheila, ed. 1992. *Visions for the 21st Century*. Westport, CT: Praeger.

Moore, Christopher W. 1996. *The Mediation Process*. San Francisco: Jossey-Bass.

Morgan, G., and R. Remirez. 1984. Action Learning: A Holographic Metaphor for Guiding Social Change. *Human Relations* 37:1–28.

Morrison, Roy. 1991. *We Build the Road as We Travel*. Philadelphia: New Society.

Muller, Birgit. 1991. *Toward an Alternative Culture of Work*. Boulder, CO: Westview.

Murray, Charles 1994. Affirmative Racism. In *Debating Affirmative Action*, ed. Nicolaus Mills. New York: Bantam.

Myers, Isabel, Briggs. 1962. *The Myers Briggs Type Indicator*. Palo Alto, CA: Consulting Psychologist Press.

Myrdal, Gunnar. 1944. *An American Dilemma: The Negro Problem and Modern Democracy*. New York: Harper and Row.

Nachmias, David, and Chava Nachmias. 1976. *Research Methods in the Social Sciences*. New York: St. Martin's Press.

Naisbitt, John. 1984. *Megatrends: Ten New Directions Transforming Our Lives*. New York: Warner.

———. 1995. *Global Paradox*. New York: Morrow.

Nash, Paul. 1980. Humanism and Humanistic Education in the 1980s: The Lessons of Two Decades. *Journal of Education* 161:5–17.

National Conference of Christians and Jews. 1994. *Taking America's Pulse: The National Conference Survey on Inter-Group Relations*. Washington, DC: Louis Harris Associates.

Newman, Frank. 1985. *Higher Education and the American Resurgence*. Princeton, NJ: Carnegie Foundation for the Advancement of Teaching.

Neibuhr, Reinhold, ed. 1964. *Marx and Engles on Religion.* New York: Schocken Books.

Neumann, Erich. 1969. *Depth Psychology and the New Ethic.* New York: Putnam.

Nhat Hanh, Thich. 1991. *Peace Is Every Step.* New York: Bantam.

Njeri, Itabari 1993. Sushi and Grits: Ethnic Identity and Conflict in a Newly Multicultural America. In *Lure and Loathing: Essays on Race, Identity and the Ambivalence of Assimilation,* ed. Gerald Early. New York: Penguin.

O'Brien, Jim. 1983. Environmentalism as a Mass Movement. *Radical America,* 17(2–3):39–50.

Odajnyk, V. W. 1976. *Jung and Politics.* New York: New York University Press.

Ohiyesa (Eastman, Charles). 1971. *The Soul of the Indian,* quoted in Tracy McCluhan, *Touch the Earth: A Self Portrait of Indian Existence.* New York: Promontory Press.

Ollman, Bertell. 1993. *Dialectical Investigations.* New York: Routledge.

Olson, Mancur. 1971. *The Logic of Collective Action: Public Goods and the Theory of Groups.* Cambridge, MA: Harvard University Press.

Onuf, Nicholas Greenwood. 1989. *World of Our Making: Rules and Rule in Social Theory and International Relations.* Columbia: University of South Carolina Press.

Ophuls, William. 1992. *Ecology and the Politics of Scarcity Revisited: The Unraveling of the American Dream.* New York: W. H. Freeman and Co.

Ornstein, Norman J., and Shirley Elder. 1978. *Interest Groups, Lobbying and Policymaking.* Washington, DC: Congressional Quarterly Press.

Orr, David. 1994. *Earth in Mind.* Washington, DC: Island Press.

Osborne, David, and Ted Gaebler. 1992. *Reinventing Government.* Boston: Addison-Wesley, 1992.

———, and Peter Plastrick. 1997. *Banishing Bureaucracy: The Five Strategies for Reinventing Government.* Reading, MA: Addison-Wesley.

OSHA/Environmental Network. 1984. *OSHA/Environmental Watch* 3(2).

Overton, Shan, and Christine Caron. 1993. The Possibility of Diversity Emerging From Communities of Care: Hearing Voices Within the Academy. Presented at the Annual Meeting of the Southeastern Women's Studies Association. Nashville, TN.

Page, Clarence. 1996. *Showing My Color: Impolite Essays on Race and Identity*. New York: HarperCollins.

Park, Peter. 1993. *Voices of Change*. New York: Bergin and Garvey.

Parkin, Sara. 1989. *Green Parties: An International Guide*. London: Heretic Books.

Pateman, Carole. 1987. *Feminist Challenges*. Boston: Northeastern University Press.

———. 1988. *The Sexual Contract*. Stanford, CA: Stanford University Press.

———. 1989. *The Disorder of Women*. Stanford, CA: Stanford University Press.

———. 1991. *Feminist Interpretations and Political Theory*. University Park, PA: Pennsylvania State University Press.

Paul, Richard. 1990. *Critical Thinking: What Every Person Needs to Survive in a Rapidly Changing World*. Sonoma, CA: Sonoma State University Center for Critical Thinking.

Paulsen, Beldon. 1983. Scenarios for Milwaukee—Citizen Participation in Projecting Futures. *World Future Society Bulletin* 17:191–98.

Peat, F. David. 1991. *The Philosopher's Stone*. New York: Bantam.

Pehrson, John B. 1995. *Creative Imagery Workbook*. Unpublished manuscript. Signal Mountain, TN.

Pfeiffer, William J., Leonard D. Goodstein, John E. Jones, eds. 1995A. *Annual Handbook: Developing Human Resources, 1972–1995*. San Diego: University Associates.

———. 1986b. *A Handbook of Structured Exercises*, Vols. I-X, San Diego: University Associates.

Phillips, Kevin. 1989. *The Politics of the Rich and Poor*. New York: Harper.

———. 1994. *Arrogant Capital: Washington, Wall Street, and the Frustration of American Politics*. Boston: Little, Brown.

Pinchot, Gifford, and Elizabeth Pinchot. 1993. *The End of Bureaucracy and the Rise of the Intelligent Organization*. San Francisco: Berrett-Koehler.

Pitkin, Hannah. 1984. *Fortune Is a Woman*. Berkeley, CA: University of California Press.

Plant, Judith, ed. 1989. *Healing the Wounds*. Philadelphia: New Society Publishers.

Polkinghorne, Donald. 1983. *Methodology for the Human Sciences*. Albany, NY: State University of New York Press.

Pool, K. T. 1981. Dimensions of Interest Group Evaluation of U.S. Senate, 1969–1978. *American Journal of Political Science* 25:49–67.

Porter, Larry. 1983. Giving and Receiving Feedback, in *The NTL Managers Handbook*, ed. Roger A. Ritvo and Alice G. Sargent. Arlington, VA: NTL Publications.

Prell, Riv Ellen. 1989. *Prayer and Community: The Havurah in American Judaism*. Detroit: Wayne State University Press.

Prigogine, Ilya, and Isabelle Stengers. 1984. *Order out of Chaos*. New York: Bantam.

Quinn, Daniel. 1992. *Ishmael: An Adventure of the Mind and Spirit*. New York: Bantam.

Ramsden, Paul. 1992. *Learning to Teach in Higher Education*. London: Routledge.

Randall, Vicky. 1994. Feminism and Political Analysis. In *Different Roles, Different Voices: Women and Politics in the United States and Europe*, eds. Marianne Githens, Pippa Norris, and Joni Lovenduski. New York: HarperCollins.

Rapoport, Robert N. 1970. Three Dilemmas in Action Research. *Human Relations*, 23, 488–513.

Ray, Paul. 1996. The Integral Culture Study: A Study of the Emergence of Transformational Values in America. *AHP Perspective*, (July/August):9–14.

Rayman, Paula. 1981. *The Kibbutz Community and Nation Building*. Princeton, NJ: Princeton University Press.

Reinharz, Shulamith. 1979. *On Becoming a Social Scientist: From Survey Research and Participant Observation to Experiential Analysis*. San Francisco: Jossey-Bass.

Reissman, Frank. 1986. The New Populism and the Empowerment Ethos. In *The New Populism: The Politics of Empowerment*, eds. Harry C. Boyte and Frank Reissman. Philadelphia: Temple University Press.

Renner, Michael. 1990. A Promise of Economic Conversion. *Utne Reader*, (March–April): 42–45.

———. 1992. Saving the Earth, Creating Jobs. *World Watch Journal* 5(1):10–17.

Rensenbrink, John. 1988. What Marx Forgot, Liberals Have Never Known, and Conservatives Find Frightening: The Ecology of Democracy. Presented at the Annual Meeting of the American Political Science Association. Washington, DC.

———. 1992. *The Greens and the Politics of Transformation*. San Pedro, CA: R. and E. Miles.

Ricci, David M. 1984. *The Tragedy of Political Science: Politics, Scholarship and Democracy*. New Haven, CT: Yale University Press.

Richardson, Dick, and Chris Rootes. 1995. *The Green Challenge: The Development of Green Parties in Europe*. London: Routledge.

Rifkin, Jeremy. 1995. *The End of Work: The Decline of the Global Labor Force and the Dawn of the Post-Market Era*. New York: Tarcher/Putnam.

———. 1991. *Biosphere Politics: A New Consciousness for a New Century*. New York: Crown.

Riker, William H. 1962. *The Theory of Political Conditions*. New Haven, CT: Yale University Press.

———, and Ordeshook, Peter. 1973. *An Introduction to Positive Political Theory*. Englewood Cliffs, NJ: Prentice-Hall.

Robertson, James. 1990. *Future Wealth*. London: Cassell.

Roelofs, H. Mark. 1994. Two Ways to Political Science: Critical and Descriptive. *PS: Political Science & Teaching* 27:264–8.

Rohter, Ira. 1992. *A Green Hawaii*. Honolulu: Na Kane O Ka Malo.

Romzek, Barbara S., and J. Stephen Hendricks. 1982. Organizational Involvement and Representative Bureaucracy: Can We Have It Both Ways? *American Political Science Review* 76:1–32.

Rosen, Jay. 1990. Missing Havel's Message. *World Monitor*, (November).

Roszak, Theodore, Mary Gomes, and Allen Kanner, eds. 1995. *Ecopsychology: Restoring the Earth, Healing the Mind*. San Francisco: Sierra Club Books.

Rothschild, Joseph. 1993. *Return to Diversity: A Political History of East Central Europe Since World War II*. New York: Oxford University Press.

Rourke, John, Richard Hiskes, and Cyrus Zirakzadeh. 1992. *Direct Democracy and International Politics: Deciding International Issues through Referendums*. Boulder, CO: Lynne Rienner.

Rubenstein, Richard. 1978. *The Cunning of History*. New York: Harper and Row.

————. 1990. Unanticipated Conflict and the Crisis of Social Theory. In *Conflict: Readings in Management and Resolution*, eds. John Burton and Frank Dukes. New York: St. Martin's Press.

Ruck, Carl A. P. 1981. Mushrooms and Philosophers. *Journal of Ethnopharmacology*, 4:179–205.

Rudig, Wolfgang, ed. 1995. *Green Politics Three*. Edinburgh: Edinburgh University Press.

Rummel, Rudolf J. 1994. *Death By Government*. New Brunswick, NJ: Transaction.

Russell, Julia Scofield. 1993. The Evolution of an Ecofeminist. In *Environmental Ethics: Divergence and Convergence*, eds. Susan Armstrong and Richard Botzler. New York: McGraw Hill.

Sachs, Stephen M. 1993. A Transformational Native American Gift: Reconceptualizing the Idea of Politics for the 21st Century. Presented at the Annual Meeting of the American Political Science Association. Washington, DC.

Sahlins, Marshall. 1972. *Stone Age Economics*. Chicago: Aldine Atherton.

Said, Abdul Aziz. 1978. *Human Rights and World Order*. New Brunswick, NJ: Transaction.

Sakamoto, Yoshikazu. 1994. *Global Transformation: Challenges to the State System*. Tokyo: United Nations University Press.

Sale, Kirkpatrick. 1985. *Dwellers on the Land: The Bioregional Vision*. San Francisco: Sierra Club.

Salisbury, Robert, John Heinze, Edward Laumann, and Robert Nelson. 1987. Who Works with Whom?: Interest Group Alliances and Opposition. *American Political Science Review* 81:1217–34.

Sandin, Robert. 1992. *The Rehabilitation of Virtue*. Westport, CT: Praeger.

Sanford, John. 1978. *Dreams and Healing*. New York: Paulist Press.

Sartori, Giovanni. 1994. *Comparative Constitutional Engineering*. New York: New York University Press.

Satin, Mark. 1979. *New Age Politics: Healing Self and Society*. New York: Dell Publishing.

————. 1990. You Don't Have to Be a Baby to Cry. *New Options*. September:1.

Schein, Edgar, H. 1980. *Organizational Psychology*. 3rd edition. Englewood Cliffs, NJ: Prentice-Hall.

————. 1969. *Process Consultation: Its Role in Organization Development*. Reading, MA: Addison-Wesley.

Schnaiberg, Allan. 1980. *The Environment: From Surplus to Scarcity*. Oxford: Oxford University Press.

———, and Kenneth Gould. 1994. *Environment and Society*. New York: St. Martin's Press.

Schohl, Wolfgang. 1985. Recovery through Ecology? *World Press Review*, July:25–27.

Schon, Donald A. 1983. *The Reflective Practitioner*. New York: Basic Books.

Schroyer, Trent. 1983. Critique of the Instrumental Interest in Nature. *Social Research* 50:158–184.

Schubert, Glendon A. 1989. *Evolutionary Politics*. Carbondale, IL: Southern Illinois University Press.

———. 1991. *Primate Politics*. Carbondale, IL: Southern Illinois University Press.

Schumacher, E. F. 1973. *Small Is Beautiful*. New York: Harper and Row.

Schwerin, Edward. 1995. *Mediation, Citizen Empowerment, and Transformational Politics*. Westport, CT: Praeger.

Sclove, Richard. 1995. *Democracy and Technology*. New York: Guilford.

Scully, Vincent. 1994. *The New Urbanism: Toward an Architecture of Community*. New York: McGraw Hill.

Seabrook, Jeremy. 1993. *Pioneers of Change: Experiments in Creating a Humane Society*. London: Zed.

Sears, Thomas. 1993. Toward a Human Economy. *In Context* 41(March):4–8.

Sessions, George, ed. 1995. *Deep Ecology for the 21st Century*. Boston: Shambala.

Shaffer, Carolyn, and Kristin Anundsen. 1993. *Creating Community Anywhere*. New York: Tarcher.

Sharan, Shlomo, ed. 1994. *Handbook of Cooperative Learning Methods*. Westport, CT: Greenwood.

Sheldrake, Rupert. 1991. *The Rebirth of Nature: The Greening of Science and God*. New York: Bantam.

Shiva, Vandana. 1993. Women in Nature. In *Environmental Ethics: Divergence and Convergence*, eds. Susan Armstrong and Richard Botzler. New York: McGraw Hill.

Sheng, Fulai. 1995. *Real Value for Nature: An Overview of Global Efforts to Achieve True Measures of Economic Progress*. Gland, Switzerland: WWF International.

Shepherd, Linda Jean. 1993. *Lifting the Veil*. Boston: Shambala.

Shor, Ira. 1980. *Critical Teaching and Everyday Life*. Boston: South End Press.

———, and P. Friere. 1987. *A Pedagogy for Liberation*. Hadley, MA: Bergin and Garvey.

Sikes, Walter, Allen Drexler, and Jack Gant. 1989. *The Emerging Practice of Organizational Development*. Arlington, VA: NTL Publications.

Simon, Sidney B., Howe, Leland, and Kirschenbaum, Howard. 1972. *Values Clarification: A Handbook of Practical Strategies for Teachers and Students*. New York: Hart.

Singer, June. 1990. *Seeing Through the Visible World*. San Francisco: Harper and Row.

Skocpol, Theda. 1994. The Choice. In *Debating Affirmative Action*, ed. Nicolaus Mills. New York: Bantam.

Skolimowski, Henryk. 1981. *Eco-Philosophy*. New York: Marion Books.

———. 1985. *Eco-Theology*. Eco-Philosophy Publication No. 2. Adyar, Madras, India: Vasanta Press.

Slaton, Christa Daryl. 1992. The Failure of the United States Greens to Root in Fertile Soil. In *Research in Social Movements, Conflicts and Change*, ed. M. Finger. Greenwich, CT: Fair Press.

———. 1992. *Televote: Citizen Participation in the Quantum Age*. New York: Praeger.

———, and Becker, Theodore. 1990. A Tale of Two Movements: ADR and the Greens. In *Conflict: Readings in Management and Resolution*, eds. John Burton and Frank Dukes. New York: St. Martin's Press.

———. 1997. The Community Mediation Service: A Model for Teaching Democracy and Conflict Resolution. In *Teaching Democracy by Being Democratic*, eds. Theodore Becker and Richard Couto. Westport, CT: Praeger.

Slavin, Robert. 1990. *Cooperative Learning: Theory, Research and Practice*. Englewood Cliffs, NJ: Prentice-Hall.

Smit, Jorgen. 1988. *How to Transform Thinking, Feeling, and Willing*. Stroud, U.K.: Hawthorn Press.

Smith, Eric. 1984. Advocacy, Interpretation and Influence in the U.S. Congress. *American Political Science Review* 78:44–63.

Sniderman, Paul. 1975. *Personality and Democratic Politics*. Berkeley, CA: University of California Press.

————, and Thomas Piazza. 1993. *The Scar of Race*. Cambridge, MA: Harvard University Press.

Sowell, Thomas 1994. *Race and Culture: A World View*. New York: Basic Books.

Spangler, David. 1988. *The New Age*. Issaquah, WA: Morningtown Press.

Spiro, Melford E. 1958. *Children of the Kibbutz*. Cambridge, MA: Harvard University Press.

Spretnak, Charlene. 1986. *The Spiritual Dimension of Green Politics*. Santa Fe, NM: Bear.

————. 1991. *States of Grace*. San Francisco: Harper.

Springston, Rex. 1995. Environmental Rules Are Not Bad for Jobs. *The Richmond Times/Dispatch*, October 24.

Standing Bear, Chief Luther. 1978. *Land of the Spotted Eagle*. Lincoln, NE: University of Nebraska Press.

Starhawk, 1993. *The Fifth Sacred Thing*. New York: Bantam.

Stavrianos, Leften S. 1971. *Man's Past and Present: A Global History*. New York: Prentice-Hall.

Steele, Shelby. 1990. *The Content of Our Character: A New Vision of Race in America*. New York: St. Martin's Press.

Stein, Diane. 1990. *Casting the Circle: A Women's Book of Ritual*. Freedom, CA: The Crossing Press.

Steiner, Rudolf. 1981. *The Stages of Higher Knowledge*. Spring Valley, NY: Anthroposophic Press.

————. 1988. *Goethean Science*. Spring Valley, NY: Mercury Press.

Stevens, John O. 1971. *Awareness: Exploring, Experimenting, Experiencing*. New York: Bantam Books.

Stewart, Ian. 1994. *Roasting Chestnuts: The Mythology of Maritime Political Culture*. Vancouver, B.C.: University of British Columbia Press.

Stewart, Jr., J. F. 1987. Does Interest Group Litigation Matter? The Case of Black Political Mobilization in Mississippi. *Journal of Politics* 49:780–800.

Storm, Hyemeyohsts. 1972. *Seven Arrows*. New York: Harper and Row.

Stouffers, Samuel. 1949. *The American Soldier: Adjustment during Army Life*. Princeton, NJ: Princeton University Press.

Stretton, Hugh. 1976. *Capitalism, Socialism and the Environment*. Cambridge: Cambridge University Press.

Swain, Carol. 1995. *Black Faces, Black Interests: The Representation of African Americans in Congress*. Cambridge, MA: Harvard University Press.

Swimme, Brian. 1984. *The Universe is a Green Dragon: A Cosmic Creation Story*. Santa Fe, NM: Bear and Company.

———. 1987. The Resurgence of Cosmic Storytellers. *Revision* 9(2):83–88.

———, and Berry, Thomas. 1992. *The Universe Story: A Celebration of the Unfolding of the Cosmos from the Primordial Flaring Forth to the Ecozoic Age*. San Francisco: Harper.

Tandon, Rajesh. 1988. Social Transformation and Participatory Research. *Convergence* 21(2–3):19–27.

Taylor, Charles. 1992. *Multiculturalism and the Politics of Recognition*. Princeton, NJ: Princeton University Press.

Taylor, Jeremy. 1983. *Dream Work*. New York: Paulist Press.

———. 1992. *Where People Fly and Water Runs Uphill*. New York: Warner.

Tehranian, Majid. 1979. Developing Theory and Communications Policy: The Changing Paradigms. *Progress in Communications Sciences* 1:120–166.

Tenner, Edward. 1996. *Why Things Bite Back: Technology and the Revenge of Unintended Consequences*. New York: Alfred A. Knopf.

Thomas, Clarence. 1994. Affirmative Action Goals and Timetables: Too Tough? Not Tough Enough! In *Debating Affirmative Action*, ed. Nicolaus Mills. New York: Bantam.

Thompson, William Irwin. 1971. *At the Edge of History: Speculations on the Transformation of Culture*. New York: Harper and Row.

———. 1981. *The Time Falling Bodies Take to Light*. New York: St. Martin's Press.

———. 1985. *The Pacific Shift*. San Francisco: Sierra Club.

———. 1987. The Cultural Implications of the New Biology. In *Gaia, A Way of Knowing: Political Implications of the New Biology*. ed. William Irwin Thompson. Great Barrington, MA: Lindisfarne Press.

Thurow, Lester. 1996. *The Future of Capitalism*. New York: William Morrow.

Tien, Chang-Lin. 1994. Diversity and Excellence in Higher Education. In *Debating Affirmative Action*, ed. Nicolaus Mills. New York: Bantam.

Titmuss, Christopher. 1988. *Spirit for Change: Voices of Hope for a World in Crisis*. London: Green Print.

Tobias, Michael, ed. 1985. *Deep Ecology*. San Diego, CA: Avant Books.

Toffler, Alvin. 1970. *Future Shock*. New York: Random House.

————, and Heidi Toffler. 1980. *The Third Wave*. London: William Collins Sons.

Tollefson, T. 1993. Is a Hero Really Nothing but a Sandwich? *Utne Reader*, May/June.

Trainer, F. E. 1985. *Abandon Affluence*. London: Zed Books.

Tribe, Laurence H. 1991. The Curvature of Constitutional Space: What Lawyers Can Learn from Modern Physics. In *Quantum Politics: Applying Quantum Theory to Political Phenomena*, ed. Theodore L. Becker. New York: Praeger.

Troxel, James, ed. 1995. *Government Works: Profiles of People Making a Difference*. Alexandria, VA: Miles River.

Truman, David B. 1951. *The Governmental Process*. New York: Alfred A. Knopf.

Trzyna, Thaddeus. 1995. *A Sustainable World: Defining and Measuring Sustainable Development*. Sacramento, CA: International Center for the Environment and Public Policy.

Uphoff, Norman Thomas. 1992. *Learning from Gal Oya: Possibilities for Participatory Development and Post-Newtonian Social Science*. Ithaca, NY: Cornell University Press.

Van den Bergh, J., and Jan van der Straaten, eds. 1994. *Toward Sustainable Development*. Washington, DC: Island Press.

Vlastos, Gregory. 1991. *Socrates, Ironist and Moral Philosopher*. Ithaca, NY: Cornell University Press.

Voegelin, Eric. 1952/1987. *The New Science of Politics: An Introduction*. Chicago: University of Chicago Press.

————. 1987. *Order and History, Vol. 5: In Search of Order*. Baton Rouge, LA: Louisiana State University Press.

————. 1990. *Published Essays 1966–1985*, Vol 12. Baton Rouge, LA: Louisiana State University Press.

von Franz, Marie-Louise. 1991. The Realization of the Shadow in Dreams. In *Meeting the Shadow*, eds. Connie Zweig and Jeremiah Abrams. Los Angeles: Jeremy Tarcher.

Wachtel, Paul. 1993. Health Care, Jobs, and the Environment: Unrecognized Connections. *Human Economy* 1:10–11.

Waldrop, M. Mitchell. 1992. *Complexity*. New York: Simon and Schuster.

Wallace, Aubrey. 1993. *Eco-Heroes*. San Francisco: Mercury House.

Wallis, Jim. 1994. *The Soul of Politics*. New York: New Press.

Ward, Barbara. 1966. *Space Ship Earth*. London: H. Hamilton.

Warren, Karen J. 1993. The Power and Promise of Ecological Feminism. In *Environmental Ethics: Divergence and Convergence*, eds. Susan Armstrong and Richard Botzler. New York: McGraw Hill.

Wascow, Arthur. 1983. *These Holy Sparks: The Rebirth of the Jewish People*. San Francisco: Harper and Row.

Webster's Ninth New Collegiate Dictionary. 1983. Springfield, MA: Merriam-Webster.

West, Cornell. 1993. *Beyond Eurocentrism and Multiculturalism*. Monroe, ME: Common Courage Press.

————. 1994a. *Keeping Faith: Philosophy and Race in America*. New York: Routledge.

————. 1994b. *Race Matters*. New York: Vintage.

————, and hooks, bell. 1991. *Breaking Bread: Insurgent Black Intellectual Life*. Boston: South End Press.

Wheatley, Margaret. 1992. *Leadership and the New Science*. San Francisco: Berritt-Koehler.

Whitmyer, Claude, ed. 1993. *In the Company of Others: Making Community in the Modern World*. Los Angeles: Tarcher.

Whyte, David. 1994. *The Heart Aroused*. New York: Bantam.

Whyte, W. D., D. Greenwood, and P. Lazes. 1989. Participatory Action Research. *American Behavioral Scientist* 32:513–551.

Whyte, William Foote. 1981. *Street Corner Society: The Social Structure of an Italian Slum*. 3rd ed. Boston: Little, Brown.

Wiener, Harvey S. 1986. Collaborative Learning in the Classroom: A Guide to Evaluation. *College English*: January:52–61.

Wilson, Edward, O. 1992. *The Diversity of Life*. New York: W. W. Norton & Co.

Wilson, James Q. 1974. *Political Organizations*. New York: Basic Books.

Wilson, John H. 1995. *The Myth of Political Correctness*. Durham, NC: Duke University Press.

Wilson, William Julius. 1987. *The Truly Disadvantaged*. Chicago: University of Chicago Press.

Wilson, William Julius. 1994. Race-Neutral Programs and the Democratic Coalition. In *Debating Affirmative Action*, ed. Nicolaus Mills. New York: Bantam.

Bibliography 279

Winner, Langdon. 1986. *The Whale and the Reactor*. Chicago: University of Chicago Press.

Wright, John R. 1989. PAC Contributions, Lobbying, and Representation. *Journal of Politics* 51:713–29.

Wolin, Sheldon. 1968. Paradigms and Political Theories. In *Politics and Experience*, eds. Preston King and B. C. Parekh. Cambridge: Cambridge University Press.

Woolpert, Stephen. 1980. Humanizing Law Enforcement: A New Paradigm. *Journal of Humanistic Psychology* 20:67–81.

———. 1984. A Comparison of Rational Choice and Self-Actualization Theories of Politics. In *American Politics and Humanistic Psychology*, ed. Tom Greening. San Francisco: Saybrook.

———. 1988. Applying Humanistic Psychology to Politics: The Case for Criminal Restitution. *Journal of Humanistic Psychology* 28:45–62.

Yankelovich, Daniel. 1991. *Coming to Public Judgment: Making Democracy Work in a Complex World*. Syracuse, NY: Syracuse University Press.

Yeich, Susan. 1991. Ecological Feminism: Drawing Connections Between the Oppression of Women, Animals and Nature. *The Trumpeter* 8(2):84–87.

Young, Iris Marion. 1990. *Justice and the Politics of Difference*. Princeton, NJ: Princeton University Press.

Zahn, Gordon C. 1969. *Chaplains in the RAF: A Study in Role Tension*. Manchester, UK: University of Manchester Press.

Zimmerman, Brenda J., and David K. Hurst. 1993. Fractals: A Lens to View Organizational Change, Learning, and Leadership. *Chaos Network* 5:1–5.

Zisk, Betty. 1992. *The Politics of Transformation: Local Activism in the Peace and Environmental Movements*. Westport, CT: Praeger.

———. 1993. "Folk Singers, Theatre, and Children's Drawings: Artists and Political Change: Explorations about the Role of the Arts." Presented at the Annual Meeting of the American Political Science Association. Washington, DC.

——— 1994. Political Transformation and Oppression. Presented at the Annual Meeting of American Political Science Association. New York.

Zohar, Danah, and Ian Marshall. 1994. *Quantum Society*. New York: William Morrow.

About the Contributors

Theodore Becker. Ph.D., Northwestern University; J.D., Rutgers University. Professor of Political Science, Auburn University. Author of numerous articles and eleven books, including *Impact of Supreme Court Decisions*; *Political Trials*; *American Government Past, Present, and Future*; *Quantum Politics*; and *Live This Book: Abbie Hoffman's Philosophy of a Free and Green America*. Co-editor, *Teaching Democracy by Being Democratic*.

Marla Brettschneider. Ph.D., New York University. Assistant Professor of Political Science and Women's Studies, University of New Hampshire. Author of numerous articles and *Cornerstones of Peace: Jewish Identity Politics and Democratic Theory*. Editor of *The Narrow Bridge: Jewish Perspectives on Multiculturalism*.

Michael Cummings. Ph.D., Stanford University. Professor and Chair, Political Science Department, University of Colorado, Denver. Member of the editorial boards of *Utopian Studies* and *Communal Studies*. Author of *Political Transformation and Political Correctness*.

Jeff Fishel. Ph.D., University of California at Los Angeles. Professor of Public Affairs, American University. Former Senior Fulbright Scholar and Woodrow Wilson Fellow. Author of numerous articles and *Presidents and Promises: From Campaign Pledge to Presidential Performance*; *Political Parties and Elections in an Anti-Party Age*; and *Party and Opposition*.

Robert Gilbert. Doctoral candidate, University of South Carolina. Dissertation title: "A World in Transition: Foundations of a

Global Democratic System." Former John C. West Fellow and Sherman Smith Fellow. Former Marine Instructor in Nuclear/Biological/Chemical Warfare. Winner of the 1994 American Political Science Association Award for the best panel paper in transformational politics.

Daniel Graham. Ph.D., University of North Carolina. Adjunct Professor, Department of Political Science, North Carolina State University and Elon College. Author of several articles on Green and left politics and a regular environmental studies contributor to the interdisciplinary journal *On the Horizon*.

Manfred Halpern. Ph.D., Johns Hopkins University, School of Advanced International Studies. Professor Emeritus, Princeton University, Department of Politics and Center of International Studies. Former member of the State Department Office of Intelligence Research on the Near East, South Asia and Africa. Author of *The Politics of Social Change in the Middle East and North Africa*; "Choosing between Ways of Life and Death and between Forms of Democracy: An Archetypal Analysis"; and *Transformation: Its Theory and Practice in Our Personal, Political, Historical, and Sacred Being* (in progress).

Gail Harrison. Ph.D., Vanderbilt University. Associate Professor of Political Science, Georgia Southern University. Author of "Study Abroad: A View from the Community College," *International Studies Notes*, Spring, 1990, and "The Ethics of a Democratically-Based Classroom," *Thresholds of Education*, May, 1993. Work in progress: feminist theory and conflict resolution.

Louis Herman. Ph.D., University of Hawaii. Associate Professor and Director of Political Science Program, University of Hawaii, West Oahu. Author of "Empowering Students" in Becker and Couto (ed.), *Teaching Democracy by Being Democratic*. Winner of University of Hawaii Regents Award and Student Government Award for excellence in teaching.

Barbara Knight. Ph.D., George Washington University. Associate Professor of Government and Politics, George Mason University. Coauthor of *Responsible Government: American & British*, and *Prisoners' Rights in America*; editor, *Separation of Powers in the American System*.

Morley Segal. Ph.D., Claremont Graduate School. Professor of Public Administration, American University. Cofounder of the American University/NTL Masters Program in Organization Development. Author of *Points of Influence: A Guide to Using Personality Theory at Work.*

Edward Schwerin. Ph.D., University of Hawaii. Director of Interdisciplinary Studies and Associate Professor of Political Science, Florida Atlantic University. Recipient of several major teaching awards. Consultant and trainer in negotiation and mediation in the private and public sectors. Author of several articles on dispute resolution and global politics, and *Mediation, Citizen Empowerment, and Transformational Politics* (winner of 1996 American Political Science Association award for best book in transformational politics).

Christa Daryl Slaton. Ph.D., University of Hawaii. Associate Professor of Political Science and Director of Master of Public Administration Program, Auburn University. Coordinator of the American Political Science Association Section on Ecological and Transformational Politics from 1992 to 1995 and recipient of their 1996 Praxis Award for Distinguished Achievement in the Role of Scholar and Activist. Author of *Televote: Expanding Citizen Participation in the Quantum Age* and several articles on Green politics and participatory democracy.

Stephen Woolpert. Ph.D., Stanford University. Professor of Government, Saint Mary's College of California. Associate Editor of the *Journal of Humanistic Psychology*. Author of several articles on humanistic political psychology and criminal justice policy.

Betty Zisk. Ph.D., Stanford University. Professor of Political Science, Boston University. Coordinator of the American Political Science Association Section on Ecological and Transformational Politics from 1995 to 1998. Author of six books and many articles on interest groups and political movements, direct democracy, and methodology in political science, the most recent of which is *The Politics of Transformation: Local Activism in the Peace and Environmental Movements.*

Index

Abalos, David, 167
Adaptation, xxi
Adler, Patricia and Peter, 133
Affigne, Tony, 20
Affirmative action, xxix, 215–231; arbitrary classifications in, 220; assumptions about, 180; benefits of, 220; change in meaning of, 215–218; competition in, 225; conservatism of, 215, 220; contradictions of, 218–219; critics of, 215; defining, 216; and fullness of opportunity, 224–226; opposition to, 217–218; and preferential treatment, 216; purposes of, 221; redefining criteria for, 222; result of political power on, 217; set-asides in, 217, 218; solutions to, 221–226; stereotypes in, 221; unprotected groups in, 219–221
Affluence, Zen, 40
Aggression, 17
Alienation, 131; cultural, 106; dispelling, 179; from government, 186, 198; from nature, 172; remedying, 112; social, 79
Americans for Peace Now, 120, 124, 125, 126
Amnesty International, 52–53
Analysis: content, 100; cost-benefit, 179; critical, 30, 94; empirical data, 100; narrative, 101, 138;

political, 99–100; precision in, 93; quantitative, 93; symbolic, 101
Anaxagoras, 5
Anthropocentrism, xxi, 38, 74, 85
Apartheid, 10
Arendt, Hannah, 67–68
Aristotle, 37
Armstrong, Susan, 16–17
Atomism, 13*tab*
Audubon Society, 84
Authority: acquiescence to, 105; central, 181; challenges to, 4; ensuring, 151; political, 29; shifts in, 157
Awareness, ego, 31

Bacon, Francis, 5, 6, 14, 16, 76
Balance: ecology/economy, 82–84; gender, 74; individual/group, 67; order/chaos, 69; seeking, 17–18
Bandura, Albert, 106
Barber, Benjamin, 9, 11, 198
Becker, Theodore, 11, 20, 179, 185–200
Beer, Stafford, 143
Behavior: dysfunctional, 104; human, 60–61; inconsistent, xxiii; and learning, 156; political, 7, 14, 92–93; study of, 8; theories of, 14
Behavioralism, 93
Being: community of, 43*n1;* as emanations, 48; emerging, 45; experi-

Kitto, H.D.F., 39
Knight, Barbara, xxv, 15, 17, 57–72, 76, 95, 149, 175, 199, 228
Knowing: construction of, 95; from multiple perspectives, 95; relationship to power, 151; ways of, xxv, 144
Knowledge: absolute certain, 29; acts of, 27; attaining, 6; based on observation, 77; basic, 107; capability for, 27; computer, 114; contexts of, 144; empirical, 144; enhancing, 153; fixed state of, 158; human, 27; love of, 40; metaphors for, 76; passion for, 32–33; personal, 157; political, 7; scientific, 93, 186; self, 43*n3;* of society, 43*n3;* subjective, 93; survival, 107; of universe, 27; verifiable, 93
Kuhn, Thomas, 9, 22, 25
Kushner, Tony, 3

Leadership, 69; cults of personality in, 201; development of, 100; directive, 237; ethical, 209; old-style, 69; political, 4, 62; public, 181; responsive, 178; risks of, 201; selection process, 195; transactional, 181; transformational, xxvii, 11, 22, 96, 100, 181, 201–213
Learning: active, 42; circle of, 158, 159, 159*fig;* communities, xxvii, 156–157; contexts of, 144, 157; to contribute, 49; democratic, 109; domain of, 157; effective, 157; holistic, 156; motivation for, 111; nontraditional, 156; objectives, 109; participatory, 156; process of, xxvii, 42, 156, 157; sequences, 158; service, xxvi, 108, 109, 112–114; strategies for, 42; styles, 163–164
Lerner, Michael, 227

Lewin, Kurt, 102, 140
Liberalism, xxiv, 8, 12, 21, 29; authoritarian, 50; classical, 9; dismantling, 19; and objectivity, 9; rejection of, 4
Liberation, 9, 38
Locke, John, 7, 29
Logic, 79
Logos, 57, 58, 60, 61, 65

Machiavelli, Niccolo, 7, 62, 233
MacKinnon, Catherine, 11
Mandela, Nelson, 201
Mansbridge, Jane, 11
Marx, Karl, 79, 83, 88*n1*
Masculine: attributes, 61; dominance, 16; science as, 17
Maslow, Abraham, 8–9, 22, 223
Materialism, 9, 13*tab,* 40, 79, 175; instrumental, 84
Mayhew, David, 132
Meaning: cognition in, 28; constructing, 30; of life, 47; search for, 28
Media technology, 10
Medicine Wheel, 33–34
Memories, 46
Mercantilism, 7
Metaparadigm, 25
Metaphor, 15, 16, 47, 57, 65, 76
Metaphysics of modernity, 30
Metaxy, 27, 29, 31, 35
Milbrath, Lester, 11, 17
Models. *See also* Theories; critical pedagogy, 145–146; dominator, 68; feminist democratic, xxvii; partnership, 68–69, 69, 70, 229; research, 119–129; transformational teaching, 108–116
Modernity, metaphysics of, 30
Morality, xxiii
Movements: antigovernment, 4; communitarian, 21, 108; environmental, xxvii, 22, 83–84, 134, 233–244; feminist, 22, 182–183;